breakdown

Deadly Technological Disasters

Also from
Visible Ink Press

Crisis Response

"Interesting and sometimes chilling insiders' perspective ... enough ... to keep any executive up at night." —Orange County Register

Twenty-five first-hand stories of major business disasters and how they were handled—such as the *Challenger* explosion and the Drexel Burnham Lambert securities fraud violations—provide insight, sound planning strategies, and useful advice for public relations, communications, and management professionals. By Jack A. Gottschalk, 7.25" x 9.25" paperback, 485 pages, 50 photos, ISBN 0-8103-9130-9.

Great American Trials

"This book is fascinating, entertaining and dependable." —The Arizona Republic

Two hundred historically significant, legally important, and notorious trials that have captured the interest of the world are told through lively text, captivating photos, and succinct coverage. Such trials as Lizzy Borden, Roe *v.* Wade, Chicago Seven, Lenny Bruce, Oliver North, and Rodney King are included along with other courtroom dramas. By Edward W. Knappman, 7.25" x 9.25" paperback, 872 pages, 175 photos, ISBN 0-8103-9134-1.

breakdown

Deadly Technological Disasters

Foreword by

Henry Petroski

Neil Schlager

VISIBLE INK
PRESS

Detroit • Washington, D.C.

breakdown

Deadly Technological Disasters

Published by Visible Ink Press™
a division of Gale Research Inc.
835 Penobscot Building
Detroit, MI 48226-4094

Visible Ink Press is a trademark of Gale Research Inc.

Cover photos of *Challenger* explosion courtesy of AP Worldwide.

Most Visible Ink Press™ books are available at special quantity discounts when purchased in bulk by corporations, organizations, or groups. Customized printings, special imprints, messages, and excerpts can be produced to meet your needs. For more information, contact Special Markets Manager, Visible Ink Press, 835 Penobscot Bldg., Detroit, MI 48226. Or call 1-800-776-6265.

Art Director: Tracey Rowens

ISBN 0-7876-0478-X

Printed in the United States of America
All rights reserved

10 9 8 7 6 5 4 3 2 1

Contents

Foreword by Henry Petroski . . . . **xi**

Introduction . . . . **xv**

Contributors . . . . **xix**

Acknowledgments . . . . **xxi**

Air & Space Disasters

Hindenburg crash

Lakehurst, New Jersey (1937) **3**
Last and largest commercial airship destroyed by hydrogen fire while landing. Thirty-five of the ninety-seven people aboard the airship died in the blaze.

TWA Super-Constellation and United Airlines DC-7 collision

Grand Canyon, Arizona (1956) **11**
Two airliners collided in empty airspace—an "impossible" accident that led to the creation of the Federal Aviation Administration.

Apollo 1 capsule fire

Cape Canaveral, Florida (1967) **17**
A wiring malfunction led to a flash fire that caused the deaths of three astronauts during a ground test and exposed the need for higher design, manufacturing, and safety standards at NASA.

Soyuz 11 reentry disaster

(1971) **23**
A cabin seal malfunction led to the deaths of three Soviet cosmonauts during reentry and represented a significant technical setback for the Soyuz manned spacecraft program.

Challenger explosion

(1986) **29**

An explosion shortly after launch caused by faulty solid rocket booster seals destroyed the shuttle and killed its crew of seven, forcing a retrenchment of NASA's shuttle program.

United Airlines Boeing 747 explosion

Hawaii (1989) **37**

A flawed design caused a cargo door to fly open, which led to an explosive decompression that punched a gaping hole above the door. Nine passengers vanished out of the cavity.

United Airlines DC-10 crash

Sioux City, Iowa (1989) **43**

The crash of a DC-10 aircraft due to an engine explosion and the subsequent loss of hydraulic power led to a massive National Transportation Safety Board investigation.

Lauda Air Boeing 767-300 crash

Thailand (1991) **49**

An inadvertent thrust reverser deployment flipped a jetliner into a crash dive that killed all 223 people on board.

El Al Boeing 747-200 crash

Amsterdam, The Netherlands (1992) **57**

Separation of both engines from the right wing caused a 747 to plunge out of the sky and into an Amsterdam apartment complex, taking the lives of six El Al crew members and more than fifty people on the ground.

Disasters at Sea

Sinking of the *Titanic*

off Newfoundland (1912) **65**

A "practically unsinkable" state-of-the-art ocean liner sank after hitting an iceberg, causing the deaths of more than fifteen hundred people.

Andrea Doria-Stockholm collision

off Massachusetts (1956) **73**

Misinterpretation of radar signals led two ocean liners into a deadly game of "chicken" off the coast of Massachusetts. The *Andrea Doria* rolled over on its side and sank, killing forty-three passengers and crew members, after the resulting collision with the *Stockholm,* which lost many of its own crew.

Thresher sinking

Atlantic Ocean (1963) **79**

An advanced nuclear-powered submarine plunged beneath its "crush depth" and sank, killing all 129 crew members.

Scorpion sinking

Atlantic Ocean (1968) **86**

Four months after the nuclear-powered submarine vanished with its crew of ninety-nine in May of 1968, portions of the *Scorpion* were found, but the cause of the sinking remained a mystery. The accident raised concerns about the safety of powering submarines with nuclear reactors.

Ocean Ranger oil-drilling rig sinking

North Atlantic (1982) **92**

A broken window on an offshore oil-drilling rig precipitated a catastrophic chain of events that caused the sinking of the rig and the death of all eighty-four people on board.

Exxon Valdez oil spill

Prince William Sound, Alaska (1989) **98**

An oil tanker ran aground in Prince William Sound, Alaska, resulting in a catastrophic oil spill that killed many thousands of birds, fish, and sea otters.

Automobile Failures

Ford Pinto rear-impact defect

(1971–1976) **109**

A flawed automobile design gave rear-impact collisions the potential to set the entire car aflame and led to the deaths of at least fifty-nine people. A comprehensive recall and prolonged negative publicity and legal entanglements ensured for Ford.

Firestone 500 steel-belted tire failure

(1972–1978) **117**

Seven-and-a-half million Firestone-built tires were recalled when it was discovered their treads were likely to separate from the main structure, especially when driven underinflated. Forty-one highway deaths may have resulted in part from the defective tire model.

Audi 5000 sudden acceleration

(1978–1986) **124**

Beginning in the late 1970s, Audi received more than 1,400 reports of accidents—which injured 330 people and killed seven—that resulted from sudden acceleration. The allegations led to the development of the automatic shift lock.

Chemical & Nuclear Disasters

Windscale reactor complex fire

England (1957) **133**

The world's first major commercial nuclear power plant disaster took place in 1957 at Great Britain's lone plutonium-making facility. A report twenty-six years later estimated that thirteen people died of thyroid cancer that was caused by the Windscale accident, while others suggested long-term damage to the populace surrounding the reactor.

Three Mile Island accident

Middletown, Pennsylvania (1979) **140**
The worst accident in the history of American commercial nuclear power generation caused a partial meltdown of the reactor core. No one was killed or injured, but expert opinion remains divided about possible future health problems that might result from the accident.

Tsuruga radioactive waste spill

Tsuruga, Japan (1981) **147**
Due to human error, nearly four thousand gallons of radioactive wastes escaped from a nuclear power plant in Japan. Although officials attempted to hide the accident from public notice, the subterfuge was discovered six weeks later during a routine study of seaweed in the area.

Ginna power plant radioactive release

Ontario, New York (1982) **153**
Failure of a pipe in a nuclear power plant caused shutdown of the reactor and release of radioactive gas to the atmosphere.

Bhopal toxic vapor leak

Bhopal, India (1984) **159**
A toxic vapor leak that released fifty thousand pounds of deadly gas over the Indian countryside resulted in massive loss of life and widespread injury.

Institute, West Virginia, toxic vapor leak

Institute, West Virginia (1985) **166**
An explosive failure of a temporary storage tank containing an aldicarb oxime mixture caused a toxic vapor leak at a chemical plant, injuring 135 people.

Chernobyl accident

Ukraine (1986) **173**
The world's worst nuclear power plant disaster eventually resulted in a level of fallout ten times that of the atomic bomb dropped on Hiroshima, Japan, during World War II. At least thirty-one workers and emergency personnel were killed immediately or died soon after the accident, some two hundred thousand residents of the area were evacuated, and clouds of radioactive material were carried over most of northern Europe.

Bridge, Building & Other Structural Collapses

Molasses spill

Boston, Massachusetts (1919) **183**
A giant, five-story-high steel tank suddenly fractured, releasing millions of gallons of deadly molasses that engulfed people, animals, and property.

Tacoma Narrows Bridge collapse

Washington State (1940) **189**

The bridge failure that brought an abrupt end to create "a slender ribbon bridge deck" also introduced the importance of considering wind dynamics in bridge design.

Ronan Point tower collapse

London, England (1968) **196**

Inadequate connections between walls and floors caused the progressive collapse of one corner of a prefabricated high-rise apartment building. More than a dozen residents were injured, five fatally.

MGM Grand Hotel fire

Las Vegas, Nevada (1980) **200**

The second most deadly hotel fire in United States history led to the deaths of eighty-five people and the injury of more than 600 others, and resulted in a nationwide revaluation of fire codes.

Hyatt Regency Hotel walkways collapse

Kansas City, Missouri (1981) **208**

The collapse of two suspended walkways caused by a simple design change resulted in the worst structural failure to date in the United States, killing 114 people and injuring nearly 200 others.

East Chicago, Indiana, highway ramp collapse

East Chicago, Indiana (1982) **216**

Poor quality scaffolding and numerous safety violations led to the fatal collapse of a portion of a highway ramp during construction. In addition to the thirteen workers who died, fifteen workers were injured severely as the ramp crashed onto the banks of an adjacent industrial canal.

Mianus River Bridge collapse

Greenwich, Connecticut (1983) **221**

The collapse of one bridge span was caused by several factors, including lack of proper maintenance over twenty-five years. Three people were killed and another three severely injured when the 100-foot-long section, three lanes wide, fell out of the Mianus River Bridge.

Stava Dam failure

Stava, Italy (1985) **228**

The failure of two mining dams in Italy unleashed a flood that killed 269 people, buried villages under tons of mud, and drew attention to several national policy issues.

Schoharie Creek Bridge collapse

New York State (1987) **234**

Two long-standing bridge engineering problems—scour and lack of redundancy— converged to destroy a New York State Thruway bridge. When the center span of the 540-foot Schoharie Creek Bridge suddenly collapsed without warning, ten people plunged to their deaths in the water below.

L'Ambiance Plaza collapse

Bridgeport, Connecticut (1987) **241**
The twin towers of a half-completed apartment building collapsed during construction and fell like a gigantic stack of concrete pancakes, killing twenty-eight workers and injuring sixteen.

Index **249**

breakdown

Foreword

by Henry Petroski

Technology is supposed to work, and by and large it does. We can drive our automobiles for hundreds of miles on interstate highways without incident and without stopping, passing thousands of automobiles going the other way, also without incident.

When our trip is going well, we tend not to marvel at how wonderfully reliable all the speeding machines (and their drivers) are; we tend to enjoy the scenery or listen to some pleasant music. It is only when we encounter something out of the ordinary that we may reflect upon the technology itself.

Once in a while, especially on a hot day, we may see an overheated car on the other side, and this may give us pause. Soon, however, we tend to forget that incident or put it out of our minds, perhaps rationalizing that it was the fault of the driver or of an automobile inferior to ours. On another occasion, we might get caught in stop-and-go traffic and wonder what is going on up ahead. We can look for clues from the traffic on the other side: If it is moving normally, we can guess there is a stalled car or something gone wrong on our side; if the other side is empty of traffic, we can guess there is an accident over there. Sometimes both directions are equally at a standstill, and only after hours of waiting and inching ahead do we pass by the scene of a terrible collision. We may wonder if the machines or their operators malfunctioned, but the thought of the carnage causes all of us to drive a bit more slowly and alertly—at least for the next several miles, during which we may reflect upon the chance we take that one of those drivers coming the other way will not lose control and head straight for us. It is not comfortable to drive with such thoughts, and we tend to blot them out, somehow accepting the odds or believing that we can steer our own automobile out of the way of another.

Even when we cannot control it in any sensible way, we tend to take for granted technology of all kinds, as long as it is working. The better and more reliably it works, the more invisible and uninteresting it is to us as we go about our daily lives. There is no front-page news value to the fact that traffic was moving along at the usual clip on the freeway yesterday, or that our water, electric power, and telephone service all remained uninterrupted for the three-hundredth day straight. Such would be a dog-bites-man story, and it does not sell newspapers or cause viewers to tune into the evening news on television.

However, when technology breaks down, no matter how benignly, we tend to take note, and we may even exaggerate its consequences. It takes just an inexplicable traffic jam encountered on our way to work to make us a bit more irritated over coffee that morning, perhaps going on and on about how inadequate the roads are and about how something should be done about them. If we are frequent flyers, even though we may in fact miss an airplane connection only once in dozens of trips, when we talk about it we tend to tell the story as if it happens every other time we fly. But such annoyances and inconveniences can be expected to happen in technological systems that rely not only upon the workings of machines but also upon the vagaries of their human operators and the weather. While such incidents serve as icebreakers for conversation and provide material for stand-up comics on late-night television, they are of little consequence in the whole scheme of things.

On occasion, technology breaks down in catastrophic ways, and when this happens it is no joking matter. The sudden collapse of a bridge over which a hundred thousand cars may travel every day, or the separation of an engine from an airliner during takeoff, can and has resulted in great losses of life and raised fundamental questions about the reliability of technology in which millions of people trust day in and day out. Unlike in the case of an oncoming car, there is little we can do to control our destiny when we find ourselves on a bridge that is collapsing beneath us or when we are a passenger on an airplane that is out of control. It is this sense of helplessness that underlies our demand that some technologies be more reliable than others.

More than technologies that are operated on a personal level, technologies over which ordinary people do not have any direct control and for which the consequences of breakdown potentially affect great numbers of lives tend to be held to a much higher standard of reliability. Not only is it a remarkable catastrophe when something of some magnitude fails, it is also a man-bites-dog story—precisely because it is such an unusual and unexpected occurrence. The potentially great consequences of a technological breakdown necessarily causes considerable care to be taken in the design, construction, maintenance, and operation of the artifact in the first place—precisely to obviate any breakdown from occurring.

Those most directly responsible for conceiving, building, and operating the large and complex technological systems upon which we have come to depend have as their foremost objective the safe and predictable functioning of their design. The whole technological enterprise, including the profit motive, is founded upon an understanding of what could go wrong with a given design, and the proper development of any artifact or system incorporates safeguards to insure that operation takes place within prescribed limits of safety. The long and deliberate conceptualization and detailed design process that precedes the realization of our more complex technologies can include seemingly endless "what-if" questions that engineers are expected to answer to everyone's satisfaction.

When technology developed this way fails, it is more than news to the engineers that designed it, for an unexpected breakdown calls into question the very process by which they design and develop systems of all kinds. Every breakdown raises fundamental questions about what went wrong: Was there a physical phenomenon than was unknown or unaccounted for in the design? Were there incorrect assumptions or calculations made? Were faulty materials or manufacturing processes employed? Were there forces applied beyond those anticipated? Was the system abused or improperly maintained? Was the system improperly operated?

When technology works, such questions are naturally assumed to have been answered satisfactorily during the process of design, development, and demonstration of the system. Having passed through a rigorous period of critical testing, a technological system confirms the claims of its designers that it will work as intended. Because it is impossible to test fully something so large as a bridge or a jumbo jet airliner until the artifact is actually built, the successful pursuit of advanced technology depends to a large extent upon the validity of the design process and its assumptions. These assumptions become embodied in the artifacts and systems and become fully tested only with their use.

When technology breaks down, we are presented with an undesired but incontrovertible test that can provide information heretofore unavailable, and whose study can provide answers to the very questions the breakdown raises. Because of the often unique insights that can result from a close study of how and why a breakdown occurred, there is always considerable need to recover and preserve the physical debris of an accident and to interview any witnesses or survivors. In especially tragic breakdowns, such as that of the space shuttle *Challenger*, there is often a highly visible and distinguished committee that conducts the investigation in full public view. It is during such proceedings that the true nature of technology and the technological process are often made clear in stark detail.

The breakdown case studies presented in this book have the value not only of providing details about the particular incidents described, but also of providing in their collectivity a means of understanding the technological process. Breakdowns generally occur in a climate of technological complacency or hubris: The *Challenger* was launched against the better judgment of some engineers in part because of the robustness that two dozen earlier space shuttle launches had demonstrated. In the wake of a breakdown, there tends to be renewed conservatism about the technology involved: After *Challenger* exploded, space shuttle flights were suspended for a considerable period so that numerous design and procedural changes could be made.

The success-failure dichotomy exhibited in the case of the *Challenger* is not a new phenomenon. While *Breakdown: Deadly Technological Disasters* provides an excellent selection of recent catastrophes, there have been countless examples throughout the history of technology of catastrophic failures occurring in the wake of prolonged success, and of renewed cautions and new departures occuring in the wake of failures. If we do not become aware of and sensitive to this larger cyclic phenomenon in the technological process, we can expect technology to continue to break down at its present rate.

Introduction

Overview

Technology, as defined in *Webster's Dictionary*, is "the totality of the means employed to provide objects necessary for human sustenance and comfort." These objects can take the form of small, simple items—like a pencil—or large, complex systems—like a jumbo jet—but regardless of the form, breakdown is always a possibility. As technology expert Henry Petroski points out in his eloquent foreword to this work, technological breakdown can result in something as relatively innocuous as a traffic jam or as devastating as a bridge collapse that claims many lives or a spaceship explosion that stuns an entire nation. The impact of a spectacular breakdown often transcends its immediate consequences: At the same time we mourn the victims of the disaster, we may begin to doubt the safety of the technological systems that provide the very foundation of our society.

It is these large breakdowns of technology that are the focus of this book. *Breakdown: Deadly Technological Disasters* includes discussions of three dozen such breakdowns from a variety of fields, ranging from transportation to civil engineering to the environment. While the events chronicled in this book produced devastating consequences, they also often led to improved standards and safer, better technological systems. *Breakdown* explores not just the tragedy inherent in the events but the valuable lessons learned—albeit the hard way—from them.

Scope

Breakdown: Deadly Technological Disasters covers significant technological disasters from the twentieth century. Events caused by deliberate human actions—such as terrorist bombings—are not included here. Nor does this book discuss purely natural disasters such as hurricanes and earthquakes, although natural phenomena did play a role in some of the events included here, such as the stormy weather that contributed to the sinking of the *Ocean Ranger* oil rig in the North Atlantic in 1982.

The qualifier "significant" is somewhat problematic for its vagueness. Admittedly, we did not apply the term evenly to every event included in this collection. Some events were chosen because they resulted in large losses of life, while others were selected for the extensive press coverage they received and the impact they had on public opinion. Still others in this book led to no loss of life and received little press coverage, but were included because they offer valuable lessons.

In general, the disasters detailed in *Breakdown* were caused by poor design, planning, testing, or construction rather than simple human error. Here again, though, exceptions can be found, since many disasters were caused by a combination of the above-mentioned factors. A primary example is the Exxon *Valdez* oil spill in 1989. While human error—including alcohol use and fatigue—was the immediate cause of the accident, technical elements such as the ship's single- rather than double-hull construction and the failure of oil containment booms both contributed heavily to the magnitude of the disaster.

You'll find specific disasters arranged chronologically within broad subject categories. To find a particular topic, you can check the **Table of Contents** at the front of the book or the **Index** at the back. In addition to listing the events included in the book, the subject index lists key terms, concepts, and people.

Acknowledgments

The material in *Breakdown* was culled from *When Technology Fails,* a library reference work published by Gale Research Inc. We wish to thank the following individuals who assisted in the formulation of *When Technology Fails:*

George M. A. Cumming, Jr.
Librarian
Science Reference Department
Boston Public Library

Larayne J. Dallas
Librarian
McKinney Engineering Library
University of Texas at Austin

John Loss, FAIA
Architect, Whitehall, Michigan, and
Former Professor of Architecture and Executive Director,
Architecture and Engineering Performance Information Center
University of Maryland at College Park

We would also like to thank **Henry Petroski**, who composed the book's foreword; **Leonard C. Bruno**, who performed a myriad of duties, from providing research to writing many entries in the airship, spaceship, and submarine sections; Kevin Hillstrom and Laurie Collier Hillstrom of Northern Lights Writers Group, whose editorial expertise made this volume's publication possible; Margaret Chamberlain and Pam Hayes, who skillfully handled this book's illustrations; and Visible Ink Press editor Christa Brelin and associate editor Dean Dauphinais.

Contributors

Henry Petroski, who wrote the Foreword, is Aleksandar S. Vesic Professor of Civil Engineering at Duke University and author of *To Engineer Is Human: The Role of Failure in Successful Design, Design Paradigms: Case Histories of Error and Judgment in Engineering, Engineers of Dreams: Great Bridge Builders and the Spanning of America,* and *The Pencil.*

Byron Acohido is a journalist at the *Seattle Times* specializing in aerospace-related news. He received the 1993 Premier Award of Excellence for Aviation Safety Coverage from the Aviation/Space Writers Association for "Jet Engine Pins: How Big a Risk" and "Flight 811, Terror in the Sky."

Leonard C. Bruno is Senior Science Specialist in the Science and Technology Division at the Library of Congress. He has written several books on science and technology, including *The Landmarks of Science, On the Move,* and *The Tradition of Technology.*

Virginia Kent Dorris is a free-lance writer specializing in construction design and development. Between 1989 and 1992, she was an assistant editor for the construction industry trade weekly *Engineering News-Record.* She has also contributed to *Architecture, Infrastructure Finance,* and *Civil Engineering.*

James M. Flammang is a free-lance writer specializing in automotive topics, including the history and technology of modern and classic cars. His books include *Understanding Automotive Specifications & Data* and *Great Book of Dream Cars.*

David N. Ford is an instructor in the Department of Civil and Environmental Engineering at Massachusetts Institute of Technology. He has extensive experience in designing and managing building expansion and renovation projects.

Neal J. Gruber is a civil engineer affiliated with Dames & Moore in Cincinnati, Ohio. He has extensive experience in the areas of hydrology, hydraulics, hydropower, coastal engineering, and environmental engineering. His work has recently appeared in *Hydro Review.*

Loretta Hall is a free-lance writer and regular contributor to *Southwest Contractor.* She has written several articles in the areas of construction design and techniques.

Lamont Ingalls is a technical writer and researcher. He has done consulting work for the Oak Ridge National Laboratory and Chevron Chemical Corporation, among others.

Greg Janicki is a free-lance writer and syndicated columnist covering developments in the automotive industry. He is the author of *Cars Europe Never Built* and the editor of *Cars Detroit Never Built,* both available from Sterling Publishing.

Robert Mark is a journalist, teacher, and pilot who has written for magazines including the *Chicago Tribune Magazine, Family Circle,* and *Airline Pilot.* He writes a monthly column for *General Aviation News and Flyer* and is the author of *The Joy of Flying,* available from McGraw-Hill.

David E. Newton was formerly Professor of Chemistry at Salem State College in Massachusetts and Adjunct Professor of Professional Studies at the University of San Francisco. He is the author of more than 50 books, including *Taking a Stand Against Environmental Pollution, Environmental Chemistry,* and *Global Warming.*

Rita Robison is a free-lance writer specializing in issues related to civil engineering. Formerly, she worked for *Civil Engineering Magazine, Progressive Architecture,* and *Architectural & Engineering News.*

Robert J. Serling is an accomplished author of over 20 books and the recipient of several Best Non-Fiction awards from the Aviation and Space Writers Association. His areas of interest include airline histories and air safety.

William B. Shapbell, Jr., is a launch and flight systems manager at the National Aeronautics and Space Administration's Kennedy Space Center. He has participated in launch operations management of all manned spaceflight programs at NASA since the Gemini program.

Sally Van Duyne is a free-lance writer who has written articles on various topics, including psychology, medicine, natural history, and naval engineering.

Richard Weingardt is the president of Richard Weingardt Consultants, a structural engineering firm located in Denver, Colorado, and the Vice President of American Consulting Engineers Council. He lectures internationally and is the author of three books and numerous articles on creativity, leadership, business, and engineering.

Acknowledgments

Photographs and illustrations appearing in Breakdown *were received from the following sources:*

UPI/Bettmann: **pp. 1, 6, 14, 47, 63, 76, 102, 121, 145, 165, 170, 181, 192, 207, 212, 220, 224, 231, 245.**

Archive Photos/Lambert: **p. 4.**

The Bettmann Archive: **pp. 9, 15, 67, 69.**

AP/Wide World Photos: **pp. 19, 20, 31, 39, 46, 52, 54, 62, 72, 83, 96, 103, 107, 110, 114, 136, 155, 177, 195, 205, 214, 237.**

Tass/Sovfoto: **p. 24.**

NASA: **pp. 32, 35.**

Reuters/Bettmann: **pp. 61, 175, 194.**

U.S. Navy: **pp. 81, 88.**

UPI/Bettmann Newsphotos: **pp. 104, 131, 142, 161, 213.**

Kyodo Photo Service: **p. 150.**

The Boston Globe: **p. 186.**

Rex USA Ltd: **p. 199.**

breakdown

Deadly
Technological Disasters

Air and Space Disasters

Hindenburg crash (1937) 3

TWA Super-Constellation and

   United Airlines DC-7 collision (1956). 11

Apollo I capsule fire (1967). 17

Soyuz 11 reentry disaster (1971) 23

Challenger explosion (1986) 29

United Airlines Boeing 747 explosion (1989). 37

United Airlines DC-10 crash (1989) 43

Lauda Air Boeing 767-300 crash (1989) 49

El Al Boeing 747-200 crash (1992). 57

Hindenburg crash

Lakehurst, New Jersey **1937**

Last and largest commercial airship destroyed by hydrogen fire while landing. Thirty-five of the ninety-seven people aboard the airship died in the blaze.

Background

On May 6, 1937, the German airship *Hindenburg* exploded and burst into flames as it prepared to land following a flight across the Atlantic. The spectacular conflagration lit up the New Jersey sky and in only thirty-two seconds, the entire ship—the largest airship ever built—lay crumpled and smoldering on the ground. Of the ninety-seven people aboard, sixty-two survived the fiery crash.

Since the end of World War I, German airship designer Hugo Eckener had dreamed of building the perfect airship. He hoped to be able to translate the years of experience that his firm, the Zeppelin Company, had accumulated into producing an airship of unparalleled size, speed, comfort, and above all, safety. Such an airship, he reasoned, could be profitable as well. Eckener also had more practical concerns that fed his desire to produce a new generation of airships. By 1934 his very successful *Graf Zeppelin* had been pushed to the limits of its performance. Although it had braved the Atlantic several times, it

by Leonard C. Bruno

The Hindenburg *flying over New York City. The airship made the trans-Atlantic journey between Europe and the United States several times before it crashed.*

was suited neither in size nor speed for such a route, and Eckener wanted to build an airship specifically designed for this rigorous long-distance flight.

By the end of 1934, when Eckener was about to begin actual construction of his new airship, every major nation of the world that had an airship program of its own had abandoned it or was about to do so. Each of these countries, save Germany, had suffered disastrous and humiliating fatal crashes over the course of the past several years. Not only was Germany uniquely untouched by serious accidents, but its record in commercial airship flying was spotless—there had never been a passenger fatality on any German airship. The *Graf Zeppelin* alone had flown over one million miles in passenger service without serious incident.

As Eckener's new ship took shape, it became apparent that it would fulfill his grand dreams. Designated the LZ 129 and later christened the *Hindenburg* after Germany's respected war hero and president, Field Marshal Paul von Hindenburg, its dominant feature was its immense size. At eight hundred and three feet, it was only twenty-nine feet longer than the old *Graf Zeppelin*; but with a maximum diameter of one hundred and thirty-five feet, it was fatter by far than that slim airship. Its design allowed it to hold nearly twice as much gas, providing it with greater lifting power, increased resistance to bending forces, and greater maneuvering efficiency. This leviathan incorporated

breakdown

the latest technology in all of its systems, best exemplified by its four Daimler-Benz diesel engines. These efficient, powerful, and lightweight eleven hundred-horsepower engines turned enormous, reversible propellers that could drive the ship to eighty-five miles-per-hour.

Traveling time on the new *Hindenburg* between Frankfurt and Lakehurst would prove to be fifty-two hours eastbound and sixty-five hours westbound—a pace far faster than that of any ocean liner. Passengers on the *Hindenburg* didn't have to sacrifice any perks associated with oceangoing vessels, either, for the *Hindenburg* was in fact a flying luxury liner. For a one-way fare of $400, a passenger could enjoy a comfortable private cabin with hot and cold running water, plus a fifty-foot long dining room that boasted an adjoining fifty-foot promenade deck with wide, sloping picture windows. The lounge on the starboard side was thirty-four feet long and was furnished with tables and comfortable upholstered chairs. Other features of the airship included a writing room, another promenade deck, and spacious toilets, washrooms, and showers, as well as a separate smoking room (sealed and protected by pressurization and an airlock). In this room an electric lighter was secured by a chain for cigarette smokers, while cigar and pipe smokers had their choice of tobacco lit by stewards. As one might guess, passengers were strictly searched for matches upon boarding.

Eckener's marvelous airship had one weakness, however. Designed to be lifted by helium, it was forced to use hydrogen—seven million cubic feet of this flammable gas—when the United States refused to sell any of its scarce supply of helium to Germany. Suspicious of Adolf Hitler, a controversial political figure in Germany who had recently ascended to power, the United States feared that Germany might one day fly its helium-filled airships for military purposes. At about the same time, Eckener found that his grip on his company was not as secure as in the past. Although he was a popular figure in Germany, Eckener was an avowed anti-Nazi, a stance unlikely to endear him to Hitler and his political allies. Hitler had the industrialist moved upstairs, where he became the company's powerless chairman of the board. Hitler's government insinuated itself into the company in other ways as well. Soon the government was half owner of Eckener's company.

The politicized atmosphere transformed the *Hindenburg*'s maiden flight, on March 4, 1936, into a propaganda mission over Germany. The airship spent four days and three nights broadcasting speeches and dropping leaflets that championed Hitler's policies. Its first commercial flight was a March 31, 1936, trip to Rio de Janeiro that carried thirty-seven passengers. Eckener was unhappy about this long-distance flight, since the airship had not flown its test trials due to the propaganda flights. The round-trip journey to Rio de Janeiro was completed, but not without some tense moments. Two of its

Passengers on the *Hindenburg* didn't have to sacrifice any perks associated with oceangoing vessels, for the *Hindenburg* was in fact a flying luxury liner.

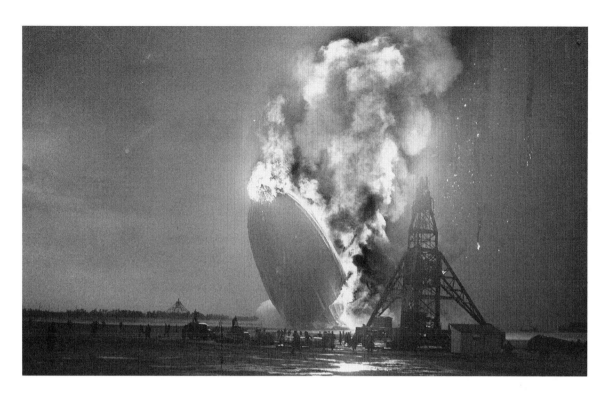

The Hindenburg *bursts into flames, lighting up the Lakehurst, New Jersey, sky.*

Daimler engines failed and the ship barely made it back home. Repairs took a month to complete.

In February 1936, Germany obtained permission from the United States to make ten round-trip treks to Lakehurst, New Jersey, during that year. The *Hindenburg* completed all of these flights on schedule and experienced no further difficulties. The first flight to Lakehurst took two and a half days, while the return leg of the journey took only two days, one hour, and fourteen minutes. That year the *Hindenburg* made not only those ten transatlantic flights to America, but also six more journeys to Rio. By the end of the year the remarkable airship had carried more than fifteen hundred transatlantic passengers and twenty tons of mail and freight. By year's end, it had won the enthusiastic endorsement of most of the traveling public, and was beginning to interest American financiers. Eckener's dream of a perfect airship had been realized, it appeared. A year's worth of Atlantic flights had proved the ship amazingly stable. Gale force winds elicited not the slightest tremor; on one occasion, in fact, the vessel weathered a hurricane without disturbing its passengers. Accommodations were plush, the meals—served on fine china, naturally—were sumptuous, and no one ever got seasick. Prospects for the future of the airship seemed so bright that a German-American international company was formed, with plans to put four Zeppelins into weekly service across the Atlantic.

breakdown

Details of the Crash

The 1937 flying season began for the *Hindenburg* in March with the first of twenty planned flights to Rio de Janeiro. The United States had agreed to a May-through-November schedule of eighteen round-trip flights between Frankfurt and Lakehurst, and the first of these was booked for a May 3, 1937, departure. Despite its past full bookings, the passenger list for this flight totaled only thirty-six, with an unusually large contingent of German officers and trainees aboard. At the same time, the Zeppelin company continued with plans to launch the *Hindenburg*'s sister ship, the LZ 130, in October 1937.

Max Pruss, a former captain of the *Graf Zeppelin*, was in command as the *Hindenburg* cast off at 8:15 P.M. from the newly completed Rhein-Main World Airport near Frankfurt. The airship headed north and reached a cruising speed of nearly ninety miles-per-hour, but encountered a strong headwind off the coast of Ireland. The ship did not fly over France or England for political reasons. It reached the North Atlantic by flying over The Netherlands and then gliding down the English Channel. Its arrival time at Lakehurst was to be May 6 at 6:00 A.M., but with its speed cut to sixty miles-per-hour by headwinds, the arrival time was rescheduled. The airship's progress was further delayed as the weather deteriorated around Newfoundland. By the time the ship reached the New England coast, its speed had slowed to thirty-seven miles-per-hour. By this time its expected arrival time had been pushed back to 6:00 P.M. on May 6, a full twelve hours behind schedule.

Finally, after an unusually tedious voyage during which bad weather shrouded most of the spectacular sights below, the *Hindenburg* came upon the field at Lakehurst from the southwest just after 7:00 P.M., after hovering along the coastline for several hours in order to wait out poor local weather conditions, including an approaching cold front. This front was followed by heavy showers and a thunderstorm, but by 7:00 P.M., conditions had improved and Lakehurst told the ship to come in.

At 7:08 P.M., the *Hindenburg* emerged from the clouds at six hundred and fifty feet, roaring over Lakehurst at full speed. The looming behemoth passed over the field and made a sweeping turn to the left so it could approach the mooring from the west. As the airship returned over the field at 7:10, the shifting winds induced Pruss to make another, much sharper turn to the right, for a northerly approach. With the cloud ceiling at between two thousand and three thousand feet and a light rain falling, lightning was noticed in the distant south and southwest. Pruss then valved off some hydrogen, which lowered the ship a bit, and dropped some water ballast. By maneuvering his four engines, he skillfully brought the huge ship to a complete, dead-level stop in midair at 7:20 P.M.

At 7:21, with the ship at about two hundred feet altitude and about seven hundred feet from the mooring mast, crewmen first dropped the

With the cloud ceiling at between two thousand and three thousand feet and a light rain falling, lightning was noticed in the distance.

starboard rope handling lines for the ground crew. The port lines tumbled out of the sky shortly thereafter. The landing proceeded normally as the ground crew continued to couple the manila rope lines to the corresponding lines on the ground. Hovering between one hundred and thirty-five and one hundred and fifty feet of altitude in the night air, the airship's outer cover suddenly began to flutter and its skin seemed to ripple. About fifteen seconds later—at 7:25 P.M.—a small tongue of flame emerged from where the fluttering had occurred and a reddish glow was noticed by the spectators below. In the control car, the crew felt a shudder in the ship's frame, while at the same time, one of the crew in another part of the ship heard a muffled pop that sounded like a gas burner igniting on a stove.

Flames shot up through promenades that acted like chimneys, shooting flames out the airship's nose "as from a blowtorch."

Within seconds, all of these subtle phenomena were followed by a geyser of flaming hydrogen that erupted out of the *Hindenburg's* top, just forward of the upper fin. In a few more seconds, almost the entire stern was engulfed in flames and began to drop. Inside the control car, Pruss reached instinctively to drop the ballast and raise the ship, but instead made the split-second decision to let the ship's tail section crash to the ground, reasoning that reaching the ground was the only hope for the passengers to scramble out alive. As the great ship's tail dropped to the ground, its nose pointed skyward. Flames shot up through promenades that acted like chimneys, shooting flames out the airship's nose "as from a blowtorch." As the entire ship dissolved in flames, its framework quickly collapsed. To horrified onlookers the ship had been transformed with mind-numbing speed. From the time the first flame was noticed until the entire ship lay smoldering on the ground, only thirty-two seconds had elapsed.

The inferno that ensued killed thirteen passengers, twenty-two crewmen, and one civilian ground handler. Of the ninety-seven people on board, sixty-two amazingly survived. Life or death was simply a matter of chance. Some men in the tail walked out virtually untouched as the flames in that section went upward. A cabin boy was saved by a deluge of ballast water. An acrobat used his professional skills to hang from a window as the ship fell, letting go at a safe height. Others were saved by the heroic actions of the American ground crew. Captain Pruss performed gallantly as well, returning to the inferno several times to help survivors get out. The flames of the *Hindenburg* burned amidst the chaos of Lakehurst for three hours.

More than any other airship disaster, the *Hindenburg* crash remains the most mysterious and most controversial. Explanations abound as to what caused the calamity, but over the years they have narrowed down to two major theories: ignition of hydrogen by sabotage or by some natural source of electricity. Investigations by both the Germans and Americans yielded no evidence of sabotage, although some argue that it was in the interest of both countries to downplay any embarrassing hint of sabotage. A book published in 1962 even gave the name of the individual on board who supposedly did the deed.

But to this day, no conclusive proof has been offered that the airship was destroyed in this manner.

The skeleton of the Hindenburg after it crashed. This disaster effectively ended airship travel.

There are several, more natural explanations that attempt to account for the disaster, and it was one of these that the German and American investigating teams chose to endorse. Both teams of experts concluded that the airship's hydrogen was probably ignited by some type of atmospheric electrical discharge. The Americans argued that St. Elmo's Fire—a discharge of electricity that sometimes occurs and manifests itself as an eerie bluish glow that appears on the prominent parts of a ship or aircraft in stormy weather—ignited the hydrogen. The German investigators charged that the manila ropes dropped to the ground became wet, resulting in the airship "becoming a piece of ground elevated into the atmosphere." This equalization of the static charges between the ship and the ground meant that the *Hindenburg* would itself discharge electricity into the atmosphere, a phenomenon known as "brush discharge."

Finally, both natural cause arguments assume that free hydrogen was loose somewhere around the ship, available to be ignited. Investigators pointed to the fluttering cover as an indicator that hydrogen was escaping just prior to the accident. The ship's tail-heaviness, witnessed by most just before the explosion, supports this contention. This lack of lift may have indicated a possible hydrogen loss. The final, official judgment was that the

Hindenburg was destroyed accidentally by unusual but natural causes. Hugo Eckener agreed with this verdict, but Captain Pruss argued for sabotage. While the debate regarding the reason for the airship' demise continues even today, a recent bit of information favors the natural causes point of view. It has been noted that the *Hindenburg* had been painted with a different type of aircraft dope, or preparatory substance; many feel this new kind of dope may have contributed to the circumstances that created the deadly spark.

Impact

At the time of the *Hindenburg* crash, the German airship *Graf Zeppelin* was flying back from Rio. On its arrival in Germany, the ship was grounded until the cause of the crash in New Jersey could be determined. No Zeppelin ever made another flight. The end of the *Hindenburg* marked the end of hydrogen as a lifting medium and the end of airship travel.

On radio, the heartbreaking, raw emotion expressed by newsman Herb Morrison— "Oh, the humanity and all the passengers!"— conveyed the horror and pity felt by all the onlookers on that scorched airfield.

Despite the fact that for more than a quarter century commercial Zeppelins had carried fifty thousand passengers without a fatality, airship travel quickly came to be regarded as untenable. Much of the impact of the crash must surely be attributed to the fact that the disaster was the most thoroughly documented crash of its time. The sights and sounds of that terrible evening were graphically documented on film and quickly disseminated over and over again in every movie newsreel. On radio, the heartbreaking, raw emotion expressed by newsman Herb Morrison—"Oh, the humanity and all the passengers!"—conveyed the horror and pity felt by all the onlookers on that scorched airfield.

The spectacular burning of the *Hindenburg* had an impact on public opinion that far exceeded the fatality count. Despite the fact that nearly two-thirds of the people on board survived, its name became linked forever with tragedy and sudden, terrifying technological disaster. The newsreel footage of those towering flames guaranteed that the stain on the image of airship travel would be a permanent one. Two years after the *Hindenburg*'s last flight, an airplane carried its first paying passenger across the Atlantic.

Where to Learn More

Dick, Harold G. *The Golden Age of the Great Passenger Airships, Graf Zeppelin and Hindenburg.* Smithsonian Institution Press, 1985.

Hoehling, Adolph A. *Who Destroyed the Hindenburg?* Little Brown, 1962.

"Sky Horror: Hindenburg Crash." *Literary Digest*, May 15, 1937, pp. 10–12.

Payne, Lee. *Lighter Than Air: An Illustrated History of the Airship.* Orion Books, 1991, pp. 218–29.

"Oh, the Humanity! Hindenburg Disaster." *Time*, May 17, 1937, p. 35ff.

Vaeth, J. Gordon. "What Happened to the Hindenburg?" *Weatherwise*, December 1990, pp. 315–22.

breakdown

TWA Super-Constellation and United Airlines DC-7 collision

Grand Canyon, Arizona **1956**

Two airliners collided in empty airspace—an "impossible" accident that killed 128 people and led to the creation of the Federal Aviation Administration.

Background

by Robert J. Serling

On June 30, 1956, the Civil Aeronautics Administration's inadequacies—which stemmed largely from its lack of independent status and rather feeble budget requests—were laid bare in a few terrifying seconds over the Grand Canyon when two airliners collided. All of the 128 people aboard the two planes perished. At the time, it was the highest single-accident death toll in the history of commercial aviation.

Back in the early days of commercial aviation, the nation's airlines operated their own air traffic control system, which was a relatively simple task. As late as 1932, the entire U.S. airline industry—twenty-four carriers, most of them minuscule—operated fewer than 700 daily flights with a fleet of only 450 planes, 80 percent of them single-engine aircraft. (By comparison, some 2,000 transports now operate more than 14,000 daily flights.)

It was not until 1936 that the federal government took over responsibility for America's civilian air traffic control, under an agency called the Bureau of Air Commerce. In 1941, jurisdiction over the nation's civil airways came into the hands of the Civil Aeronautics Administration (CAA), which, like the old Bureau of Air Commerce, was part of the Department of Commerce.

As a relatively small subordinate agency, the CAA was beholden to Commerce for all funding, a budgetary dependency that worried the entire airline industry. With air traffic booming after World War II, more than one air safety expert warned that the money-starved CAA was trying to operate a hopelessly antiquated and potentially dangerous air traffic control system. "We're tracking three hundred mile-an-hour airplanes with radar designed to track twenty-knot battleships," one official complained.

Details of the Collision

The aircraft involved in the crash that first alerted the country to the dangers of the air traffic control system were a Trans World Airlines triple-tailed Super-G Constellation and a United Airlines DC-7. Both flights had left Los Angeles within minutes of each other, heading east and flying "off airways"—using airspace uncontrolled by Air Route Traffic Control (ARTC) centers. Both captains had chosen such routing because the controlled airways were either too clogged or not as direct, and their decision was not unusual given ARTC's lack of personnel and proper facilities. Their flight plans, therefore, specified that they would be operating under visual flight rules (VFR), which meant they would assume the responsibility for avoiding other traffic themselves.

The TWA captain had filed a flight plan that put him at a lower altitude than the United plane. But after his Constellation reached its assigned cruising altitude, it flew into clouds and the captain received permission to go one thousand feet higher. This put the TWA "Connie" above the cloud cover, at 21,000 feet—which also happened to be United's assigned cruising altitude.

TWA was told the United DC-7 also was at 21,000 feet, but the undermanned ARTC centers along the route failed to warn United that another flight had been cleared to the same altitude. ARTC, busy with traffic in controlled airspace, could not accept responsibility for flights using uncontrolled airways, so the two airliners ended up bisecting an angle of death. One controller admitted later he had noticed that the estimated arrival time of both flights over a checkpoint near the Grand Canyon was identical. But the harassed controller, occupied with handling his own traffic, gave the fatal coincidence no further thought.

The two planes, each traveling at approximately three hundred miles per hour, collided at an estimated angle of thirty-five degrees. Searchers later found one of the Constellation's tails with red, white, and blue paint marks, obviously from a DC-7 propeller, which had such colors on its tips. Another search party located a rear cargo door from the TWA plane that also carried red, white, and blue gouges. Civil Aeronautics Board (CAB) investigators deduced that the DC-7 had hit the Connie, although no blame was attached to this finding—the unsuspecting United pilots did not know TWA had been cleared to their own altitude.

Because the collision occurred in wide-open airspace and in relatively clear weather, it was considered to have been an "impossible accident." But it was far from that—it was an accident just waiting to happen. In fact, the CAB's subsequent investigation steered clear of putting the majority of blame on the two flight crews, and indirectly put it where it belonged: the CAA, Commerce, and a parsimonious Congress—all of whom had allowed aviation technology to outpace an obsolete, overworked air traffic control system.

Impact

The CAB spent almost ten months investigating the Grand Canyon collision. Its final, understated verdict—"that the pilots did not see each other in time"—was akin to saying that the accident happened because it happened.

But the board went far beyond this mundane conclusion in listing six definite or possible contributing factors that told the real story of the Grand Canyon catastrophe:

1. Limited cockpit visibility.

2. Intervening clouds that may have temporarily obscured vision.

3. Preoccupation with normal cockpit duties.

4. Physiological limits to human vision.

5. Insufficient en route air traffic advisory information due to inadequate facilities and lack of personnel in Air Traffic Control.

6. Preoccupation with unrelated cockpit duties, such as trying to provide passengers with a more scenic view.

The last seemed an unfair charge against the TWA and UAL flight crews alike; the Grand Canyon that day was covered by low-hanging clouds and haze, and it was hardly likely that either flight crew were engaged "in unrelated cockpit duties." However, this did not prevent one congressman, who arrived on the scene a few days after the accident, from flatly announcing that "the collision was caused by one or both pilots sightseeing."

The CAB's other suggested causal factors made far more sense. Airline pilots had frequently and fervently complained about poor cockpit visibility in the transports of that era, and the DC-7 and Constellation were no exceptions to such criticism. "You might as well be trying to see out of a phone

booth," one captain remarked. And the high speeds of airliners flying under visual flight rule conditions were another invitation to disaster: a 600 mile-per-hour combined closure speed is faster than the velocity of a .45 caliber bullet as it leaves a gun muzzle.

The board had plenty of evidence on the potential hazards of distracting cockpit workload, inadequate cockpit visibility, and the limitations of the human eye—which, in effect, has the same constricted vision as the cockpit itself. There is no way to see directly above, below, or behind from an airplane flight deck, just as you cannot see the top, base, or back of your head.

In addition, Air Force tests demonstrated that if a DC-7 pilot spotted a Constellation two miles away coming at him head-on at 300 miles per hour, he had only one-tenth of a second to decide on evasive action. At a distance of one mile, there was no time left. The Air Force tests disclosed another phenomenon: at high altitudes in clear weather, a pilot actually suffers "empty field myopia," which means he becomes temporarily nearsighted and tends to concentrate on a location less than six feet in front of the cockpit. But the CAB's fifth suggested contributing factor—the inadequacies of the ATC system—was the most damning of all, and the one that had the most repercussions. The CAB's final report on the collision merely referred to the system's inadequacies without pinpointing why they existed. It was not necessary,

however, because the airlines, air safety experts, responsible lawmakers, the White House, and the media were in unanimous agreement on the real reason for the Grand Canyon tragedy.

The CAA had been too long starved for adequate funding to modernize the air traffic control system. Subservient to its parent Department of Commerce, its budget requests were often too modest, and what money it did ask for usually fell under Commerce's economy axe. Even while Congress was debating solutions, two more mid-air collisions occurred—a United DC-7 and an Air Force fighter over Las Vegas, and a Capital Viscount and National Guard fighter near Brunswick, Maryland. Both military planes were operating under VFR, and the accidents exposed another ARTC weakness—the danger of mixing VFR and controlled traffic, especially when the VFR flights involved swift military planes.

At the time of the Grand Canyon collision, the U.S. airlines were only two years away from inaugurating jet service. They would soon be operating aircraft with closure speeds upward of 1,000 miles per hour, and they justifiably asked that something be done to ensure safe separation of such traffic.

In August 1958, Congress passed and President Eisenhower quickly signed into law the Federal Aviation Act, which established an independent Federal Aviation Administration (FAA) and provided it with almost total

One of the first on-scene photos, showing the fuselage of the TWA Constellation. It apparently was hit by the United DC-7 after both were cleared for the same cruising altitude.

jurisdiction over civil and military air traffic alike. The new agency was given the necessary regulatory authority and funding to modernize air traffic control and drastically expand controlled airspace. And the FAA administrator reported only to the president of the United States.

Ironically, the chief motivation behind this massive reform—the establishment of a fully independent agency with its own budget and virtually unlimited powers—was to be tossed aside only eight years later. In 1966, Congress, with the enthusiastic blessing of the Johnson administration, placed the FAA under a new Department of Transportation. Not only did this relegate the air agency to the same subordinate status as the old CAA, but in the opinion of most aviation observers, it also cost the FAA much of its effectiveness. But by then, the Grand Canyon tragedy was just another forgotten chapter in aviation history.

Where to Learn More

"All 128 on 2 Airlines Found Dead." *New York Times*, July 2, 1956, pp. 1, 14.

"Apparent United-TWA Collision Highlights Traffic-Control Problem." *Aviation Weekly*, July 9, 1956, pp. 39–40.

"CAB Begins Hearings on Mid-Air Collision." *Aviation Weekly*, August 5, 1956, p. 463.

"CAB Issues Report on Canyon Collision." *Aviation Weekly*, April 22, 1957, pp. 33–34.

"Disaster in the Desert." *Newsweek*, October 8, 1956, p. 51.

"Grand Canyon Disaster: Averages Catch Up." *Business Weekly*, July 7, 1956, pp. 28–29.

Hotz, R. "We Are All to Blame." *Aviation Weekly*, July 16, 1956, p. 21.

"Identifying Crash Bodies in Grand Canyon." *Science News*, July 14, 1956, p. 22.

"Into the Thunderhead." *Newsweek*, July 9, 1956, p. 25.

Lewis, C. "Eyewitnesses Describe TWA-UAL Crash." *Aviation Weekly*, August 13, 1956, p. 38.

"Painted Desert." *Time*, July 9, 1956, p. 18.

"Perilous Searching Operation: Grand Canyon Crash." *Life*, July 16, 1956, pp. 19–25.

"Visual Failure Blamed in Canyon Crash." *Aviation Weekly*, May 13, 1957, p. 113.

Apollo 1 capsule fire

Cape Canaveral, Florida 1967

A wiring malfunction led to a flash fire during a ground test, causing the deaths of three astronauts and exposing the need for higher design, manufacturing, and safety standards at NASA.

by Leonard C. Bruno

Background

On January 27, 1967, at the National Aeronautics and Space Administration (NASA) base in Cape Canaveral, Florida, three astronauts died during a routine ground test of the Apollo command module. Although the exact cause of the fire that killed them remained undetermined, it probably began with an electrical arc caused by poor wiring design and installation. Once some combustible materials ignited, the fire was fed by the pure oxygen under pressure in the module. The astronauts had no equipment to suppress the fire, and were unable to open the six-bolt escape hatch in the short time before the flames engulfed them.

With the successful completion of NASA's two-man Gemini program, AS-204 was to be the first manned Apollo mission. The United States was involved in a race with the Soviet Union to land men on the Moon, and the three-man Apollo capsules were a critical part of the American plan to accomplish this feat. The AS-204 crew was named in August 1966. It consisted of two space veterans, Virgil I. "Gus" Grissom and Edward H. White, and one new astronaut, Roger B. Chaffee. NASA planned for the crew to make a December 1966 "shakedown" flight of up to two weeks in Earth's orbit. This flight would test the Apollo's new command and service modules (CSM) built by North American Aviation, which had not yet been deployed on a manned mission. Following a series of mechanical problems, however, the flight date was postponed until February 1967.

In preparation for this flight, the astronauts were to complete a four-phase ground test of the CSM's systems. One phase of this process required that the astronauts enter the command module, which was perched on a *Saturn IB* launch vehicle and emptied of fuel; seal and pressurize the module; and then begin a "plugs out" test to see if the spacecraft could run on its internal power system.

The command module was designed to function in space, and therefore to be subject to greater internal than external pressure. To simulate this condition as closely as possible, NASA's engineers planned to pressurize the cabin with pure oxygen at approximately 16 pounds per square inch, rather than the normal 5 pounds per square inch of air. Although pure oxygen itself will not ignite, it can, when pressurized, rapidly feed an existing fire. No one, however, considered a cabin fire likely. There was no fire extinguisher in the capsule, and since the launch vehicle was not fueled, the fire crews were on standby rather than maximum alert. Furthermore, no one considered the 90 seconds it took to open the new six-bolt escape hatch to be excessive; in fact, most experts were convinced that the alternate quick-release hatches were accident-prone and dangerous.

NASA's apparent complacency about safety precautions stemmed from the fact that, in six years of manned space flights, no astronaut had died in the course of a mission. The "plugs out" test, conducted with an unfueled launch vehicle, seemed both routine and low-risk.

Details of the Fire

On January 27, 1967, Gus Grissom, Edward White, and Roger Chaffee undertook the "plugs out" test on the new Apollo command and service modules. By 1:00 P.M. on that Friday afternoon, the three-man crew had crawled through the open hatch and assumed their flight positions. After two hours of tests conducted with the hatch open, the capsule was sealed and the cabin pressurized to 16.2 pounds per square inch of pure oxygen. The crew then went through a practice countdown and ran simulation tests for more than three hours, regularly interrupted by minor problems.

Shortly after 6:00 P.M., fifteen minutes before lift-off was to be simulated, the spacecraft switched to internal power. NASA engineers called a hold

to check on some problem, and the astronauts waited yet again. It had been a long day—the astronauts had been strapped in their couches some five and one-half hours. Suddenly, at 6:31 P.M., telemetry from the spacecraft indicated that a major short had occurred somewhere in the nearly twelve miles of electrical wiring packed into the command module. Less than ten seconds later, Roger Chaffee made an almost casual report: "Fire, I smell fire."

The spacecraft was not equipped with internal cameras, but a camera was focused on its porthole. At the first report of fire, all the camera operator could see was a sudden bright glow. The operator then saw flames flickering across the porthole and Edward White's hands reaching above his head to get at the bolts securing the hatch. The cameraman saw a lot of movement, and then another pair of arms struggling with the hatch. Soon, dark smoke completely obscured the scene. The last sound from the astronauts was a now frantic cry from Roger Chaffee: "We've got a bad fire—let's get out . . . we're burning up!" Seconds after this last transmission, the tremendous pressure inside the cabin split the capsule open, and a blaze of flame gushed out. Only 18 seconds had passed from the first call of fire to this explosion.

Help was close at hand, but the control personnel in the White Room were momentarily held back by the explosion. Due to the thick smoke, it then

The last sound from the astronauts was a now frantic cry from Roger Chaffee: "We've got a bad fire—let's get out . . . we're burning up!" Seconds after this last transmission, the tremendous pressure inside the cabin split the capsule open, and a blaze of flame gushed out. Only 18 seconds had passed from the first call of fire to this explosion.

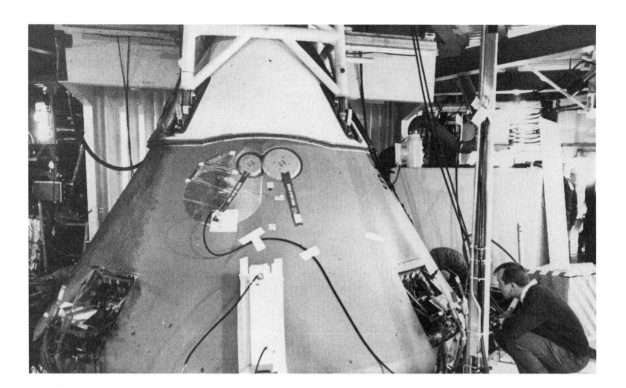

took five men working in shifts five and a half minutes to remove three separate hatches: the boost protective cover that shielded the command module during launch, the ablative hatch, and the inner hatch. Inside the capsule, once the smoke thinned, they found the three dead men. Chaffee was still strapped onto his couch, and the bodies of White and Grissom were lying close together below the hatch. White's handprint was outlined in ash on the hatch.

Official autopsies would later identify the cause of the deaths as asphyxiation, observing that although each astronaut had suffered serious burns, these were not fatal. However, the heat during those few terrible seconds had been so intense—the holes burned in aluminum tubing indicate temperatures of at least 760 degrees Celsius—that the astronauts' suits had melted and fused with the molten nylon and Velcro inside the capsule, forming a synthetic liquid that solidified as it cooled. Doctors arrived fourteen minutes after the first alarm of fire, but it took them seven hours to remove the bodies; those of White and Grissom had been welded to the capsule floor.

Impact

NASA's entire multi-billion dollar effort to put a man on the Moon virtually came to a standstill as a special Board of Inquiry sought explanations for the accident. On February 22, 1967, almost a month after the disaster, a seven-man review board issued an interim report stating that although no definite cause of the fire could be established, the most likely origin was an electrical malfunction. A fourteen-volume report of some three thousand pages came out in early April; this report specified that the fire was probably caused by an electrical arc that occurred in the vicinity of the environmental control equipment under Grissom's couch.

The full report was highly critical of the conditions that contributed to the fatal accident. It indicated that the some of the wiring unaffected by the fire revealed "numerous examples of poor installation, design, and workmanship." Moreover, the capsule was loaded with highly combustible materials such as Velcro and the nylon netting used to prevent loose objects from floating around in the zero gravity of space. In its conclusion, the report implied that disaster may have been inevitable given the substandard manufacturing procedures and the lack of safety measures.

The critique of NASA at least implicit in this report was not lost on Congress, and a House space subcommittee opened hearings on April 7, 1967, to assess the space program and the Apollo accident. Most observers decided that NASA had been pushing the Apollo program too hard and too fast; there simply had not been enough time to thoroughly test all its systems. The Apollo spacecraft was still an unproven and evolving craft, having undergone 623 changes between August 1966, when North American Aviation first delivered it to NASA, and the fatal accident in January 1967. By the end of the Congressional hearings, the prevailing view was that making limited adjustments to the Apollo capsule and allowing the space program to continue on its timetable would be ill-advised. An exhaustive review of the entire spacecraft was necessary, however long it took.

NASA was therefore obligated to step back and reassess the full scope of its systems and procedures, particularly in terms of safety standards. NASA took good advantage of this enforced break from its rivalry with the Soviet space program, and the outcome of a year and a half's worth of reevaluation was a completely redesigned Apollo command module. Some 1,500 modifications were made to the command module, resulting in a considerably more secure and fireproof vehicle.

First, NASA installed high-quality wiring. Flameproof coatings were applied over all wire connections, plastic switches were replaced by metal ones, and soldering became more meticulous. Almost all flammable materials inside the module were removed. A new, fire-resistant material known as Beta cloth was developed for spacesuits. Instead of igniting at 500 degrees Celsius, as did the old suits made of Nomex, the Beta cloth suits could withstand temperatures of more than 800 degrees Celsius.

A considerable debate over the use of pure oxygen resulted in a compromise in the favor of safety. When they were in space, the crew would breathe pure oxygen at five pounds per square-inch. For ground testing and launching, however, the cabin would be filled with a mixture of oxygen and nitrogen at sea-level pressure. To prevent this nitrogen from causing "the bends" (nitrogen narcosis or poisoning), the astronauts would breathe only through their spacesuits, which contained pure oxygen, until the cabin had been purged of nitrogen.

One irony of the Apollo accident was that Grissom, White, and Chaffee's workday was scheduled to end with a test of the new six-bolt escape hatch. This system had replaced the controversial quick-release, explosively charged hatch that had been used on both Mercury and Gemini spacecraft. In 1961, a quick-release hatch had blown prematurely and almost sank Grissom and his *Mercury Liberty Bell 7* when he landed in the Atlantic. The new Apollo design returned to a quick-escape system, but this improved hatch took only twelve seconds to release and opened outward so that internal pressure would not affect its functioning. Among the revelations of the full report on the Apollo accident was that even if the astronauts had managed to undo the six-bolt hatch, their efforts would have been futile. When the internal pressure exceeded the external pressure by more than 0.25 pounds per square inch, the hatch, which swung inward, became impossible to open.

If good can be said to come of such a disaster, it was that the American government and industry coalition became conscious of the need to raise design, workmanship, and safety standards. The fire both forced and enabled NASA to step back from its politically controlled timetables and methodically build the high-performance spacecraft that ultimately proved capable of putting a man on the Moon.

Where to Learn More

Bond, Peter. *Heroes in Space: From Gagarin to Challenger*. Basil Blackwell, 1987.

"Electrical Malfunction Termed a Likely Source of Apollo Fire." *New York Times*, February 26, 1967, p. 39.

McAleer, Neil. *The OMNI Space Almanac: A Complete Guide to the Space Age*. World Almanac, 1987.

Murray, Charles, and Catherine Bly Cox. *Apollo: The Race to the Moon*. Simon and Schuster, 1989.

Wheeler, Keith. "Disaster—The Harsh Schoolmaster." *Life*, January 26, 1968, pp. 56–59.

Wilford, John Noble. "Apollo Fire Review Board Finds 'Many Deficiencies'; Calls for Safety Moves." *New York Times*, April 10, 1967, p. 1.

> Among the revelations of the full report on the Apollo accident was that even if the astronauts had managed to undo the six-bolt hatch, their efforts would have been futile. When the internal pressure exceeded the external pressure by more than 0.25 pounds per square inch, the hatch, which swung inward, became impossible to open.

breakdown

Soyuz 11 reentry disaster

1971

A cabin seal malfunction during reentry caused the deaths of three Soviet cosmonauts and represented a significant technical setback for the Soyuz manned spacecraft program.

Background

by Leonard C. Bruno

After occupying the first orbiting space station for over three weeks and achieving many scientific and technological feats, the three-man *Soyuz 11* crew was killed in the process of reentering the Earth's atmosphere. While separating from the service module, explosive bolts misfired and caused a pressure equalization valve to open prematurely, exposing the command module to the vacuum of space. The Soviet crew—who were not wearing full spacesuits—were unable to close the valve manually before they lost consciousness and died due to the rapid decompression of the cabin. Their spacecraft was on automatic control, and its reentry and touchdown proceeded normally. The ground recovery crew, however, found the cosmonauts dead inside.

By 1971, the Soviets had given up attempts to compete with the United States in terms of manned lunar landings, and had redirected their efforts to establishing the first manned laboratory in space. To this effect, the Soviets launched the long-awaited *Salyut 1* on April 19, 1971. This 20-ton laboratory

All three crew members of the Soyuz 11 *died during reentry when a pressure equalization valve opened early, causing rapid decompression of the cabin.*

was 65.5 feet long and 13 feet wide, and was placed into a circular orbit about 200 miles above the Earth. *Salyut 1* was powered by two pairs of giant solar panels that looked like wings, and was divided into several different modules, three of which were pressurized and habitable.

Four days after launching the *Salyut 1* space laboratory, the Soviets sent *Soyuz 10* into space. Most Western observers assumed that its three-man crew would occupy the orbiting space station, but the spacecraft remained docked to *Salyut 1* for only five and a half hours, and returned to Earth just two days after it had been launched. Soviet officials characteristically claimed that the *Soyuz 10* mission had achieved its goals, but most Western experts assumed that some technical malfunction had prevented the cosmonauts from entering the space station as planned.

It was no surprise, then, when the three-man crew of *Soyuz 11* was launched at 7:25 A.M. Moscow time on June 6, 1971, and approximately 24 hours later docked beside and entered the *Salyut 1* space laboratory. The crew of Georgi Dobrovolsky, Vladislav Volkov, and Viktor Patsayev substituted for the better-trained *Soyuz 10* crew, who could not undertake the mission because one of its members was ill; of the *Soyuz 11* crew, only Dobrovolsky had previously flown in space. The *Soyuz 11* rendezvous and docking procedure was especially slow and exhausting, but this second crew either did not encounter or resolved whatever technical problems the *Soyuz 10* mission experienced, and the space station was occupied for the first time.

Once inside, the crew transferred the station to a higher, more stable orbit and spent the next three days preparing it for extended occupancy. The Soviets took great pride in deploying and manning the first successful space station, and publicized this accomplishment as more significant than the American manned lunar landings. The *Soyuz 11* crew performed a broad range of scientific experiments in space, which included cultivating a small garden and conducting medical and biological experiments on themselves. They made observations of celestial targets using a special astrophysical observatory, and took thousands of photographs of the Earth.

In their stay of more than three weeks in space, the *Soyuz 11* crew had carried out a highly successful mission in terms of both achieving scientific goals and enhancing Soviet prestige. The cosmonauts were immediately transformed into national heroes. When the crew were instructed by ground control to leave the station they had occupied and worked in for a record span of nearly 24 days, they could look back on a mission that had proceeded almost flawlessly. With complete confidence, the Soviet government organized official celebrations for the cosmonauts' return to Earth.

Details of the Disaster

On June 29, the *Soyuz 11* crew prepared the *Salyut 1* space station for automatic operation and transferred back to their spacecraft. At 9:28 P.M. on June 29, they undocked from the station and changed from full-pressure suits into space-saving woolen flight suits and leather helmets. At 1:35 A.M. on June 30, the crew strapped themselves into their couches and fired their retrorockets to deorbit. Dobrovolsky reported at this time that "Everything is satisfactory on board. Our condition is excellent. We are ready to land." Twelve minutes later, additional rockets were fired to separate the spacecraft's command module, in which the crew would reenter the Earth's atmosphere, from the service module.

Twelve pyrotechnic bolts were designed to fire sequentially just before reentry to complete the separation of the two modules. These devices, however, malfunctioned and fired simultaneously. The combined explosion generated severe vibrations that in turn caused a pressure equalization valve to release a seal and open prematurely. This valve normally would open at low altitudes within the Earth's atmosphere, just prior to touchdown, to equalize the command module and external air pressures.

The opening of this valve while the *Soyuz 11* spacecraft was still 120 miles above the Earth, in the vacuum of space, caused two things to happen. First, the air shooting out from the spacecraft's base skewed the vehicle off course. This was not in itself hazardous, since the spacecraft's stabilization rockets would fire automatically to return the vehicle to a proper reentry course. The second result of the escaping air, however, was a sudden decompression of the command module that immediately endangered the cosmonauts' lives.

The cosmonauts must have become aware of the leak almost instantly, and one crew member attempted to crank the valve shut manually. But he simply did not have enough time, and only halfway succeeded. The manual valve crank was difficult to reach because it was situated in the floor of the cabin below one of the crew member's couches. Once the crank was located, it would take well over 60 seconds to close the valve manually. Fifteen seconds after the valve had opened, half the cabin air had vented out. When only thirty seconds had passed, all the air was gone from the cabin. The three men at this point would succumb to anoxia (lack of air) and suffer the fatal effects of the "bends," which would cause their blood to boil as the nitrogen in their tissues turned into gas. Once these physical reactions set in, the *Soyuz 11* crew lost consciousness and died. The air pressure in the cabin remained at zero for eleven and a half minutes.

During this time, the spacecraft's other systems operated automatically and took the cabin through reentry as planned. After the build-up of G forces abated, a drogue parachute opened and the main canopy deployed. A recovery beacon sent signals to the ground crews. Braking rockets then slowed the spacecraft's descent even further, and *Soyuz 11* fell gently on the flat ground of Kazakhstan at 2:17 A.M. on June 30, 1971. The record-setting space flight had lasted 23 days, 18 hours, 21 minutes, and 48 seconds. Although air had by now seeped back through the open valve into the command module, it was much too late to save the three men inside.

Helicopter recovery crews sped to the landed craft within minutes, aware that an ominous silence had been maintained since the command module separated from the service module. Despite this omen, the recovery crews were unprepared for what they discovered after they climbed aboard the eight-foot, bell-shaped capsule and opened its hatch. Expecting to greet three jubilant heroes, they found instead the dead men—two still in their couches, and another huddled in a corner. After hours of silence, the Soviet news agency announced the cosmonauts' deaths—the first human casualties in outer space—to the world. The effect of this disaster on the Soviet people has been compared to America's reaction to the Kennedy assassination.

breakdown

Impact

Although the Soviets would not ordinarily release details about such an accident, a planned cooperative space venture with the United States compelled them to divulge what had happened to the National Aeronautics and Space Administration (NASA). In this cooperative program, called the Apollo-Soyuz Test Project (ASTP), American and Soviet spacecraft were to link up in space and exchange crews. The Americans demanded to know what went wrong because they would be occupying a Soyuz spacecraft; the Soviets ultimately acquiesced and gave NASA a detailed report on the disaster. NASA then verified this information by analyzing the telemetry data provided by the Soviets.

As a result of the accident, the Soyuz spacecraft once again became a two-man craft. The use of spacesuits had been eliminated earlier in the Soyuz program to add room for a third cosmonaut. Making room for an extra man by dispensing with a redundant life-support system proved to be a fatal expediency; had the crew of *Soyuz 11* been wearing full spacesuits, they would have survived the loss of their cabin environment.

With the Soyuz program returning to two-men crews, the cosmonauts would wear full-pressure spacesuits during ascent and reentry. This change implied a complete reconceptualization of the Soyuz spacecraft (including a redesigned pressure valve system) that delayed the Soviet manned space program for approximately one year. The *Soyuz 11* disaster also led to a top-echelon personnel change: General Nikolai Kamanin was forced to retire as head of the Soviet manned space program, and his position was filled by Vladimir A. Shatalov, a former cosmonaut.

The delay in the Soyuz space flight program eventually doomed the orbiting *Salyut 1* space station. Although the station had been boosted into a higher, longer-life orbit before the *Soyuz 11* accident, it could remain self-sufficient only for a limited period of time. Once the Soyuz program had been put on hold and there was no way to occupy the space station and replenish its propellant supply, the *Salyut 1*'s orbit inevitably decayed. The Soviets waited as long as they safely could, but then reluctantly intervened in the station's orbit so that it would reenter the atmosphere and burn up over the Pacific Ocean. This reentry occurred on October 11, 1971; *Salyut 1* had orbited the Earth for 175 days.

In 1972, the Soviets tested their redesigned Soyuz spacecraft in an unmanned flight. *Soyuz 12* finally flew in September 1973, with a two-man crew. It was not until November 1980 that the Soviets would again send a three-man crew into space.

Making room for an extra man by dispensing with a redundant life-support system proved to be a fatal expediency; had the crew of *Soyuz 11* been wearing full spacesuits, they would have survived the loss of their cabin environment.

Where to Learn More

Bond, Peter. *Heroes in Space: From Gagarin to Challenger.* Basil Blackwell, 1987.

"Cause Sought in Soyuz Tragedy." *Aviation Week and Space Technology,* July 5, 1971, pp. 12–15.

Magill, Frank N., ed. *Magill's Survey of Science: Space Exploration Series.* Salem Press, 1989.

Newkirk, Dennis. *Almanac of Soviet Manned Space Flight.* Gulf, 1990.

Oberg, James. "Volkov: Space Engineer." *Space World,* January 1976, pp. 2–21.

"Triumph and Tragedy of *Soyuz 11.*" *Time,* July 12, 1971, pp. 38–39.

breakdown

Challenger explosion

1986

An explosion shortly after launch caused by faulty solid rocket booster seals destroyed the shuttle and killed its crew of seven, forcing a retrenchment of NASA's shuttle program.

Background

On January 28, 1986, the National Aeronautics and Space Administration (NASA) launched STS 51L, the twenty-fifth mission of its space shuttle program, from Cape Canaveral in Florida. The *Challenger* launch received considerable publicity because it carried the first Teacher-in-Space, Christa McAuliffe, who was to broadcast a series of lessons to schoolchildren throughout America. Seventy-three seconds after its launch, however, the shuttle's solid rocket O-rings failed, triggering an explosion that shattered the *Challenger* within full view of thousands of NASA personnel, relatives and friends of the crew, and spectators. The live television broadcast of the launch carried the shock and grief across the nation. After further investigation, it was revealed that the seven-person crew evidently survived the explosion inside a module that detached from the shuttle, but died at impact after a nine-mile free-fall into the Atlantic Ocean.

by Leonard C. Bruno

In 1982, four years before the disastrous *Challenger* mission, a National Security Decision Directive indicated that NASA's highest priority would be to make its shuttle program "fully operational and cost-effective in providing routine access to space." Subsequent directives called for a schedule of up to twenty-four flights a year. But by the end of 1985, NASA had been unable to manage more than nine shuttle flights in any given year. Although the United States was already dispensing with its expendable rockets and scheduling all of its satellites to be launched by shuttle, the nine-billion-dollar shuttle had not yet proven itself to be a cost-efficient, reliable space transportation system or achieved anything like the performance desired.

NASA intended 1986 to be the shuttle program's breakthrough year, reporting in January that it would launch fifteen missions, using all four of its shuttles, during the next twelve months. This total would be the largest to date, and in order to realize this goal NASA would have to initiate the year's launches without delays. The year did not, however, get off to the desired start. After at least seven separate postponements, the first shuttle mission, 61-C, was launched on January 12. When the *Columbia* returned from space on January 18, with bad weather having prolonged the flight, NASA's tight 1986 schedule was already in jeopardy.

In the days that followed, everyone worked feverishly to get the *Challenger* (which had completed its last space mission on November 6, 1985) ready for its January mission. This ambitious mission involved not only the much-publicized Teacher-in-Space broadcasts, but also launches of a Data-Relay Satellite (TDRS) and the high-priority Spartan-Halley comet research observatory. The mission was scheduled to last six days, during which time the Spartan observatory would be recovered from orbit. Because of launch window requirements, the Spartan could be orbited no later than January 31. This inflexible deadline, as well as the sequence of missions in line to follow, led NASA to prepare contingency plans to skip the *Challenger* mission if it could not launch by the end of the month.

Although an afternoon launch was originally planned for the *Challenger*, as recommended by the Spartan project scientists, a mid-morning launch was ultimately scheduled. Ironically, this shift was due to safety considerations. If the *Challenger* was to suffer an "engine-out" during launch, the shuttle would glide to its planned emergency landing site at Casablanca, on the west coast of Africa. NASA argued that an afternoon launch off Florida meant that the emergency landing in Africa would occur at night, a situation that should be avoided because the Casablanca runway was not equipped with lights.

On January 15, 1986, NASA held a Flight Readiness Review for the upcoming *Challenger* mission, linking up the various centers involved with the

breakdown

project via teleconference. All systems were reviewed in detail, from the engineering of the spacecraft to the in-flight responsibilities of the Johnson Space Center in Houston and the Marshall Space Flight Center in Huntsville, Alabama. The conference concluded with a "Go" for launch.

During its earliest moments in flight, the Challenger exhibited no problems or complications.

The seven-person crew chosen for the mission was commanded by Francis Scobee, who had piloted a 1984 shuttle mission. His pilot, Michael Smith, had not previously flown in space. Ellison Onizuka, Ronald McNair, and Judith Resnick, the mission specialists who ran the satellites and experiments, were all experienced space travelers. The payload specialist in charge of the TDRS satellite was Gregory Jarvis, who had no previous space-flight experience. The crew also included the 37-year-old Christa McAuliffe, the Teacher-in-Space from Concord High School in New Hampshire.

The launch of the *Challenger* was originally set for January 22, 1986. The first delays postponed the flight schedule to January 24 and then to January 25. A forecast of bad weather for the 26th held up the mission until Monday the 27th. On this date, a problem with a hatch bolt developed, and by the time this problem was corrected, crosswinds had built up to a dangerous 30 knots. Liftoff had to be rescheduled for Tuesday, although the crew was ready to launch and the shuttle had been fueled.

Details of the Disaster

During the night of January 27, 1986, the temperature at Cape Canaveral dropped to well below freezing. This prompted a late-night review of the prospects for the Challenger launch by NASA managers and contractors, who were becoming increasingly concerned about the cold weather. In fact, no shuttle had ever been launched at a temperature lower than 53 degrees Fahrenheit. During these prelaunch discussions, engineers from Morton Thiokol, a NASA contractor, expressed concern about the O-rings on the shuttle's solid rocket boosters stiffening in the cold and thereby losing their ability to act as a seal. The engineers apparently were unable to make a fully convincing case, particularly since the O-rings had never been tested at low temperatures. With NASA managers pushing for an unequivocal go or no-go, Thiokol managers overruled their own engineers and signed a waiver stating that the solid rocket boosters were safe for launch at the colder temperatures.

During the final hours before launch on January 28, 1986, NASA turned its attention to the ice that had formed on the shuttle and launchpad overnight, when temperatures had ranged from 19 to 29 degrees Fahrenheit. The icicles formed could potentially break off during launch and damage the insulating tiles required to protect the shuttle's reentry into the Earth's

breakdown

atmosphere. The launch was therefore delayed from 9:38 A.M. to 10:38, and then to 11:38. During those hours, inspection teams surveyed the craft's condition and reported no anomalies due to the ice build-up. Finally, at precisely 11:38:00.010 Eastern Standard Time, the *Challenger* launched off from Complex 39B at Cape Canaveral to begin its tenth flight into space.

As the *Challenger* rose into a clear but cold blue sky, no one on the ground or in the shuttle realized that a tongue of flame was extending from the right-hand booster rocket to the giant fuel tank. The crowd of spectators, which included Christa McAuliffe's husband and two children as well as a group of her pupils, cheered at the shuttle's majestic ascent. The vehicle then rolled to align itself on the proper flight path and throttled back its engines. At about 59 seconds into the launch, the plume of flame became evident.

After 64 seconds, a gaping hole had formed in the casing of the booster from which the flame was escaping. At 72 seconds into the flight, the flame loosened the strut that attached the booster to the external tank. At that moment, the cockpit's voice recorder captured the only indication that anyone onboard was ever aware of any serious trouble: pilot Michael Smith uttered, "Uh oh." One second later, the loosened booster rocket slammed into and detached the *Challenger*'s right wing; it then crashed into the fuel tank and set off a massive explosion. The explosion occurred at an altitude of 48,000 feet, with the shuttle traveling at twice the speed of sound.

To many spectators unfamiliar with shuttle launches, the accident seemed like a spectacular staging, or separation of the booster rockets. But the disaster became apparent when the fireball widened and debris began to scatter. The spectators fell silent, spellbound with disbelief. The shuttle itself was no longer visible. Although NASA began rescue operations immediately, the chances of finding survivors were very remote. During the segment of a flight when the solid rocket boosters are thrusting, the crew has no survivable abort options. There was nothing anyone could do if something went wrong at that critical launch moment.

The *Challenger* exploded twenty miles off the coast of Florida, and the force of the explosion pushed its debris to an altitude of twenty miles. For the next hour, incendiary fragments of the shuttle continued to rain down on the recovery forces. Among the worst accidents in the twenty-five year history of manned spaceflight, the *Challenger* disaster marked the first time that American astronauts were lost during a mission. Footage of the explosion, replayed continuously on television, sent shock waves through the nation.

Impact

Within a few days of the *Challenger* disaster, then-President Ronald Reagan eulogized the crew during a nationally televised memorial ceremony at

During these prelaunch discussions, engineers from Morton Thiokol, a NASA contractor, expressed concern about the O-rings on the shuttle's solid rocket boosters stiffening in the cold and thereby losing their ability to act as a seal.

Recalling that fateful morning, Christa McAuliffe's mother wrote "Everyone wondered why a liftoff should be scheduled in such freezing weather. We could see icicles hanging from the shuttle. How could they lift off like this?"—*A Journal for Christa,* 1993.

the Johnson Space Center in Houston. On February 3, 1986, Reagan established a Presidential Commission to investigate the accident, appointing former Secretary of State William B. Rogers as the commission chair.

Six weeks after the disaster, the shuttle's crew module was recovered from the Atlantic ocean floor; the crew members were subsequently buried with full honors. There was considerable speculation as to whether the crew had survived the initial explosion. The evidence gathered by NASA indicates that the crew did survive the breakup and separation, and had begun to take emergency action inside the module. Whether the entire crew remained conscious throughout the two minute, forty-five second free-fall into the ocean remains unknown, but at least two crew members were breathing from emergency air packs that they had activated. The crew module has never been exhibited publicly, but the cabin was essentially unrecognizable in the photographs that were eventually released. The force of the module's impact with the surface of the ocean has been estimated at a 200-G deceleration from 207 miles per hour. This impact compressed the sixteen-and-a-half foot high cabin into a solid mass half its original size and certainly killed anyone still alive in the module. The module's thick windows were shattered, but there was no evidence of fire.

The story of the *Challenger* mission continued in public investigations of NASA and the disaster. The Rogers Commission, which had been charged with assessing the accident and recommending preventative measures, conducted a three-month investigation that involved more than 6,000 people. The commission recorded 15,000 pages of testimony during public and closed hearings, collected 170,000 pages of documents as well as hundreds of photographs, and sponsored independent technical studies. In its methodical review of the events, the commission also evaluated flight records, film evidence, and recovered debris.

On June 6, 1986, the Rogers Commission released its determination that the immediate physical cause of the *Challenger* disaster was "a failure in the joint between the two lower segments of the right Solid Rocket Motor," and specifically "the destruction of the seals that are intended to prevent hot gases from leaking through the joint during the propellant burn." In attributing the disaster to the destruction of these seals, the commission focused on the O-rings. The shuttle's large strap-on booster rockets were built in four sections, and the rubber O-rings were required to seal the sections together. A zinc chromate putty was also used to keep the hot combustion gases on the inside from coming into contact with the rubber rings.

When it checked into the history and performance of this O-ring sealing system, the Rogers Commission was amazed to find that the O-rings had failed regularly, if only partially, on previous shuttle flights. Although both NASA

breakdown

and Thiokol were concerned about the frailty of the seals, they chose to forgo a time-consuming redesign of the system. Both had come to regard O-ring erosion as an acceptable risk because the seal had never completely failed. But when the *Challenger* flew on January 28, the frigid temperatures made the O-rings so brittle that they did not even provisionally seal the joint. Even before the shuttle had cleared the launch tower, hot gas was already "blowing by" the rings.

The Rogers Commission's 256-page report concluded that "the decision to launch the *Challenger* was flawed," and blamed the management structures of both NASA and Thiokol for not allowing critical information to reach the right people. This assessment was seconded by the U.S. House of Representatives' Committee on Science and Technology, which spent two months conducting its own hearings. The congressional committee determined that although the technical problem had been recognized early enough to prevent the disaster, "meeting flight schedules and cutting cost were given a higher priority than flight safety."

These public indictments of NASA had grave consequences. Not only was the nation's confidence in NASA shaken, but its own astronaut corps was extremely disturbed—they had never been consulted or even informed about

This segment of the Challenger's right wing, along with other debris, was recovered by Navy divers about 12 nautical miles northeast of Cape Canaveral and in 70 feet of water.

the dangers that the current sealing-system exposed them to. Allowing astronauts and engineers a greater role in approving launches was among the nine recommendations the Rogers Commission made to NASA. The commission's other recommendations included a complete redesign of the solid rocket booster joints, a review of the astronaut escape systems towards achieving greater safety margins, regulation of the rate of shuttle flights to maximize safety, and a sweeping reform of the shuttle program's management structure.

Following these revelations, several key people left NASA. The loss of personnel included a number of experienced astronauts who resigned due to disillusionment with NASA and frustration over their chances to fly, given the long redesign process now pending. Ultimately, it was not until September 29, 1988, that an American shuttle would again fly in space. NASA also built a shuttle to replace the *Challenger*; this vehicle, the *Endeavour*, first flew on May 7, 1992.

Since the *Challenger* disaster, NASA has been launching small American and foreign satellites with expendable rocket vehicles, and the shuttle's days as the sole deployer of unmanned satellites are past. The *Challenger* disaster also eroded the public's perception of NASA as a "can-do," high-achieving agency that justified the public expenditure involved. The funding problems NASA has encountered since, particularly with its new space station plans, indicate that NASA may face an uphill struggle to reassert its special status as a federal agency and scientific program.

Where to Learn More

"NASA Identifies Failure Scenarios." *Aviation Week and Space Technology*, March 17, 1986, pp. 25–26.

Bell, Trudy E. and Karl Esch. "The Fatal Flaw in Flight 51-L." *IEEE Spectrum*, February 1987, pp. 36–51.

Boffey, Philip M. "NASA Had Warning of a Disaster Risk Posed by Booster." *New York Times*, February 9, 1986, p. 1.

Broad, William J. "Thousands Watch a Rain of Debris." *New York Times*, January 29, 1986, p. 1.

Lewis, Richard S. *Challenger: The Final Voyage*. Columbia, 1988.

McConnell, Malcolm. *Challenger: A Major Malfunction*. Doubleday, 1987.

"A Fatal 'Error of Judgment.'" *Newsweek*. March 3, 1986, pp. 14–19.

Report of the Presidential Commission on the Space Shuttle Challenger Accident, 5 volumes. The Commission, June 6, 1986.

Sanger, David E. "Shuttle Changing in Extensive Ways to Foster Safety." *New York Times*, December 28, 1986, p. 1.

Smith, Melvyn. *Space Shuttle*. Haynes, 1989, pp. 264–285.

Smith, R. Jeffrey. "Inquiry Faults Shuttle Management." *Science*, June 20, 1986, pp. 1,488–1,489.

United Airlines Boeing 747 explosion

Hawaii **1989**

A flawed design caused a cargo door to fly open, which led to an explosive decompression that punched a gaping hole above the door. Nine passengers vanished out of the cavity.

by Byron Acohido

Background

On February 24, 1989, about eighteen minutes after takeoff from Honolulu, Hawaii, a United Airlines 747-100 passenger jet bound for Auckland, New Zealand, underwent explosive decompression with tragic results. The forward cargo door flew open, disrupting the even distribution of pressure in the airplane's cabin and cargo hold. The subsequent effect of this interruption to the pressure was not unlike that of a truck tire blowout. A massive rush of air punched a gaping hole in the fuselage above the door, and nine business-class passengers vanished out of the cavity.

The accident triggered a three-year investigation that ultimately revealed how a stray electrical signal could overcome an elaborate system of latches and locks to open a 747's cargo door without being commanded to do so. It also resulted in extensive improvements in the 747's cargo door system.

Designed in the late 1980s, the Boeing 747 jumbo jet, with its distinctive humped fuselage, is one of the most successful jetliners ever built. More

37

than 900 of the jets are in commercial service, and production is scheduled to continue into the foreseeable future. Each 747 has two nine-foot-square cargo doors located on the starboard (right) side of the airplane's belly, one forward and one aft. Unlike inward-opening "plug doors," which wedge into the passageway as the airplane pressurizes, the cargo doors on a 747 swing out and up in gull-wing fashion.

DEVELOPMENT OF THE 747 CARGO DOOR. Until the 747 came along, plug doors were used almost exclusively for both passenger entry and cargo access doors on commercial jetliners. This was considered an extra measure of safety against the possibility of breaching the integrity of the fuselage while the airplane was pressurized. But with the 747, designers wanted to avoid the heavy tracks and wide inside clearances implied by a giant plug door.

Engineers thus designed a relatively light door (about eight hundred pounds) that swung out and up and did not obstruct any cargo space. To assure that the door would always hold fast against enormous pressurization forces, an intricate system of electromechanical latches and locks was devised. The system permits a ground worker to lower and shut a door in about fifteen seconds by depressing a toggle switch that sets into motion a series of electrical motors. As a final step the worker locks the door manually by depressing a handle in the middle of the door.

The 747's outward-opening cargo door proved so successful that it became the standard for the ensuing generation of jetliners. Yet soon after the 747 entered commercial service in the early 1970s, a vexing trend emerged. One by one, the door's complicated system of sequential electronic actuators began to fail: locks became battered and bent, clutches and motors stripped, sensors and switches burned out, and latches and locks jammed. Boeing advised airline companies how to rectify each problem, but an incident in England added to the puzzle.

On March 10, 1987, the forward cargo door of a Pan Am 747-100 about to depart London for San Francisco was lowered and shut—manually—by a ramp worker using a speed wrench to do the work of the electrical motors. This was a routine procedure prescribed for instances when the door's electrical system malfunctions. Shortly after takeoff, though, the pilot found he was unable to pressurize the cabin. He returned to London, where the worker discovered that the forward cargo door was open 1.5 inches. The door was shut and locked and the plane sent on its way.

A closer inspection in San Francisco revealed severe damage to eight boomerang-shaped door locks designed to secure eight door latches in a closed position during flight. The C-shaped latches work by engaging and then rotating to a closed position around latch pins fastened to the door sill. The locks then swing into place over the open end of the latches, blocking them from reverse-rotating to the open position.

breakdown

Lab tests conducted by Boeing after this incident revealed that a switch designed to cut all electrical power from the door once the locks are set had the potential to jam. Such a development could leave the door's mechanisms vulnerable to stray electrical signals that might inadvertently actuate the latch motor. The motor could then "backdrive" the latches to an open position, bending the locks out of the way in the process. Tests showed that the locks, made of aluminum, were too weak to prevent the latches from rotating open should something activate the latch motor. Testing also showed that a stray electrical signal could almost instantly "backwind" the latches past weak locks to a fully open position. An inspection of Pan Am's 747 fleet revealed numerous damaged locks, suggesting a chronic pattern of backwinding of latches against weak locks.

Rather than search for the possible source of stray electricity activating the latch motor, officials blamed the London incident on the ground worker who manually operated the door. They accused the worker of using his speed wrench to backwind the latches after setting the locks in place, a charge the worker heatedly denied. Officials theorized that this was a shortcut procedure devised by ground workers to confirm that the latches were snugly secured against the locks. They chose to disregard the fact that the mechanic would have had to make ninety-five full turns of his speed wrench to fully open the latches, a task the latch motor could accomplish in 1.5 seconds.

The rupture on the starboard side of the plane, under examination here, exposed passengers and cabin attendants to a hurricane-force blast of cold air.

About one month after the Pan Am incident, Boeing alerted airlines worldwide that opening of a cargo door in flight "could result in rapid decompression . . . resulting in collapse of the passenger cabin floor and the possible damage to airplane electrical and hydraulic systems." Boeing's warning was accompanied by a call for airlines to reinforce the weak aluminum locks with special steel braces. Pan Am immediately fabricated the braces and installed them on its 747 fleet. Meanwhile, the Federal Aviation Administration (FAA) assigned a low priority to the matter, giving airlines up to two years to make the upgrade.

Details of the Explosion

On the morning of February 24, 1989, all was routine during preparations for United Airlines Flight 811. Two months earlier, in December 1988, maintenance logs showed the aircraft's forward cargo door's electrical system had malfunctioned repeatedly, necessitating manual operation in fourteen separate instances. Since that time, though, there had been no "write-up" on the door. Flight 811's ground crew used the toggle switch to routinely lower and latch the door, and a ground worker noticed nothing unusual when he depressed the lock handle to swing the weak aluminum locks into place over the closed latches. United had not yet installed the steel braces.

The flight, carrying 337 passengers, 15 cabin attendants, a pilot, a co-pilot, and a flight engineer, was cleared for takeoff at 1:52 A.M. The airplane climbed past 22,000 feet at more than 500 miles per hour. Pressurization, accomplished by continually pumping compressed air into the cabin and cargo hold, proceeded as usual.

At 2:09 A.M., all on board were stunned by a loud thump. Captain David Cronin remarked, "What the hell was that?" The thump was followed 1.8 seconds later by a tremendous boom, the sound of eleven million pounds of force—to this point distributed evenly on each square inch of the aircraft's interior—gushing explosively toward a breach in the fuselage. As the forward cargo door heaved away, it tore a thirteen-by-fifteen-foot opening on the fuselage alongside rows 9, 10, 11, and 12 on the starboard side.

In the blink of an eye, business class seats G and H, in rows 8 through 12, vanished out the hole along with a chunk of the floor, the starboard aisle, and the eight passengers who were sitting in those seats. Seat 9F, bordering the left edge of the starboard aisle, remained on its mounts, but its occupant, a forty-nine-year-old man, disappeared out the gaping hole as well.

At the moment of explosive decompression, passengers and cabin attendants reported experiencing a hurricane force blast of cold air. Cabin attendant Curt Christensen described it this way: "Immediately the air filled with a hazy smoke and flying debris. I felt a cold wind and sucking, if you will, but it wasn't a sucking. It was like being in the middle of a huge cannon blast, a blast of cold air. There was gray, swirling smoke and debris flying everywhere."

For the next twenty minutes terrified passengers and cabin attendants, some severely injured, waited to see if the wounded jetliner would plummet down into the Pacific Ocean. They watched in horror as the two starboard engines flamed out. Captain Cronin, though, heroically nursed the crippled aircraft to a safe landing in Honolulu.

Impact

The tragic consequences of the door failure haunted the investigative proceedings that followed. Even the survivors' rejoicing was muted, for all

breakdown

knew that—had their seat assignments been different—they might have been torn out of the plane themselves. The catastrophe prompted the FAA to order steel braces installed on locks of all 747s within thirty days. Over the next several months, Boeing developed a number of improvements to the door's warning system. As for what caused the accident, officials were stumped. The most telling evidence—the door itself—lay at the bottom of the Pacific Ocean, one hundred miles south of Honolulu.

Even so, after an intensive investigation the National Transportation Safety Board ruled on April 16, 1990, that the weak locks probably were severely damaged during the fourteen instances of manual operation two months before the accident. The safety board concluded that the ground crew somehow did not fully close the latches prior to takeoff, a conclusion that some regarded as questionable since no problems with the door lock or the use of the toggle switch to lower and shut the door had been reported.

A grim find in the Pacific Ocean several months later contradicted the board's conclusions. On September 27, 1990, the U.S. Navy deep-submergence vehicle *Sea Cliff* plucked the lower two-thirds of Flight 811's cargo door from the ocean floor. The eight locks were found in the locked position, but bent out of the way by the eight latches, which had somehow reverse-rotated to the open position. All the locks were in relatively good shape, a finding that contradicted the safety board's official explanation, which had contended that severely battered locks had been to blame. A few days later, *Sea Cliff* recovered the upper section of the door. Both parts were then shipped to a Boeing laboratory in Seattle, where they underwent thorough analysis under safety board supervision.

While the door was being examined, a related incident took place on June 21, 1991, at Kennedy International Airport on a newer model United Airlines 747-200 being prepared for a flight to Tokyo. The aft cargo door had been closed and latched, but not yet locked—and no one was touching the toggle switch—when a stray electrical signal rotated the door latches open, then lifted the door up. The powerful door-lift motor continued to run, trying to raise the door past its maximum open position, until a mechanic shut it off by popping a circuit breaker. The stray signal was subsequently traced to a cracked wire-bundle conduit that was located near the door hinges and exposed to wear and tear each time the door was opened or closed.

After that incident, United ordered its ground crews to open a pair of circuit breakers just before pushing any 747 back from the gate as an extra precaution. This removed all potential power from the cargo door area, above and beyond other power-cutting safety features.

Based on this real-life example of stray signals at work in the door and detailed analysis of Flight 811's cargo door, the safety board took the unusual step of reversing its earlier ruling. In the new report, issued on March 18, 1992, the board attributed the opening of the door to a "faulty switch or wiring in the door control system which permitted electrical actuation of the door latches toward the unlatched position after initial door closure and before takeoff."

Although the wire bundle that may have contained conclusive evidence of such a fault was never found, the board weighed other evidence uncovered by United. After the Kennedy door-opening incident, the airline found twenty-one different simple short circuits that could lead to actuation of the latch motor. Boeing maintained that steel reinforced locks now used on all 747s would prevent the latches from moving, even if a stray signal did come into play. Even so, the board called the design of the cargo door locking mechanisms "deficient" and said that a lack of timely corrective action by Boeing and the FAA after the 1987 Pan Am incident contributed to the tragedy of Flight 811.

Where to Learn More

Acohido, Byron. "Flight 811: Terror in the Sky" *Pacific Magazine* (*Seattle Times/Seattle Post Intelligencer* Sunday supplement), January 5, 1992, pp. 10–19.

"Airlines Inspect Cargo Doors in Wake of United Accident." *Aviation Week & Space Technology,* March 6, 1989, p. 22.

"Board Suggests Changing Cargo Door Latch Design." *Aviation Week & Space Technology,* August 28, 1989, p. 29.

"Close Look at Cargo Door Workings Fails to Reveal Cause of Accident." *Aviation Week & Space Technology,* May 22, 1989, p. 86.

Hackett, George. "Flight 811: A Nightmare in the Sky." *Newsweek,* March 6, 1989, p. 26.

Henderson, Breck W. "Investigators Believe Cargo Door Failed, Ripping 747 Open." *Aviation Week & Space Technology,* March 6, 1989, p. 18.

United Airlines DC-10 crash

Sioux City, Iowa **1989**

The crash of a DC-10 aircraft due to an engine explosion—and a subsequent failure of the ground crew's fire-fighting equipment—caused the deaths of 112 people and led to a massive National Transportation Safety Board investigation

by Robert Mark

Background

A regularly scheduled United Airlines DC-10 flight departed from Denver's Stapleton Airport at about 2:00 P.M. enroute to Philadelphia, with a stop scheduled at Chicago's O'Hare International Airport. After an hour of flight, the number two (tail section) engine exploded, cutting off the aircraft's hydraulic power. The crew, forced to attempt an emergency landing, almost miraculously was able to bring the aircraft in line with a runway at the Sioux City, Iowa, airport. Nonetheless, the crew had no way to slow the airliner's speed of over 240 miles per hour (m.p.h.) until immediately prior to touchdown. At this point, the captain's attempt to use the throttles to decelerate sent the aircraft into an uncontrolled spin. In landing, the DC-10 rolled over to the right and burst into flames. An equipment failure sabotaged the efforts of the Sioux City airport's emergency fire-fighting crew, and 112 of the 296 people on board the flight were killed.

Details of the Crash

About an hour into United Airlines Flight 232, the cockpit crew heard an explosion in the rear of the aircraft that was followed by a shuddering of the airframe. When the pilots checked their instruments, they learned that the number two engine, the engine mounted in the center of the vertical tail section, had failed. As the captain began the emergency shutdown procedure, the flight engineer noticed that the hydraulic system's quantity level as well as pressure had dropped to zero. Hydraulic power is necessary to move the aircraft's elevators, rudders, and ailerons on the wings and tail. The co-pilot, who had been flying the plane at the time of the explosion, indicated that he could no longer control the aircraft. The cockpit crew attempted to use an emergency backup power source for the hydraulic system, but to no avail.

When the captain took command, he found the only form of control he had over the 430,000-pound aircraft was to use, alternately, the throttles that controlled the two remaining engines—number one (on the left wing) and number three (on the right wing). When he pulled the number one throttle back, the remaining engine on the right wing tended to pull the aircraft around to the left; the opposite reaction occurred with use of the left engine throttle. At this point, the captain reported to air-traffic control that the aircraft was almost out of control and needed to be landed immediately. The nearest airport was in Sioux City, Iowa, where the emergency crew was put on alert.

The captain then instructed the lead flight attendant to prepare the cabin for an emergency landing. He also told her that the chances for a successful landing were not good, since he had very little control over the aircraft's flight path. Another United pilot, who by chance was travelling on the flight, came forward to the cockpit to help. After half an hour of zig-zag turns across Iowa, the crew managed to align the aircraft to land on a short runway at Sioux City; they had too little control over the DC-10 to maneuver it toward a longer runway. The cockpit crew used an emergency system to pump down the landing gear. They did not have use of any hydraulic landing flaps to slow the airliner, forcing them to maintain an aircraft speed of over 240 m.p.h. (the normal landing speed for a DC-10 is about 160 m.p.h.) until just before touchdown.

A quarter mile from the runway, the captain pulled back the throttles in a last-ditch effort to slow down the aircraft. When he did so, the aircraft began a roll to the right that could not be stopped. As the aircraft touched down, the right wing-tip struck the ground and the plane skidded, turning over to the right as it ground to a stop. The aircraft was quickly engulfed in flames that killed 112 of the 296 people on board.

The failure of a critical piece of emergency fire equipment at the Sioux City Airport, which was not prepared to cope with a fire as large as that pro-

When the captain took command, he found the only form of control he had over the 430,000-pound aircraft was to use, alternately, the throttles that controlled the two remaining engines— number one (on the left wing) and number three (on the right wing).

breakdown

duced by the Flight 232 crash, contributed to the loss of life after the DC-10 landing. The airport's Kovatch P-18 water-supply vehicle developed a supply hose blockage soon after the crash, which prevented the pumping vehicles from receiving a fresh supply of fire retardant to use against the blaze. Although the fire crew vigorously attacked the fire immediately after the crash, the fire flourished after the supply vehicle failure and burned strongly for another two hours.

As with most aircraft accidents, the crash of United Airlines Flight 232 was the result of a combination of problems, any one of which might have been manageable, but which in conjunction proved almost insurmountable. Flight 232 crashed after the failure of all the aircraft's hydraulic systems left the cockpit crew virtually helpless in its attempts to direct the flight. The hydraulic systems failed because the number two engine had not only failed, but exploded.

The first stage fan, a device within the opening of the engine that draws in fresh air to help produce the engine's thrust, had failed. The failure of a section of the fan disc unbalanced the remaining portion, causing it to tear itself loose. As the bits of shrapnel-like metal from the fan disc shot through the tail section of the DC-10, they severed the hydraulic lines, which ran through the tail section near the center engine, draining all control fluid from the system.

McDonnell-Douglas had not planned for a total hydraulic failure when it designed the DC-10.

McDonnell-Douglas had not planned for a total hydraulic failure when it designed the DC-10. Moreover, since the forces required to control an aircraft as large as the DC-10 were beyond manual control by a single individual, the aircraft was not equipped with a manual backup to the flight controls. A large portion of Flight 232's tail section was reconstructed after the accident in a hanger at the Sioux City Airport, from pieces of the aircraft gathered during an intensive search across hundreds of square miles of farmland near the airport. The reconstruction proved that pieces of the titanium fan disc had, in fact, punctured the skin of the rudders and horizontal stabilizers in at least 75 different places, as well as cut the hydraulic lines. Although a shroud is installed around the outside of the fan assembly to catch parts that might fly loose from an engine, the shroud could not contain the explosive force of this kind of breakup.

The catastrophic failure of the fan assembly on the number two engine occurred because of a fracture to the metal fan disc induced during its production eighteen years earlier by ALCOA. The engine, produced by General Electric Aircraft Engines of Evendale, Ohio, in 1972, had flown a total of 40,266 hours. In the life of a turbine aircraft engine, 40,000 hours is old but not unusable, thanks to the hundreds of maintenance inspections that are performed during an engine's lifetime, in which worn-down components are

replaced with serviceable parts. The fan disc (serial number MPO 00385) that would eventually fail on Flight 232 was installed on the DC-10 in July 1988, during one of these maintenance stops. Although routine write-ups on this DC-10 aircraft were submitted to the United maintenance department between July 1988 and July 1989, none indicated any problems with this particular component of the engine.

Impact

The crack in the fan disc initiated a great deal of controversy after the Flight 232 accident—not only because a defective disc had been shipped out from the ALCOA factory, but also because the crack was never detected over the course of nearly eighteen years of maintenance inspections. During those inspections, the disc was repeatedly tested through the use of a fluorescent penetrant (FPI), an industry-accepted method for checking nonmagnetic material for cracks too small to be seen by the unaided human eye. A penetrant fluid is applied to and allowed to flow over the

Two investigators examine the tail piece of the United Airlines DC-10 that crashed in Sioux City after an engine explosion resulted in the loss of hydraulic power.

part. The fluid will seep into any cracks in the material and leave a trace later detectable under ultraviolet light. Although metallurgists believe the crack—which was almost half an inch in length—should have been detected, it was not.

During the post-crash investigation, it also emerged that ALCOA had manufactured two discs with the same serial number, MPO 00385. One was discarded due to a defect, and another given the same part number. Experts initially believed that the two discs had been switched, so that the defective part was shipped out. This theory proved to be erroneous, but only after much investigative work, because GE's records for the manufacture of this part were so poorly maintained. Metallurgists ultimately concluded that the final machining (known as shot-peening) of the fan disc at ALCOA was responsible for the crack that caused the accident.

The Federal Aviation Administration (FAA) specifies that the owner of an aircraft—in this case United Airlines—is responsible for the proper maintenance of that craft. Although the aircraft and its engines were indeed maintained in accordance with FAA and GE procedures, United's maintenance department failed to detect the crack on the fan disc during any of its routine checks of the engine parts, the latest of which was performed about a year before the crash.

breakdown

The fan disc is round and has a large shaft hole in its center. When the fan disc is removed from the engine for the required FAA maintenance, this hole becomes convenient to string the part up for inspection. It was inside this hole, where the cable to hang the part passed through, that the crack was located. Most people familiar with the GE engine believed this spot to be a next to impossible location for a crack to develop, which is why the National Transportation Safety Board (NTSB) concluded that the United Airlines mechanic gave the part only a cursory inspection.

The NTSB determined that the cause of the Flight 232 accident was the inadequate inspection of the fan disc and the fan disc's subsequent breakup in flight. However, one dissenting NTSB member believed the cause to be three-fold: the poor manufacturing of the disc at ALCOA; the failure by United Airlines inspectors to detect the crack; and the failure by McDonnell-Douglas to recognize the vulnerability of the DC-10 airframe to a complete hydraulic malfunction after an explosion of the number two engine. The FAA determined, however, that McDonnell-Douglas had indeed complied with all certification regulations in effect when the DC-10 was built.

The Flight 232 accident did initiate the formation of a Systems Review Task Force (SRTF) to explore design solutions that would prevent this kind of accident from recurring. Additionally, it was held that "where applicable, the concepts developed by the SRTF should be considered for retrofit of current

The crash of United Flight 232 during an emergency landing attempt resulted in the deaths of 112 people on board.

fleet aircraft." The SRTF includes representatives from Boeing, McDonnell-Douglas, Airbus, Lockheed, General Electric, Pratt & Whitney, and Rolls-Royce.

The NTSB also recommended that the FAA search for new inspection methods to automate procedures and eliminate human inspection error (possibly by using a second, back-up inspector). They requested that the FAA issue an Airworthiness Directive removing from service any aircraft equipped with engine discs manufactured by ALCOA that were similar to the failed Flight 232 disk and made during the same time period. The NTSB also asked the FAA to require that all occupants, even those under two years old, be secured in their seats with an approved restraint device during landing and takeoff. In the initial moments of the Flight 232 crash, the mother of one of the four infants onboard the aircraft could not hold the child in her lap, and he eventually died of post-crash asphyxiation.

While 112 people onboard Flight 232 died in the crash, 184 survived. Those individuals owe their lives to the cockpit crew, who used their combined experience to devise a method of flying an airplane whose normal flight controls no longer had any effect. The captain, a thirty-three year veteran of United Airlines, relied on a sometimes controversial plan called Cockpit Resource Management (CRM)—in which all the pilots truly work as a team to solve a problem—to save those 184 lives.

The McDonnell-Douglas Corporation, the manufacturer of the DC-10, had assumed that the triple hydraulic failure that occurred in Flight 232 was impossible. After the accident, company representatives spent hundreds of hours in a DC-10 simulator trying to develop a procedure to help a crew cope with this particular systems failure. McDonnell-Douglas discovered, as had the pilots of Flight 232, that control of a DC-10 with no hydraulic systems becomes "very limited." The McDonnell-Douglas simulations underscored how much the Flight 232 crew had achieved in maneuvering the DC-10 back to earth.

Where to Learn More

Fotos, Christopher P. "Sioux City Hearings Focus on History of Failed Disk." *Aviation Week & Space Technology*, November 6, 1989, p. 56.

Hughes, David. "DC-10 Accident Leads to Basic Review of Jet Engine Rotating Parts Treatment." *Aviation Week & Space Technology*, May 20, 1991, p. 35.

—, and Michael Dornheim. "United DC-10 Crashes in Sioux City, Iowa." *Aviation Week & Space Technology*, July 24, 1989, p. 96.

Ott, James. "Investigators Find Reconstructed Tail of DC-10 Riddled with Damage." *Aviation Week & Space Technology*, July 31, 1989, p. 30.

—. "Probe Focuses on Failure of Fan Disk in DC-10 Crash." *Aviation Week & Space Technology*, July 31, 1989, p. 30.

Springen, Karen. "The 'Fear of Death' Lawsuits; Taking Legal Action after the Flight 232 Crash." *Newsweek*, August 7, 1989, p. 27.

Lauda Air Boeing 767-300 crash

An inadvertent thrust reverser deployment flipped a jetliner into a crash dive that killed all 223 people on board.

Background

On May 26, 1991, an eighteen-month-old Boeing 767-300ER (extended range) jet-liner operated by Lauda Air was climbing out of Bangkok bound for Vienna when an engine-braking device inadvertently deployed, throwing the left engine into reverse thrust. The airplane instantly flipped into a supersonic crash dive and began to break up even before it slammed into the jungle floor, killing all 213 passengers and ten crew members on board.

This air disaster raised questions about the reliability of electronically controlled thrust reversers put into wide use on all Boeing models starting in the late 1980s. The tragedy also illustrated with stunning finality the fallibility of aircraft designers, who had offered previous assurances that reversers deployed in flight would not result in loss of life. The wreckage of the Lauda Air Boeing 767-300 offered mute but powerful testimony suggesting otherwise.

Reversers slow a jetliner by diverting an engine's forward thrust. On most modern jetliners this feature is designed to be used only on the ground as a supplement to the wheel brakes. Air travelers hear the reversers at work

by **Byron Acohido**

49

moments after a jetliner's wheels touch down on landing; the increased roar of the engines is the sound of thrust being reversed to slow the aircraft down. When Boeing designed the 767 twin jet in the late 1970s, it followed a principle for the reversers that had been used successfully on its older 747 model. The rear portion of the engine casing slid aft, swinging panels into position to block the engine airflow. Thrust was diverted out the opening in the casing at a forward angle.

Power to operate the reverser was supplied by the engine's hydraulic system and was controlled by a series of valves, including a directional control valve, or DCV, designed to sit in two positions. In one position, the DCV directed pressurized fluid to open the reverser. In the other position it directed fluid to close the reverser. On 767s built through the mid-1980s, operation of the reversers was controlled by a mechanical cable linked to a lever in the cockpit. During flight, mechanical locks kept the engine casing secured in the closed position. Another safety feature was found on the reverser actuation lever in the cockpit. The lever was designed to remain in the closed position whenever the throttle was open, powering the engines. The lever could not move to the deploy position unless the throttle was first moved to the idle setting.

REFINEMENTS PROVE DEADLY. In the late 1980s, more sophisticated electronic engine controls became available and Boeing made several major refinements to this system. Boeing initiated installation of the upgraded reverser system on all of its models, including 747s, 737s, and 757s. This refinement replaced the mechanical link to the cockpit actuation lever with electronic controls. Under the new arrangement, when the pilot moved the reverser lever in the cockpit, he was not physically actuating the system, but setting into motion electronic signals to perform that function.

An elaborate safety feature called the auto-restow was added to the system as well. Sensors were installed on the casing to gauge any instances where the casing, despite the locks, might somehow begin to slip open in flight, thus starting the reverser deployment sequence. At the first sign of such a development, the auto-restow sensor was designed to signal the electronic controls to send pressurized fluid into the reverser. Since the DCV should always be in the closed position in flight, the DCV would direct the fluid to drive the casing shut, thus automatically restowing the reverser.

Back in the cockpit, an amber "REV ISLN" light was designed to illuminate when the auto-restow activated during flight, and extinguish when the restow process was completed. Pilots were told in the cockpit handbook to expect normal landing if the REV ISLN light came on during flight. While pilots reported seeing the REV ISLN light flickering from time to time, a more common sight was the separate "REV" light, designed to keep pilots advised of various stages of reverser operation upon landing. The REV light was designed

breakdown

to be blank when the reversers were locked, amber when they were partially extended, and green when the reversers were fully deployed.

In certifying the electronically controlled 767 reverser system and this auto-restow feature with the Federal Aviation Administration (FAA), Boeing asserted that there were no known ways the reverser could open in flight. Even so, the FAA asked Boeing to show in a test flight what would happen if a reverser deployed in flight. For this test, Boeing took a 767 up to a relatively low altitude of ten thousand feet. At a moderate speed of about two hundred fifty knots, test pilots were instructed to deliberately slow one engine to idle before deploying the reverser on the idled engine. When they did this, the airplane buffeted and began to swerve, or yaw, in the direction of the reversed engine, but the pilots were able to maintain control. The data from this test was programmed into 767 simulators, and the FAA approved the 767's electronically controlled reverser and auto-restow system. What would happen if a reverser somehow deployed at high altitude and high speed? The FAA never asked and Boeing never checked.

Details of the Crash

Shortly after 11:00 P.M. the night of May 26, 1991, a packed Lauda Air Boeing 767-300ER jetliner took off from Bangkok airport with 213 passengers and eight cabin attendants on board. At the controls were Captain Thomas Welch, an American, and co-pilot Josef Thurner, of Austria.

At 11:21 P.M., as the jet climbed under near full thrust, the cockpit voice recorder recorded Welch's comment to Thurner that the REV ISLN light kept flickering on and off. Thurner asked if he should alert ground staff. Welch told him not to bother, noting that the REV ISLN light is "an advisory thing" and that it was probably flickering because of "moisture in there or something." At 11:26 P.M. the airplane began to yaw to the left and Thurner told Welch to add rudder trim to the left to compensate.

At 11:30:37 P.M., the airplane was at 25,000 feet and climbing at a speed of 320 knots. Thurner spotted the REV light illuminate amber, then green—a signal that a pilot should only see on the ground—and exclaimed, "Ah, reverser's deployed." At 11:30:39, an audible snap was heard followed by Welch's oath, "Jesus Christ!" at 11:30:41. At 11:30:44, a series of warning alarms began.

The thrust reverser on the left engine had deployed. Because the large-diameter engine was mounted close to the wing and jutted out well in front of the leading edge, the sudden blast of reverse thrust interrupted the air flow over the wing, disrupting lift, the steady flow of air over the curved top of the wing that kept the airplane aloft. This sudden loss of lift on the left wing caused the airplane to twist and roll to the left.

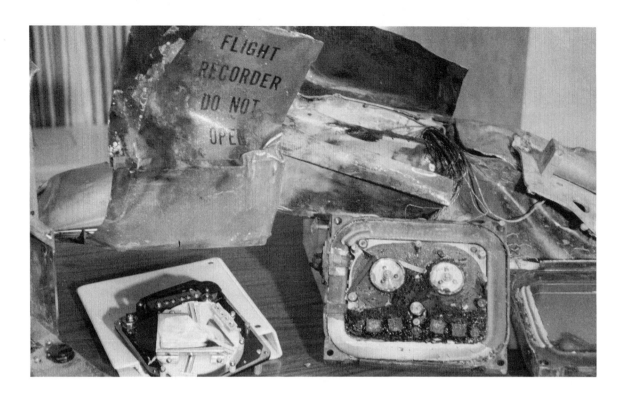

As the airplane rolled with the left engine, the right engine's high forward thrust further pushed the airplane into its roll. This combination of roll and yaw snapped the right wing forward into the air stream, which produced even more lift on the right wing. With no lift on the left wing and an abundance of lift on the right wing, the airplane's roll was accentuated, and it began a twisting dive to earth. Careening to the earth at ten miles per minute, the jet fell 8,000 feet in less than thirty seconds and began to break up under speed and forces it was not designed to withstand. The fury and helplessness of these final seconds was captured on the cockpit voice recorder. At 11:30:58 Welch's final words, "Damn it," were recorded. At 11:31:05 there was the sound of a bang. At 11:31:06, the recording ended.

The flight recorder of the Lauda Air 767 was analyzed in Washington after it was released by Thai officials. As the plane careened to the ground, the recorder captured the fury in the cockpit.

Impact

This dramatic air disaster revealed the auto-restow to be an overly complex safety device that probably caused the accident. It also showed that Boeing and the FAA had inadequately examined the possible repercussions if a thrust reverser deployed at a high altitude under high thrust on a modern two-engine jetliner.

Several months passed before authorities reached consensus that the auto-restow was to blame, however. In the weeks following the accident, speculation on the cause ranged from a detonated terrorist bomb, to catastrophic engine failure, to spontaneous combustion of a crate of lithium wristwatches in the cargo hold. The location of the crash site added to the confusion surrounding the investigation. The plane had crashed into a remote jungle hillside 130 miles from Bangkok. By the time investigators reached the site, nearby villagers had looted the wreckage and made off with a number of items, including the bright metallic directional control valve from the left engine. The engine itself was recovered with the reverser in a fully deployed position a few days after the accident.

In the early stages of the investigation, the widespread belief was that, even though hard evidence showed the reverser had deployed, the pilots should have been able to handle the accompanying roll and yaw. After all, Boeing's test pilots had done so in their low-altitude, low-speed test flight. Airline owner Niki Lauda, a seasoned pilot, accepted that line of reasoning after flying through a reverser deployment in a 767 simulator programmed with flight parameters derived from the flight test data. A week after the accident, Lauda said he thought that a bomb or fire caused the crash.

Eventually, though, authorities homed in on the auto-restow system, surmising that something must have shifted the DCV to the wrong position in flight. In such a scenario, the engine casing could have slipped or an out-of-adjustment sensor could have signaled the auto-restow to activate. In either case, the auto-restow would activate and illuminate the REV ISLN light. Perhaps the DCV was in the proper position the first couple of times this happened, directing the hydraulic fluid to restow the reverser. Such a series of events, investigators reasoned, would explain Captain Welch's early nonchalant comments. Then something, perhaps a stray electrical signal or quirky vibration, might have moved the DCV to the open position, so that when the auto-restow activated again the reverser deployed.

In mid-August 1991, Boeing lab technicians were probing this theory when one of them decided to place a worn seal on the DCV and see what would happen when the auto-restow mechanism was activated. The technicians were alarmed to discover that during the test bits of the seal contaminated the hydraulic lines and the DCV deployed the reverser. The worn-seal tests prompted the FAA to order a ban on use of reversers on 767s that used the same electronically controlled restow valve as the Lauda airplane. The agency noted that out-of-adjustment sensors, which could have been unnecessarily activating the auto-restow system in flight, had been discovered on nine out of ten airplanes checked to that point. The inspections also turned up chafed wires and short circuits in the wiring bundles integral to operation of the DCV.

Careening to the earth at ten miles per minute, the jet fell 8,000 feet in less than thirty seconds and began to break up under speed and forces it was not designed to withstand. The fury and helplessness of these final seconds was captured on the cockpit voice recorder. At 11:30:58 Welch's final words, "Damn it," were recorded. At 11:31:05 there was the sound of a bang. At 11:31:06, the recording ended.

Still, the FAA was not yet willing to completely blame the auto-restow because Boeing continued to maintain that the aircraft should have been flyable, even with the left reverser deployed. The earlier test flight, they noted again, supported this view.

Finally, under pressure from the National Transportation Safety Board, Boeing agreed in early September 1991 to throw out the limited flight test data and run fresh aerodynamic calculations. These calculations, based on new high-speed wind-tunnel tests, would hopefully provide some insight into the behavior of the Lauda jet after the reverser deployed. The results chilled and shocked the officials.

The fresh data were fed into a 767 simulator in Seattle. Airline owner Niki Lauda flew the simulator himself. Afterwards, a grim Lauda told news reporters that, upon deploying the left reverser, the simulator twisted and flipped completely over to its left in a couple of seconds. A few seconds more and it was careening, nose aimed at the darkened jungle below. It hurtled to the earth at more than 600 miles per hour, a speed greater than the speed of sound. Designed to withstand pressures present at up to 86 percent of the speed of sound, the simulator was helpless in the grip of the dive. It plummeted three miles—from 24,700 feet to 8,000 feet—in less than half a minute and then began breaking apart.

breakdown

"You're suddenly upside down in a dive," Lauda said sadly. "There's nothing you can do. It turns over, then it goes nose down. You go right into overspeed and then you lose all of your controls. The airplane broke up exactly seventeen seconds after it went out of control."

The Lauda Air crash served as a grisly reminder to aircraft designers that the ever-increasing reliance on electronic controls and computers to operate modern aircraft can have dangerous consequences that can be very difficult to anticipate. Ultimately, the accident prompted the FAA to order extra locks for reversers on 2,000 late model 767s, 737s, and 757s—all Boeing's twin jet models—as well as upgraded DCVs for some 757s. The agency also ordered substantially modified wiring and DCVs for about fifty-seven 767s with the same type of engine as the Lauda airplane.

Where to Learn More

Acohido, Byron. "Agencies Clash on Jet-Safety Rule: Crash in Thailand Spurs Call for Emergency Action." *Seattle Times*, July 23, 1991, p. C1.

—. "Air Disasters: Critics Question FAA's Response." *Seattle Times*, September 1, 1991, p. E3.

—. "FAA: Don't Use 767 Thrust Reversers—Boeing Expands Call for Inspections for Other Jets." *Seattle Times*, August 16, 1991, p. A1.

—. "FAA Scrutinizes Reversers: Agency Orders Changes in Faulty Valve System on Some 757s." *Seattle Times*, September 12, 1991, p. F1.

—. "Flaw in the Fleet: Boeing Executive Says Precautions Adequate for Jets with Suspect Reverser." *Seattle Times*, September 15, 1991, p. E1.

—. "No Worst-case Test for 767 Part: FAA Accepted Boeing Assurances on Thrust Reversers." *Seattle Times*, June 14, 1991, p. A1.

—. "Safety Board Wants 767 Part Banned: Agencies Fight over Safety of Reverser." *Seattle Times*, August 8, 1991, p. A1.

Daly, Kieran. "FAA Narrows Thrust-Reverser Directive." *Flight International*, September 4–10, 1991, p. 10.

Lane, Polly, and Byron Acohido. "Boeing Tells 757 Owners to Replace Part—Faulty Thrust Reverser Valve Blamed in 767 Accident That Killed 223." *Seattle Times*, September 9, 1991, p. A1.

—. "Interpreting Last Words of Doomed Crew: Boeing Part Occupied Final Minutes as 767's Pilots Struggled with Riddle." *Seattle Times*, June 6, 1991, p. A1.

"New Boeing Lock Targets Unwanted Reverser Activity," *Aviation Week & Space Technology*, June 1, 1992, p. 32.

Norris, Guy. "FAA Lauda 767 Reply Inadequate, Says NTSB." *Flight International*, August 14–20, 1991, p. 4.

—. "FAA Queries Thrust-Reverser Designs." *Flight International*, August 28–September 3, 1991, p. 4.

Norris, Guy and Kieran Daly. "FAA Orders Review of All Thrust-Reverser Designs." *Flight International*, September 18–24, 1991, p. 4–5.

Ott, James. "Lauda Crash Probers Focus on Midair Thrust Reversal." *Aviation Week & Space Technology*, June 10, 1991, pp. 28–29.

Proctor, Paul. "Sabotage Feared in Destruction of Lauda Air 767-300ER over Thailand." *Aviation Week & Space Technology*, June 3, 1991, pp. 29–30.

Richards, Bill. "FAA Calls for Shutdown of 767 Thrust Reversers." *Seattle Post-Intelligencer*, August 17, 1991, p. A1.

El Al Boeing 747-200 crash

Amsterdam, The Netherlands **1992**

Separation of both engines from the right wing caused a 747 to plunge out of the sky and into an Amsterdam apartment complex, taking the lives of six El Al crew members and more than fifty people on the ground.

Background

On October 4, 1992, after a year-old Boeing 747-200F (freighter) operated by El Al Israel Airlines had taken off from Amsterdam's Schipol Airport at 6:22 P.M. carrying its commercial cargo, the inboard engine came loose from the right wing. Veering sideways, the loosened engine smashed into the outboard right engine, crippling that one as well. The jetliner lurched to the right and, steadily losing altitude, made two wide clockwise circles over the city. The terrifying flight finally ended when the giant airplane plowed into a low-income ten-story apartment complex filled with residents who were just sitting down to dinner. The disaster took the lives of six El Al crew members and more than fifty people on the ground at the crash site.

The El Al Boeing 747 catastrophe brought to public light a hazard that air safety officials had been trying to solve since 1978: the potential for corroded or cracked engine mounting safety bolts—called fuse pins—to fail during flight. The disaster also revealed that aircraft designers had miscalculated

by Byron Acohido

how an engine under high thrust would behave if it came loose in flight. Instead of safely falling down and away from the aircraft, as designed, the El Al jet's inboard right engine veered forcefully to the side and into the outboard right engine.

FUSE PINS HAD HISTORY OF PROBLEMS. The Boeing 747's fuse pins were hollow cylinders of cadmium-plated steel four inches long and 2.25 inches in diameter. These fuse pins were designed to be sturdy enough to endure enormous stress from multiple directions throughout the flight's trajectory—as the airplane takes off, climbs, banks, bounces, descends, and lands. Four fuse pins connect the engine strut to the wing. The pins slip through lug fasteners then through parallel lugs on the wing.

Like automobile electrical fuses, these Boeing fuse pins are designed to be fragile enough to break under certain circumstances. For example, engineers designed the fuse pins so that they would snap if an engine began to fall apart in flight. The designers felt that this would enable the damaged engine to shear cleanly away without damaging the wing. Similarly, if a 747 were forced to belly land, the design specifications called for the engines, upon striking the runway, to shear away from the wings. This would greatly reduce the possibility of a hot engine igniting any fuel that might spill from ruptured storage tanks in the wings.

From 1969 through 1980, Boeing mounted its 747 engines with fuse pins that machinists honed to just the proper strength by boring an intricate hourglass shape across the interior surface of the pin. But this original technique turned out to be flawed. Officials discovered that the machining process sometimes left tiny nicks where corrosion could develop. Under stress, the corroded nicks developed into cracks that made the pins dangerously weak. Therefore, in 1979, the Federal Aviation Administration (FAA) ordered airlines to periodically inspect these "old-style" fuse pins for corrosion and cracks.

Boeing attempted to correct the problem by designing a "new-style" pin that featured a simplified hourglass core supported by inserts wedged permanently into the two open ends of the fuse pins. Factory installation of the new-style pins on new jetliners began in 1980. In 1982 the FAA advised airlines operating older 747s that regular inspections of fuse pins would no longer be required if the old-style fuse pins were replaced with the newer version.

The issue remained troublesome, though. Disquieting reports soon reached Boeing that the new-style pins were also corroding and cracking. On one occasion, an alert ground inspector averted a possible tragedy when he spotted an engine drooping on a 747 passenger jet just minutes before it was to take off. The flight was aborted, and inspectors discovered that the droop was caused by a cracked new-style fuse pin. Over the next few years, several more cases of weakened new-style pins came to light. In May 1991, therefore, the FAA ordered airlines operating 747s equipped with the new-style pins to

On one occasion, an alert ground inspector averted a possible tragedy when he spotted an engine drooping on a 747 passenger jet just minutes before it was to take off. The flight was aborted, and inspectors discovered that the droop was caused by a cracked new-style fuse pin.

breakdown

perform a one-time check to determine whether the anti-corrosive primer on the inside core of the pins was intact. If corrosion or cracks were discovered, the airlines were instructed to install fresh pins.

Nonetheless, the FAA made no provisions to formally tally or assess the cases of corroded or cracked pins uncovered by their call for inspection. Moreover, some airlines balked at the requirement, which meant that they had to squeeze a time-consuming task into a rigorously tight maintenance routine. Mechanics were not pleased with the requirement, either. The inspection procedure called for the tightly wedged inserts to be yanked loose with a special tool to check for corrosion or cracks inside the pin. As it turned out, the inserts were the reason why the new-style pins proved susceptible to corrosion. Upon being wedged into place in the ends of the pins, the inserts scraped away small amounts of the anti-corrosive primer coating the internal bore. Moisture, probably from intense condensation, then seeped into the bore and corroded the scraped area.

On December 29, 1991, eight months after the FAA authorities determined that a one-time examination of the new-style pins and periodic inspections of old-style pins would ensure the safety of the 747 fleet, a twelve-year-old China Airlines 747-200 jet freighter crashed near Taipei, Taiwan, killing all five crew members. The 747's original, old-style fuse pins had recently been replaced with the new-style pins. Even so, a few minutes after take-off from Taipei, the airplane's right inboard engine ripped loose and slammed into the right outboard engine, knocking it loose as well. Both right-side engines fell into the sea, and the airplane, stuck in a right hand turn, smacked into a cliffside.

For several months, very little information was made public about this crash in Taiwan. Then, on September 11, 1992, an inspector checking an Argentina Aerolineas 747-200 passenger jet prior to take off noticed that the aircraft's right inboard engine was sagging. Mechanics called to the plane discovered the droop was caused by a cracked new-style pin. A week later, Boeing convened a meeting in Seattle, Washington, with several major 747 operators to discuss the fuse pin problem. An advisory was agreed upon that would request that airlines once again perform an inspection of the new-style fuse pins on all airplanes. The operators at the mid-September meeting agreed to issue the advisory on October 8, 1992.

Details of the Crash

At 6:22 P.M., October 4, 1992, the El Al Boeing 747-200 jet freighter, laden with 114 tons of commercial cargo, took off from Amsterdam. Heading southeast over the Dutch city, the airplane was bound for Tel Aviv, with

Captain Isaac Fuchs at the controls. At around 6:25, the jet reached 4,000 feet and continued climbing under high thrust.

A minute later, Captain Fuchs reported to the control tower that a fire warning light for the right inboard or No. 3 engine had come on. An engine in the process of separating from the wing had the potential to trigger this warning light, and evidence from the wreckage later confirmed that a fuse pin had failed on the No. 3 engine, setting the accident into motion. At 6:28, Fuchs reported that the right outboard or No. 4 engine was out. It was later determined that the No. 4 engine was operating properly until it was knocked off the wing by the loosened No. 3 engine.

Fuchs had no way of knowing from these control panel indications that the jet had completely lost its two right-side engines. At 6:34, after flying a wide right-hand circle over Amsterdam, Fuchs reported a "problem with the flaps," the movable control surfaces on the trailing edge of the wings. Only at this point did Fuchs acknowledge that "We have a control problem." A minute later, at 6:35, Fuchs radioed: "going down, 8162 going down, going down." The jetliner roared out of the sky and slammed into the center of the ten-story apartment building at 6:35:53 P.M., obliterating the middle section of the complex. Along with the six-member El Al crew, more than fifty people at the apartment building site were casualties of the crash.

The El Al jetliner was one of about two hundred older model 747s that had continued to use the old-style pins. Airline records showed that El Al mechanics inspected the pins four months before the accident, per regulations, and reported no problems. In January 1993, Israeli authorities, citing evidence uncovered in the wreckage, blamed the broken fuse pin on the inboard right engine for causing the engine to tear off and veer into the outboard engine. El Al officials indicated there were no signs of sabotage and that the crew did everything possible to maintain control of the damaged airplane. An El Al director reported that he would demand payments from Boeing for the victims' families and, given the damage to its reputation, to the airline itself.

Impact

The El Al Boeing 747 catastrophe, coupled with the crash of the China Airlines 747 freighter in Taiwan eleven months earlier, indicated that airline authorities probably should have acted more quickly and decisively to address the long-recognized dangers posed by both versions of the Boeing 747 fuse pins. After the Amsterdam accident, the FAA and Boeing did take more aggressive steps to identify and replace weak fuse pins in the 747 fleet of more than nine hundred jets. However, it remains to be seen whether the design of the 747 engine mount systems will continue to pose an air safety hazard.

The day after the crash, Boeing hastily issued the advisory written in mid-September that called for a one-time re-inspection of new-style pins. Boeing exempted the newer model 747-400 from the advisory, however, and gave no recommendations regarding 747s still equipped with old-style pins. A few days later, the FAA widened the call for inspection by including the 747-400 model and requiring more frequent inspections of 747s still using the old-style pins. Inspections of the first 300 jets turned up 499 corroded pins and fourteen cracked pins, a defect rate of 20 percent. Airlines were permitted to refurbish lightly corroded pins, but were required to replace heavily corroded and cracked pins.

During this period Boeing continued its development, initiated several months before the El Al crash, of a corrosion-proof fuse pin for use on all models of its planes. Like other exterior parts, the fuse pins are exposed to intensive condensation as a jet rapidly ascends to and descends from the sub-Arctic levels of cold found in jetliner cruising lanes seven miles above the Earth. Other potential sources of corrosive moisture include de-icing agents and various types of liquid cleaners and polishers routinely sprayed on the wings near the engine mounts.

Inspection of the first 300 jets turned up 499 corroded pins and fourteen cracked pins, a defect rate of 20 percent.

A large piece of the 747's wreckage is guarded by police in Amsterdam. Investigations showed that corroded engine mount systems allowed the two right engines to drop from the plane, causing the catastrophe.

Boeing officials declined to publicly discuss the separate phenomenon of the loosened engine—which should have fallen harmlessly to the earth according to designers—and its destructive role in the El Al Boeing disaster. Aeronautical experts theorize that substantial gyroscopic forces could cause a suddenly loose engine to rocket forward in an arc either to the right or the left, depending on which direction the engine fan blades were rotating. This new information about the trajectory of loose engines has raised a separate concern about the increasing use of jetliners with only one powerful, wide-diameter engine under each of the two wings. These models include the Airbus A321, A300, A310, A330, and A340 and the Boeing 737, 757, 767, and 777. Critics contend that a loose engine on such an airplane could devastate the fuselage, or central portion, of a passenger-carrying airplane.

Where to Learn More

"Fuse Pins Suspect in El Al Crash." *Aviation Week & Space Technology*, October 12, 1992, pp. 30–33.

Egozi, Arie. "El Al Crash Centered on 'Engine-pylon Fittings.'" *Flight International*, October 28–November 3, 1992, p. 5.

Hornblower, Margot. "Death from the Sky." *Time*, October 19, 1992, pp. 50–52.

Mecham, Michael. "El Al Strut Shows Possible Fatigue." *Aviation Week & Space Technology*, October 26, 1992, p. 30.

Disasters at Sea

Titanic sinking (1912) 65

Andrea Doria–Stockholm collision (1956) 73

Thresher sinking (1963) 79

Scorpion sinking (1968) 86

Ocean Ranger oil-drilling rig sinking (1982) 92

Exxon *Valdez* oil spill (1989) 98

Titanic sinking

off Newfoundland 1912

A "practically unsinkable" state-of-the-art ocean liner sank after hitting an iceberg, causing the deaths of more than fifteen hundred people.

Background

On the night of April 14, 1912, the White Star Line's *Titanic,* on her maiden voyage from Southampton to New York, struck an iceberg off Newfoundland. The vessel sank just two hours and forty minutes after the collision at 11:40 P.M., with a loss of over fifteen hundred lives. The *Titanic*, the largest and most luxurious ship afloat, was also believed to be the safest—"practically unsinkable." Heralded as a symbol of the triumph of technology, after the sinking it became a notorious symbol of human presumption.

The *Titanic* was conceived in 1907 by Lord Pirie, head of Harland & Wolff, a shipbuilding firm that enjoyed a reputation as the builder of the sturdiest and best ships in the British Isles, and J. Bruce Ismay, chairman of the White Star Line. Several years before, in 1902, the White Star Line had been swallowed up by the monster trust International Mercantile Marine. This acquisition made the American financier J. Pierpont Morgan the principal owner of the *Titanic*. The venture was thus a marriage of American money and British technology. But in many respects, the *Titanic* was thought of as a British

by Sally Van Duyne

vessel: it was registered as a British ship, was manned by British officers, and would revert to the British Navy in time of war.

The beginning of the century was a time of great rivalry among steamship companies. Pirie and Ismay felt they couldn't match the speed of the Cunard liners so they focused on creating a vessel of tremendous size and grandeur. Cognizant of the growing tide of passengers emigrating to America as well, they made plans to greatly increase the accommodations available to steerage or low-fare passengers. The *Titanic* was thus built in Belfast alongside its sister ship, the *Olympic*, a vessel that the *Titanic* exceeded in gross tonnage but not in length.

The *Titanic* was 882 feet in length, ninety-two feet in width, and weighed 46,328 gross tons; its nine steel decks rose as high as an eleven-story building. The stability afforded by its vast size was deemed to be one of many safeguards against its foundering. It also embodied a greater proportionate mass of steel in its structure than had been used in previous ships. It was built with a double bottom, two layers of steel of tremendous weight and thickness. The outer skin of the bottom was a full inch thick. No other vessel could boast of such a level of protection.

As one eyewitness noted, she had "a rudder as big as an elm tree ... propellers as big as a windmill. Everything was on a nightmare scale."

As the ship neared completion, observers marveled at its size. Three million rivets were pounded into the hull. The *Titanic's* gigantic anchors weighed a total of thirty-one tons. As one eyewitness noted, she had "a rudder as big as an elm tree ... propellers as big as a windmill. Everything was on a nightmare scale."

The huge hull was divided by fifteen transverse bulkheads, or upright partitions, that extended the width of the ship into sixteen "watertight" compartments, any two of which might flood without affecting the safety of the ship. The six compartments that contained boilers had their own pumping equipment. The doors between watertight compartments could be closed all at once by a switch on the bridge, or individually by crewmen. The bulkheads rose from the double bottom to five decks above forward and aft, and to four decks above amidships (the middle).

The *Titanic* was not only the biggest ship afloat but the last word in comfort and elegance. The ship was equipped with a stunning array of accoutrements: the world's first shipboard swimming pool, a Turkish bath with gilded cooling room, a gymnasium, a squash court, a loading crane and compartment for automobiles, and a hospital with a modern operating room. The dining rooms, staterooms, and common rooms were furnished in various styles and periods; there was a Parisian café, for instance. The first-class cabins were especially opulent. Several included coal-burning fireplaces in the sitting rooms and full-size four-poster beds in the bedrooms.

breakdown

Excitement mounted as the day of the *Titanic's* maiden voyage grew near. There were few detractors. Some dissenters, though, pointed out that there wasn't a dock in America of sufficient size to house the *Titanic* or the *Olympic*. Others complained that the opulence of vessels such as the *Titanic* would signal a new era of greater expense in water travel. Other critics contended that ships of such great size would concentrate so much wealth and so many lives in a single vessel that underwriters would be unable to provide insurance coverage.

The Titanic *as she set out on her voyage from Southampton.*

Such laments were ignored, though, drowned under a deluge of excited anticipation. The *Titanic* was launched on May 31, 1911, to loud hosannas, lauded as a marvel of engineering ingenuity and astonishing luxury.

Details of the Sinking

The evening of April 14, the fifth day of the *Titanic's* maiden voyage, the sea was exceptionally calm and the sky was starry but moonless. During the course of the day, the *Titanic* received seven different warnings concerning ice sightings in the region. Captain E. J. Smith saw at least four of these ice formations himself, yet he did not alter the ship's speed of about twenty-one knots. Lulled by the seemingly clear visibility, his previous experience in navigating ice fields, and the ship's reputation as an unsinkable vessel, Smith may have simply thought a drop in speed to be unnecessary. Other possible factors? The sea captains of the White Star Line had cultivated a reputation as unflinching, proud skippers, a philosophy that Smith probably shared. Finally, he may simply have been trying to make good speed on the maiden voyage.

Yet April is one of the worst months for icebergs—the seaward tips of glaciers that break off. Many of these mountainous fragments hail from the west coast of Greenland, and more than a thousand reach the shipping lanes each year. The stage was set for a tragedy of epic proportions.

The two crewmen serving as lookouts that night on the *Titanic* were posted but neither man had a pair of binoculars, which were supposed to be standard equipment on the White Star Line. They scanned the surrounding water, but the lack of binoculars had horrifying consequences. They did not see the looming iceberg until it was only a quarter mile away. The alarm was raised and the bow was swung swiftly to port (left), but it was too late. Several tons of ice clattered over the ship's decks as the ship brushed against the visible section of the iceberg. The real damage, however, occurred beneath the water's surface. The underwater shelf of the ice tore through the plating on the starboard (right) bow, shredding the exterior of the ship. Historians estimate the tear might have extended from aft to amidships. Six watertight compartments were thought to have been breached. The bow started to sink and additional compartments filled with water, which soon sloshed over the tops of the transverse bulkheads.

Yet when the collision first occurred, few were aware of the seriousness of the incident. The 46,000-ton *Titanic*, speeding along at over twenty knots, seemed to not even feel the impact. The gravity of the situation was comprehended only gradually, and many passengers had to be awakened. The collision occurred at 11:40 P.M., but the order to ready the lifeboats was not given until 12:20 A.M.

Confusion reigned as the passengers began to board the lifeboats, though the crowd remained relatively calm. Some passengers at this juncture were even reluctant to leave the ship, preferring to remain on the brightly lit ship and listen to the ship's band as it continued to play.

As the situation worsened, however, a serious problem emerged. There were only sixteen lifeboats and four emergency rafts—enough for roughly half of the passengers. Although the *Titanic* had complied with British Board of Trade rules regarding lifeboats, the regulations were based on the tonnage of the ship rather than on the passenger capacity. Moreover, a reduction in the number of boats was allowed for ships such as the *Titanic* deemed to have satisfactory watertight subdivision.

Several tons of ice clattered over the ship's decks as it brushed against the visible section of the iceberg. The real damage, however, occurred beneath the water's surface.

breakdown

Since there had been no boat drill, the crew and passengers did not know to which lifeboats they should go. Furthermore, the officers in charge of loading the boats, unaware that the boats and davits had been tested, were afraid that if they were fully loaded, either the boats would buckle as they were lowered to the water or the davits (cranes) holding the boats over the side would break. Thus they sent the boats down only partly loaded, with instructions to pull alongside the cargo ports to pick up additional passengers. The cargo ports, though, were never opened. Investigators later estimated that the boats housed on the *Titanic* could have held 1,178 persons; instead, only 711 were saved in the boats. Many crew members and passengers needlessly lost their lives in the loading mishap.

Contemporary drawing of how the Titanic *may have struck the iceberg.*

As the *Titanic's* bow sank lower and lower, those remaining on the ship frantically climbed to the stern. A desperate few jumped into the twenty-eight-degree water in their lifebelts. The ship's last moments afloat were desperate ones for the passengers stranded on board. One survivor recalled that scene sadly: "We could see groups of ... people aboard, clinging in clusters or bunches, like swarming bees; only to fall in masses, pairs or singly, as the great part of the ship ... rose into the sky." As the survivors watched spellbound, the immense stern of the vessel reared up so that it was almost perpendicular to the water's surface. It remained there for a few moments, its wet sides gleaming in the cold starlight, before it slid slowly into the sea at 2:20

"We could see groups of ... people aboard, clinging in clusters or bunches, like swarming bees; only to fall in masses, pairs or singly, as the great part of the ship ... rose into the sky."

A.M. Many survivors reported hearing sounds like thunder, or thick detonations, or a kind of "death rattle" before the stern went down. The worst sound, though, according to one passenger, was "the most terrible noise that human beings ever listened to—the cries of hundreds of people struggling in the icy cold water, crying for help with a cry we knew could not be answered." These cries became "a long continuous wailing chant," before slowly diminishing into silence.

Although some passengers asserted that the great ship broke in two, the explanation generally accepted to explain the thunderous sound was that as the stern rose, the boilers crashed down through the bulkheads. From what we know now about the position of the bow and the stern on the ocean floor— they are facing in opposite directions and are about 1,970 feet apart —it seems likely that the ship did break in two at or near the surface. As the bow sank and the stern rose, the pressure on the keel probably increased until it snapped.

The other startling discovery made by the 1985 Franco-American expedition and the 1986 American expedition led by Dr. Robert D. Ballard of the Woods Hole Oceanographic Institute concerned the gash in the hull. These expeditions located and photographed the wreck in thirteen thousand feet of water, a few miles from where it had been thought to be. Dr. Ballard observed many buckled plates below the waterline, but no gash. It is possible, however, that the gash remains hidden under the sediment.

Historians believe that mishaps in wireless communication may have also contributed to the unnecessary loss of life on the *Titanic*. On the *Californian*, a ship stopped for the night in ice fields not more than twenty miles away from the *Titanic*, the wireless operator had stopped working only fifteen or twenty minutes before the operator from the *Titanic* tried to get through with a distress call. At the time, wireless operators were employees of the Marconi company and did not follow around-the-clock shipboard watches. The next closest ship, which the *Titanic* successfully contacted, was the *Carpathia*, about fifty-eight miles away. The *Carpathia* picked up the first lifeboat at 4:10 A.M.

In 1993, a team of architects and engineers released a report in which they argued that the tragedy was caused not so much by the collision with the iceberg as by the structural weakness of the ship's steel plates. Low-grade steel such as that used on the *Titanic* is subject to brittle fracture—a phenomenon wherein the metal breaks rather than bends in cold temperatures. If a better grade of steel had been used, the group argued, the ship might have withstood the collision or, at the very least, sunk more slowly, thus allowing more passengers to be saved. The team also suggested that the roar heard by the passengers as the ship sank may have been the steel plates fracturing, not the boilers crashing through the bulkheads.

Impact

A U.S. Senate inquiry into the *Titanic* tragedy began the day after the *Carpathia* landed in New York with the survivors. It was headed by William Alden Smith. A British investigation by the Board of Trade, with Lord Mersey as wreck commissioner, followed and lasted from May through July of 1912. An international Safety of Life at Sea (SOLAS) conference met in London from November 1913 to January 1914 as well. Many new rules and regulations resulted from these and later forums.

New regulations required that the number of lifeboats be based on the number of passengers rather than on the tonnage of the ship. New rules were implemented that required that lifeboat drills take place shortly after a ship sails. Crew members and passengers were assigned to particular areas of the boat in emergencies. Other regulations addressed the training of the seamen assigned to the lifeboats and listed required equipment for lifeboats.

Shipping lanes were moved farther south, away from the ice fields. Ships approaching ice fields were required to slow down or alter their course. (If a ship is traveling at half speed, the reactive blow of a collision is reduced by one fourth, in that the energy of a moving mass increases as the square of its velocity.) The International Ice Patrol, based in Groton, Connecticut, was set up to monitor iceberg movement. It uses radar-equipped aircraft to spot icebergs and makes computer-tabulated predictions about their whereabouts. To date, no further loss of life due to iceberg collisions has occurred in North Atlantic shipping lanes monitored by this station.

New regulations were also brought to bear on wireless operations. Legislation was passed that required that a ship's wireless be manned day and night and have an auxiliary source of power. Regulations were also instituted to ensure that amateur wireless operators secure licenses. This licensing was the beginning of the Federal Communications Commission.

Over the years the loss of the *Titanic* and so many of its passengers has acquired a mythical sort of quality. Even the speed with which the ship sank has contributed to the legend. The jewel of that era of shipbuilding should not have succumbed so quickly.

The *Titanic* disaster, while it spurred much-needed regulatory action, was a stunning blow to a world that had begun to underestimate the power of nature. After a century of steady technological growth, there was widespread disillusionment. The tragedy was likened to Greek tragedies in which heroes were destroyed by their *hubris*, and to medieval morality plays. Today, the *Titanic* tragedy remains one of the most discussed events in naval history, its implications and meaning a subject of continued debate and thought.

At 13,000 feet below the surface, the Titantic *deck plays host to the Alvin submarine of the 1986 Woods Hole Oceanographic Institute expedition.*

Where to Learn More

Ballard, Robert D., and Rick Archbold. *The Discovery of the Titanic.* Madison Press Books, 1987.

Broad, William J. "New Idea on Titanic Sinking Faults Steel as Main Culprit." *New York Times,* September 16, 1993.

Davie, Michael. *Titanic: The Death and Life of a Dream.* Alfred A. Knopf, 1987.

"Scientific Aftermath of the Titanic Disaster." *Literary Digest,* May 25, 1912, pp. 1096–97.

"Tragedy of the Titanic—A Complete Story." *New York Times*, April 28, 1912, pp. 1–8.

Wade, Wyn Craig. *The Titanic: End of a Dream.* Rawson, Wade, 1979.

breakdown

Andrea Doria–Stockholm collision

off Massachusetts 1956

Misinterpretation of radar signals led two ocean liners into a deadly game of "chicken" off the coast of Massachusetts. The Andrea Doria *rolled over on its side and sank, killing forty-three passengers and crew members, after the resulting collision with the* Stockholm, *which lost many of its own crew.*

by Sally Van Duyne

Background

On July 25, 1956, the liners *Andrea Doria* and *Stockholm* collided near the Nantucket Lightship off Massachusetts. The *Andrea Doria* sank, causing the deaths of forty-three passengers and crew members and becoming the first big liner to be lost in peacetime since the *Titanic* went down in 1912. On the *Stockholm*, three crew members were never seen again, and several more later died from their injuries. Misinterpretation of radar signals was the primary cause for the collision, while faulty ballasting contributed in the sinking.

The *Andrea Doria* was the flagship of the Italian Line. Built by Ansaldo of Sestri, near Genoa, the vessel was launched in 1951—the first passenger ship to come out of Italy after World War II. The *Doria* was seven hundred feet in length, weighed 29,083 tons, had a service speed of twenty-three knots, and was known for its graceful lines. On what was to be its last voyage, the ship left its home port at Genoa on July 17, 1956, and was scheduled to arrive in New York City on July 26.

The *Stockholm*, owned by the Swedish-American Line, was built in Sweden by Götaverken of Göthenberg and launched in 1943. It was 525 feet long and weighed 12,644 tons, with a service speed of nineteen knots. On the fateful day, the ship was beginning its homeward voyage to Sweden from New York City.

Both ships were heading toward the Nantucket Lightship, a vessel anchored fifty miles off Nantucket Island to guard its offshore shoals. The Nantucket Lightship is an important focal point for the sea lanes of the world. Although the shortest great circle—a circle outlined on the Earth's surface by a plane passing through its center—track for ships traveling between New York and European ports would be to the north of the vessel, they must pass to the south of it before turning north. Certain shipping lines had agreed to have their eastbound ships pass in a track twenty miles south of the light vessel and their westbound ships pass close to it. However, neither the Italian Line nor the Swedish-American Line were a party to this agreement.

Details of the Collision

On the afternoon of July 25, 1956, the *Andrea Doria*, eight days out of Genoa and due to dock in New York the next morning, encountered fog when it was still about 150 miles from the Nantucket Lightship. Captain Piero Calamai observed the normal precautions for these conditions: closing the watertight doors, sounding regular prolonged blasts on the siren, having an officer keep a constant watch on the radar screen for any sign of approaching ships, and reducing the ship's speed. Only the last of these can be criticized, as the *Doria* had reduced its speed by only five percent, from twenty-two knots to twenty-one, when the "moderate speed" called for in the collision rules is defined as a speed that allows the ship to be stopped within its visibility distance. By 8:00 A.M., the *Doria*'s visibility was only half a mile, and stopping her would take considerably more distance than that. However, it was the custom among sea captains bound by schedules to make only token reductions in speed in bad weather, while keeping a close watch on their radar.

At 10:20 A.M., the westbound *Doria* passed one mile to the south of the light vessel. At about 10:45, Second Officer Franchini saw a "blip" on the radar screen representing a ship that appeared to be not quite due ahead, but fine, or slightly, to starboard. Captain Calamai checked the radar screen himself and judged that the rapidly approaching ship was to starboard—that is, to the right—of his heading marker. Captain Calamai felt quite certain that the two ships were on a starboard-to-starboard path, but thought that the distance between them would be uncomfortably small. He gave the order to alter course to four degrees to port (left). In so doing, he went against rule eighteen of the collision rules, which states that "when two power-driven vessels are meeting end on, or nearly end on, so as to involve risk of collision, each shall alter her course to starboard, so that each may pass on the port side of the other." He had two justifications for going against this well-known rule: he believed that the two ships were clearly on a starboard-to-starboard course, and he thought that an alteration of course to starboard might force his ship into the shoal water to the north of the light vessel.

When the two ships were less than five miles apart, the *Doria* still could not see the *Stockholm,* while the *Stockholm* could see the masthead lights, but not the sidelights denoting port and starboard, on the *Doria.* When the ships were about two miles apart—and at their combined speeds of forty knots would close in on each other in three minutes—the *Doria* could see that the first navigation lights on the *Stockholm* were not green as expected in a starboard-to-starboard passing, but red. The red lights meant that the *Stockholm* was crossing the *Doria*'s bow to make a port-to-port passing. At that moment Captain Calamai gave the fatal order, "Hard-a-port," which was consistent with his plan for a starboard-to-starboard crossing. There was nothing the crew could do as they watched the bow of the *Stockholm* coming straight toward their starboard side.

The weather encountered by the *Stockholm* as it traveled east toward the Nantucket Lightship was very different from that encountered by the *Andrea Doria.* Somewhat before 11:00 P.M., as the *Stockholm* traveled through a clear moonlit night, Third Officer Carstens-Johannsen first saw the sign of an approaching ship at the twelve-mile radius on the radar screen. He recorded the position of the approaching ship as two degrees to port of his heading marker. Another plot of the ship a short time later also showed the ship to be slightly to port. As there was no sign of fog, Carstens saw no reason to call Captain Nordensen up to the bridge. But he did post a lookout on the port wing of the bridge to spot the approaching vessel, at which time he planned to alter his course to starboard to make a safe port-to-port passing. When the bridge lookout suddenly called out "Lights to port," Carstens immediately ordered a change in course of twenty degrees to starboard. Then he went out onto the bridge and saw to his horror that an immense liner was about to cross his bow, presenting the green lights of her starboard side. He shouted "Hard-a-starboard!" to the helmsman. As Captain Calamai tried at the last moment to increase the distance in a starboard-to-starboard passing, Third Officer Carstens-Johannsen tried to increase the distance in a port-to-port passing. Then Carstens pulled the telegraphs to "Stop" and "Full Astern."

The stem of the *Stockholm,* stiffened for travel through the ice in northern oceans, plowed into the side of the *Andrea Doria* just below the bridge down to her starboard fuel tanks with a momentum of thirty million

The stem of the *Stockholm,* stiffened for travel through the ice in northern oceans, plowed into the side of the *Andrea Doria* just below the bridge down to her starboard fuel tanks with a momentum of thirty million foot-pounds.

The Andrea Doria's *severe
list, or tilt, while sinking
rendered the port-side
lifeboats useless and caused
the starboard-side lifeboats
to swing far out over
the water, making them
hard to access.*

foot-pounds. Yet only one main compartment of the *Andrea Doria* was damaged, and it would have been able to withstand the collision had it not been for the severe list that developed soon afterward. Since the *Doria* was near the end of its journey, the starboard fuel tanks contained only air. When the starboard tanks were rent in the collision, water rushed to fill them, making the starboard side much heavier and causing a list to starboard of first eighteen and soon twenty-two degrees. In its pump room, the *Doria* had valves that could have been used to flood the port tanks with sea water for stability. The narrow tunnel that ran between the fuel tanks on the port and starboard sides to the pump room, however, had not been fitted with a watertight door because it was so far inboard. As a result, the tunnel flooded quickly after the collision, and it was not possible for the crew to reach the valves to flood the port tanks and right the ship.

When the passengers and crew of the *Doria* began readying the lifeboats, they found that the davits—cranes that project over the sides of a ship— could work only if the vessel's list was less than fifteen degrees. That rendered the port lifeboats useless, while the starboard-side lifeboats could not accommodate everyone and were hard to reach because, with the list, they swung far out over the water.

Of the 1,706 passengers and crew on the *Doria*, 1,663 survivors were taken off; most of the dead were killed on impact. The surviving passengers were all off by 4:00 A.M. on June 26; at 5:30, when the list reached forty degrees, the officers also left. At 10:09 A.M., eleven hours after the collision, the *Andrea Doria* rolled over onto its side and sank.

Impact

In the legal proceedings that followed, each line claimed that the other was totally to blame and maintained that its own officers were entirely blameless. The Swedish-American Line sued the Italian Line for four million dollars and the Italian Line sued the Swedish-American Line for 1.8 million dollars. The Swedish-American Line's case was by far the stronger. Most important was the immediate eighteen-degree list of the *Andrea Doria*, which placed the responsibility for her capsizing and sinking onto the owners of the *Doria*. The fact that the *Doria* turned to port to make a starboard-to-starboard crossing, thus violating the rules of the sea, was another incriminating factor. Also at issue were the speed of the *Andrea Doria* in fog, the failure of its crew to plot the bearings of the approaching *Stockholm*, and the disappearance of the *Doria*'s ship's log.

The important elements in the Italian Line's case were Third Officer Carstens-Johannsen's delay before making a starboard turn, his youth and inexperience, and the fact that the *Stockholm* was far to the north of the recommended track for eastbound vessels.

After the hearings had gone on for about three and a half months, the two lines dropped their claims against one another and reached an out-of-court settlement. As a result, the court never did apportion blame for the collision. It seems likely, however, that the two ships were not on safe parallel courses in which they would pass either port-to-port or starboard-to-starboard, but were converging at a very small angle. A lesson reemphasized in the disaster is that in order to conform to the collision rules, officers of the watch should treat fine bearings as a head-on collision course, and should make large alterations clearly discernable to the approaching ship in ample time.

There have been considerable changes in both the average officer's understanding of radar and the technology of radar since the *Doria-Stockholm* collision. Captain Calamai probably did not understand that a four-degree change in course would not be enough to make his intention of a starboard-to-starboard passing clear to the *Stockholm*. However, today, largely as a result of this disaster, officers on ships are required to take courses in radar. In addition, by international convention, automatic radar plotting aids have been required in all large ships since the 1980s. Apparently, the crew of the *Andrea*

Doria failed to plot the *Stockholm*'s bearings, and though the *Stockholm*'s crew claimed to have plotted the *Doria*'s bearings, they could not produce records of it.

The true-motion radars in use today allow the officer of the watch to see the actual course and speed of another ship, instead of its bearing relative to a heading marker. The previous radar system could result in errors because a ship can get a few degrees off course at any time, which may explain why the *Andrea Doria* thought the *Stockholm* was fine to starboard and the *Stockholm* thought the *Andrea Doria* was fine to port.

Another lesson learned from the collision involved the ballast tanks. The designers of the *Andrea Doria* had followed the practice common at the time of stipulating that empty oil tanks be flooded with sea water to stabilize the ship in case of excessive listing. This was an unreasonable burden to lay upon the engineers, who did not want to contaminate their fuel tanks with sea water and then face a time-consuming and costly cleaning process. The 1960 Safety of Life at Sea (SOLAS) convention criticized the practice of using oil tanks for ballast, and recommended that full stability information be issued to the staff and that diagrams of ballasting arrangements be displayed on board. After the *Doria*'s experience, shipbuilders began including separate tanks for ballast water and providing remote control access to the valves.

A final effect of the *Andrea Doria-Stockholm* collision was the 1977 introduction of a traffic separation scheme for ships passing near the Nantucket Lightship. It required that eastbound ships keep to a lane south of the light vessel, and that westbound ships keep to a lane north of the light vessel. The separation zone is three miles wide, with the light vessel in between the two lanes.

Where to Learn More

Barnaby, K. C. *Some Ship Disasters and Their Causes*. A. S. Barnes, 1970.

Hoffer, William. *Saved: The Story of the Andrea Doria—The Greatest Sea Rescue in History*. Summit Books, 1979.

Marriott, John. *Disaster at Sea*. Ian Allan, 1987.

Moscow, Alvin. *Collision Course*. Grosset & Dunlap, 1981.

breakdown

Thresher sinking

Atlantic Ocean **1963**

An advanced American nuclear-powered submarine plunged beneath its "crush depth" and sank, killing all 129 crew members.

Background

by Leonard C. Bruno

On the morning of April 10, 1963, an advanced American nuclear-powered submarine, the *Thresher*, attempted to dive to its maximum operating depth of 10,000 feet. At 9:13 A.M., a short time after submersion, communication from the *Thresher* to the accompanying surface vessel became erratic. At 9:17 A.M., the surface vessel heard the words "test depth" and then a muted thud. Nothing more was ever heard from the submarine again. The entire crew of 129 men died in this accident, the worst peacetime submarine disaster ever recorded at that time. While the cause of the disaster remains shrouded in mystery, many experts believe that carelessness and rushed construction resulted in a pipe failure and possibly a power loss that crippled the *Thresher*, rendering the vessel helpless to halt its descent into fatal depths.

The USS *Thresher*, with a price tag of $45 million, was the first of an advanced class of attack nuclear-powered submarines. These were to be true submarines, designed to spend prolonged periods of time in the depths of the sea. The *Thresher* was powered by a Westinghouse S5W nuclear reactor that drove the submarine's single propeller via a steam turbine. The *Thresher* also had a small backup diesel-electric power plant. This class of submarine would eventually carry nuclear-tipped underwater-to-underwater Subroc missiles.

The *Thresher* featured an innovative tear-shaped hull which, though very efficient underwater, was primarily designed to accommodate the submarine's state-of-the-art sonar equipment, designated as BQQ-2. The vessel's design placed this sonar equipment on the specially shaped hull, far removed from the interfering noise of the submarine's machinery and propeller.

Submerged, the *Thresher* could achieve speeds of thirty knots or more and could submerge to depths greater than that posted by any previous submarine. The sub was 278 feet long and featured a beam of twenty-one feet; its displacement was 3700 tons. Built at the Portsmouth Naval Shipyard in New Hampshire, the *Thresher*'s keel was laid on May 28, 1958, and the submarine was launched on July 9, 1960.

The most striking advantage that the nuclear-powered *Thresher* enjoyed over its diesel-engine predecessors was in the realm of underwater endurance. Diesel-driven submarines stored energy in batteries, which then propelled the submarine through the use of electric motors. Since the energy storage capacity of batteries is limited, and since diesel engines required oxygen, a conventional submarine could stay submerged for only a moderate period of time. Nuclear power, however, was not handcuffed by such oxygen requirements. Through the process of electrolysis, the *Thresher* could produce oxygen from water.

During its sea trials, nonetheless, the *Thresher* was subject to several disquieting incidents. On April 31, 1961, after checking the submarine's trim (its buoyancy and ability to stay balanced) during fairly shallow dives, Commander Dean L. Axene ordered that a deeper dive be attempted. As the *Thresher* descended, its instruments suddenly indicated that the submarine was near the pressure limit that the hull could withstand, although all other indicators confirmed that the submarine was not even approaching its maximum operating depth. Axene aborted the dive and returned the submarine to the surface. At the shipyard, the instruments were checked and found to have been faulty.

The submarine then resumed its sea trials. Throughout this trial period, the *Thresher* would often make brief stops at port to conduct routine maintenance and to rest its crew. In November 1961, at one such stop in San Juan, Puerto Rico, the *Thresher* underwent its usual routine of shutting down the nuclear reactor and switching to diesel power. After about eight hours, the diesel engines stalled, and the submarine switched to backup battery power. The crew soon recognized that the diesel repairs would be time-consuming, and that the backup battery power would be inadequate. The nuclear power system was again activated, although this process would itself take several hours and risked overheating the reactor. During that time, the crew was forced to repair the diesel engines in near-darkness. Without ventilation, the

temperatures inside the increasingly tense submarine reached 140 degrees Fahrenheit before the diesel engines were repaired and the situation was brought under control.

The *Thresher* continued with the sea trials until it returned to the shipyard for Christmas. The trials resumed in February 1962, as the *Thresher* underwent shock tests to determine its ability to withstand underwater explosions. On June 3 of that year, a short distance off Cape Canaveral, Florida, the submarine was the victim of an unscheduled blow: a tugboat rammed into it accidentally. A three-foot gash in the submarine's port side resulted. After being repaired at the shipyard, the *Thresher* was subjected to two more weeks of pounding by underwater blasts. Although it suffered some damage, the submarine passed all the shock tests. The *Thresher* then went into drydock for nine months for a complete overhaul.

On April 9, 1963, following this overhaul at Portsmouth, the *Thresher* went out to sea for a series of shallow test dives under its new skipper, Lieutenant Commander John W. Harvey. Harvey was a veteran of atomic submarines with periods of service on the *Nautilus*, as well as the *Tullabee* and the *Sea Dragon*. After the shallow test trials were completed, the submarine crossed the Georges Bank area of the Atlantic to pass the continental shelf and enter truly deep waters. The vessel would never return.

The nuclear-powered Thresher *before its 1963 sinking. Priced at $45 million, the sub was seen as the first of an advanced class of nuclear-powered submarines.*

Details of the Disaster

On the morning of April 10, in water between 7,800 and 8,500 feet deep, the *Thresher* began a depth dive. The *Thresher* was accompanied by a submarine rescue ship, the *Skylark*. In coastal waters, the *Skylark* had the resources to attempt crew rescues if the need should arise. In these deeper waters off the continental shelf, however, it could provide only a communication link and navigation checks.

At 8:53 A.M., the submarine approached its test depth of nearly ten thousand feet. Communication between the two vessels continued in normal fashion. At 9:13 A.M., however, communication from the *Thresher* became garbled and sporadic. Sometime between 9:14 and 9:17 A.M., disaster struck somewhere in the depths below. During those minutes, the communications personnel on the *Skylark* heard the words "attempting to blow" and—just prior to a muted, dull thud—the words "test depth."

For one hour and forty minutes thereafter, the *Skylark* circled the area, frantically attempting to reestablish communications. It dropped hand grenades, a signal for a sub to surface, every ten minutes. There was no response to any of the *Skylark* efforts from the depths below.

For one hour and forty minutes thereafter, the *Skylark* circled the area, frantically attempting to reestablish communications. It dropped hand grenades, a signal for a sub to surface, every ten minutes. There was no response to any of the *Skylark* efforts from the depths below.

The Navy ordered an extensive air and sea rescue operation, but the effort was hindered by clouds, winds of about thirty to forty-five miles an hour, and waves five to nine feet high. Before dusk, another submarine rescue ship sent to the area spotted an oil slick and a few bits of cork and yellow plastic floating on the surface. Within a few hours, the awful fate of the submarine was clear; the *Thresher* had exceeded its design depth and imploded. Admiral George W. Anderson, the Chief of Naval Operations, notified the crew's families and scheduled a press conference to announce the loss. "To those of us who have been brought up in the traditions of the sea it is a sad occasion when a ship is reported lost," Anderson noted grimly. The Navy then prepared to mount one of the greatest searches in United States naval history.

Impact

Among the scores of vessels used by the Navy in its grim effort to locate the lost submarine was the bathyscaphe *Trieste*. This submersible had recorded the deepest dive on record, and it was the only vessel capable of going down to the depths where the wreckage of the *Thresher* was thought to be located. The *Trieste* was a vertical-movement vehicle with minimal maneuverability.

The trailing cameras of the Navy's new research ship, the *Atlantis*, had photographed a mass of debris over an area of approximately 1,000 by 4,000 yards. The *Trieste* made its first dive to that spot on June 24, 1963. Several dives followed over the next two months, until on August 29 the *Trieste* spotted a sizable deposit of fairly large pieces of metal. Using its newly installed mechanical arm, it picked up a piece of twisted and mangled brass pipe. This piece of pipe was positively identified as part of the *Thresher*, since it carried its part number, job-order number, and the numerical designation of the *Thresher*, "593."

The wreckage of the Thresher *was photographed in 1964. The hull number, "593," is partially visible at right, slightly above center.*

As the physical evidence accumulated, the Court of Inquiry set about making its determination of the cause of the tragedy. Investigators quickly ruled out any enemy involvement, and then ruled it "inconceivable" that human error had caused the disaster. The Court's final opinion painted a chilling picture of the last moments endured by the *Thresher's* crew. After accumulating 1,700 pages of testimony from 120 witnesses, the determination came that the "most likely" cause of the disaster was a cracked fitting or faulty joint in a cooling pipe. Such a break would have filled a small compartment with sea water in seconds, a development that could short out a key control panel or power circuit. This would have caused the nuclear reactor to shut down, resulting in the loss of propulsion power. As the ship filled with water, its auxiliary diesel power would be insufficient to counteract its plunge. Moreover, the system in place to expel sea-water ballast would be unable to function because of the tremendous counterpressure present at such great depth. Under the increasing water pressure, the *Thresher's* hull would have twisted and rippled like rubber before the submarine imploded.

Although most experts find this hypothesis the most reasonable, two additional explanations have been proposed. The first is that an open sea valve may have been to blame. Openings in the *Thresher's* hull allowed water to be taken in for use in the nuclear power cooling system. If the submarine's electrical system had shut down because of a leak or any other reason, this valve could not have been closed electrically; sea water would subsequently flow into the vessel. A second alternative explanation offered contend that the *Thresher* may have encountered a mammoth underwater wave. A large storm moved across the Gulf of Maine on April 8, 1963. This storm could have generated a sub-surface eddy that would raise an underwater wave of up to 300 feet in height. Such a sub-surface wave might have driven the submarine far below its crush depth.

During the Court of Inquiry's own investigation, a number of unsettling facts about the rushed construction history of the *Thresher* came to light. Its periscope control had been installed backwards. A spike was found in its air circulation system. The "open" and "close" indicators were reversed on at least 20 percent of its hydraulic valves. The most appalling discovery, though, may have been that tests on 145 of the vessel's pipe joints revealed that 14 percent were below standard. Yet the submarine was sent to sea with 2,855 other joints untested.

Although investigators ruled out human error as the source of the disaster, they did conclude, from this construction and drydock record, that "practices, conditions and standards existing at the time were short of those required to insure safe operation." The *Thresher* tragedy, although its exact cause remains undetermined, may trace back to this carelessness. The Court also acknowledged that the Navy's deployment of new design technology may have outpaced mastery of its practical application.

The *Thresher* disaster did lead to several reforms in Navy policies. First, a new quality-assurance program was implemented at naval shipyards wherein fitters were required to fill out and sign a card verifying that they had brazed each joint. Ultrasound replaced x-rays to inspect fittings and verify their integrity. Redundant hydraulic systems were installed that enabled valves to be closed without the use of electrical power. Finally, submarines were fitted with a new emergency "blow" system that introduced air directly into ballast tanks at a rate seven times faster than could the equivalent system on the *Thresher*.

The Navy also prioritized the development of highly maneuverable deep-sea submersibles. This resulted in the DSRV-1 (Deep Submergence Rescue Vehicle), a vessel that can rescue submarine crews at down to 3,500 feet; the DSRV-2, which can operate at depths to 5,000 feet; and the nuclear-powered NR-1, which operates at depths to 3,000 feet and can remain submerged for extended periods of time.

The Navy was subject to considerable political criticism for its handling of the *Thresher* disaster. The decision to classify all twelve volumes of its inquiry as secret meant that its determination could not be evaluated independently. In addition, Navy officials appeared uncooperative during the congressional hearings held by the Joint Committee on Atomic Energy.

The concerns of the Joint Committee are justifiable and shared by many others. After all, a nuclear reactor now rests on the ocean floor 220 miles off the coast of Boston. Observers note, however, that the *Thresher* underwent an extensive overhaul prior to its final voyage that might have included renewal of the reactor core. Because of this, experts hope that the fission product content of its core would be low enough to render it harmless.

While the cause of the disaster remains shrouded in mystery, many experts believe that carelessness and rushed construction resulted in a pipe failure and possibly a power loss that crippled the *Thresher*, rendering the vessel helpless to halt its descent into fatal depths.

breakdown

Where to Learn More

Bentley, John. The *Thresher* Disaster. Doubleday, 1974.

Colley, David P. "The Lessons Learned from SSN 593." *Mechanical Engineering*, February 1987, pp. 54–59.

Gannon, Robert. "What Really Happened to the *Thresher*." *Popular Science*, February 1964, pp. 102–109, 208–209.

Polmar, Norman. Death of the *Thresher*. Chilton, 1964.

"*Thresher* Post-Mortem." *Scientific American*, November 1963, pp. 66–68.

Scorpion sinking

Atlantic Ocean **1968**

by Leonard C. Bruno

Four months after the nuclear-powered submarine vanished with its crew of ninety-nine in May of 1968, portions of the Scorpion *were found, but the cause of the sinking remained a mystery. The accident raised concerns about the safety of powering submarines with nuclear reactors.*

Background

On May 27, 1968, the *Scorpion*, an American nuclear-powered submarine with a crew of ninety-nine, disappeared without a trace in the middle of the Atlantic Ocean. On October 28, 1968, following one of the most extensive searches in United States naval history, portions of the lost submarine were located about four hundred miles southwest of the Azores. While the naval Court of Inquiry failed to identify the cause of the *Scorpion* disaster, photographs of the wreckage rule out hostile action and indicate that the source of the accident was internal to the submarine.

The nuclear-powered *Scorpion* (SSN-589) was built in Groton, Connecticut, by the Electric Boat Division of the General Dynamics Corporation. Sleek and powerful, the *Scorpion* was an attack submarine of the *Skipjack* class, designed primarily to hunt down and destroy enemy submarines. Accommodating ten officers and eighty-nine crewmen, the vessel measured over 251 feet in length and thirty-one feet in beam and displaced 3,075 tons of water.

The *Scorpion* was armed with six torpedo tubes and powered by a water-cooled nuclear reactor. This reactor—a Westinghouse S5W with a thermal power of seventy megawatts—combined with the submarine's teardrop-shaped Albacore-type hull, gave the *Scorpion* an exceptionally high submerged speed of thirty knots. The S5W propulsion plant was the workhorse of the Navy until the 1970s and was equipped with a large number of redundancy features for its major components; if one component failed, another one could usually operate in its place. The majestic submarine was loaded with two steam generators, two pressurizers, two sets of turbines, and two turbo-generators. The sub also had conventional diesel engines and back-up batteries.

The *Scorpion* was launched on December 19, 1959, and joined the U.S. Atlantic Fleet in August 1960. It performed admirably during the next few years, and was overhauled from June 1963 to May 1964. Following another tour of duty, it drydocked at the Norfolk, Virginia, naval shipyard during February 1967 for another overhaul, which included refueling its nuclear reactor. During October of that year, the *Scorpion* began sea trials under a new skipper, Commander Francis A. Slattery. After a tour in the Mediterranean in early 1968, the sub left Gibraltar to return to the Norfolk naval shipyard.

Details of the Disaster

On May 21, 1968, during the voyage to Norfolk, the *Scorpion* reported its bearings south of the Azores, and noted that everything was operating normally. The submarine was never heard from again.

On May 27, 1968, the submarine was reported overdue at Norfolk. Alarm mounted quickly when the *Scorpion* failed to return at its expected time. As the hours stretched into days, the Navy devoted fifty-five ships and twenty-three aircraft to an extensive search. On June 5, 1968, the Chief of Naval Operations announced it presumed lost. Over the ensuing months, the dark mystery surrounding the *Scorpion* and its demise deepened.

Eventually, experts identified wreckage of the submarine from photographs taken by the remote-controlled undersea cameras of the *Mizar*, a naval research ship.

Impact

The *Mizar* did not happen upon the carcass of the *Scorpion* by chance. Sophisticated maritime detective work led the Navy to the site. Investigators knew that if a *Skipjack*-class submarine went down in the deep Atlantic, it

The *Mizar* did not happen upon the carcass of the *Scorpion* by chance. Sophisticated maritime detective work led the Navy to the site.

The Scorpion, *shown in a photo taken about eight years before it sank in the Atlantic Ocean. The last communication ever heard from the sub indicated that all systems were operating normally.*

would descend past its crush depth of about 2,000 feet and implode. Navy antisubmarine warfare scientists turned to the Navy's underwater listening system, called SOSUS, an elaborate array of underwater devices that monitored the movements of foreign submarines. The implosion, they suspected, would register on the SOSUS system.

A review of SOSUS tapes from the time period in which the *Scorpion* vanished revealed a peak noise event. At least two Navy listening devises detected the disturbance, which enabled investigators to settle on the general area of the Atlantic where the submarine sank. Navy personnel went to that area and detonated charges of TNT calibrated to generate acoustical energy comparable to what would have resulted from the *Scorpion*'s implosion. When the trace of these TNT noises on the SOSUS tapes matched that of the earlier event, the Navy dispatched the *Mizar*, with its trailing 35mm cameras, to photograph the area.

Several thousand undersea photographs provided a haunting view of the wreckage on the dark ocean floor. The bow appeared to have sunk partially into the sandy bottom. The submarine's "sail" or superstructure was lying intact more than 100 feet away; it had broken away from the body of the *Scorpion*. The nuclear reactor was not visible.

These photographs and various forms of testimony were considered by the naval Court of Inquiry that convened in June 1968. The seven-man court

breakdown

met intermittently for eleven weeks and heard ninety witnesses before issuing its final report on January 31, 1969. The court's report, though, reflected the continuing mystery of the *Scorpion's* final hours: "The certain cause of the loss of the *Scorpion* cannot be ascertained from evidence now available." While the court was able to eliminate several theories, it was unable to arrive at a hypothesis to explain the *Scorpion* disaster.

Before the Court of Inquiry received the *Mizar* photographs, it identified several possible causes for the loss of the *Scorpion*. Did the submarine collide with a seamount (an underwater mountain)? Was the submarine a victim of hostile action from the Soviets? Did it collide with another vessel?

A popular rumor about the disaster contended that the *Scorpion* had been on a secret mission and had been lost in waters frequented by Soviet submarines and surface vessels. At that juncture in the Cold War, such speculation held some weight. Hardly a week seemed to pass without a clash or minor incident between Soviet and American ships. In fact, the correspondence of a *Scorpion* crew member dated two weeks before the sinking indicated that the vessel had been confronted by a Soviet destroyer with its guns trained on the American submarine.

The *Mizar* photographs, however, indicated to most observers that the origin of the *Scorpion* disaster was internal. After evaluating these photographs, the court eliminated both its seamount collision and hostile action/second vessel hypotheses. As one assessment of the disaster maintained, "had the *Scorpion* been hit by a torpedo or scraped by a surface ship while she was near the surface, this would have left identifiable damage."

Another possibility addressed by the court was that the *Scorpion*, prior to the accident, was unfit or damaged. The submarine, after all, was en route to the Norfolk shipyard. The court heard testimony that the submarine had hairline cracks across its hull. Another witness stated that the submarine had a small oil leak around its propeller shaft. A crew member who was left ashore in Spain due to illness recalled that the *Scorpion* had been leaking hydraulic fluid around its periscope fitting, and that it was having trouble with its navigational equipment.

The *Scorpion* did report at least five mechanical problems before leaving Spain. Moreover, the submarine had collided with a barge during a storm in the Naples harbor one month before the *Scorpion's* final disaster. This barge had been placed between the *Scorpion* and an American warship as a buffer, and the submarine's stern had taken the brunt of the impact. Divers made a partial inspection of the docked submarine after the collision but reported no significant damage. Investigators also noted that the Navy's own "Subsafe" program had not been completely implemented on the *Scorpion*. This program, initiated in response to the *Thresher* disaster in 1963, involved a series of safety modifications.

Even so, the court determined that the submarine's overall condition was "excellent" and that none of the pending repair work was of a nature that would have had an impact on the *Scorpion*'s safety. It also concluded that the disaster could not be attributed to the delayed completion of the "Subsafe" program, and it ruled out the possibility that the *Scorpion*'s nuclear reactor had exploded. A catastrophe of such magnitude, they reasoned, would have been detected.

The court also judged that the *Scorpion*'s crew was well-trained and prepared for emergencies. The court felt it improbable that any aberrant behavior on the part of the crew might have led to the disaster, noting that no testimony or documentation was put forth to indicate that any officer or seaman was unstable or unreliable. The court therefore discounted the possibility that the loss of the *Scorpion* was caused by "the intent, fault, negligence or inefficiency of any person or persons in the naval service or connected therewith."

The court, however, to a degree refused to speculate on any such internal occurrences, and many outside observers hold that the court rejected this and other possible causes too readily. Critics point to control failure, for example, as a possible explanation that the Court of Inquiry was too quick to dismiss. According to this theory, the submarine might have been running very fast and very deep when its diving mechanism suddenly locked into the "dive" position. Proponents of this explanation note that such a development would have sent the submarine below its crush depth before correction was possible.

Another possibility raised concerned the ever-present danger of leaks, particularly in light of the allegations that were made about cracks in the *Scorpion*'s hull and a faulty propeller shaft. Under the severe pressure of great depths, such flaws could lead to a sudden, fatal breach. A possible malfunction in one of the submarine's own torpedos was discussed as well. The *Mizar* photographs do not rule this theory out, and some experts find this last hypothesis the most likely. To date, though, no exact cause for the *Scorpion* disaster has been determined.

The loss of the *Scorpion* and the failure of the U.S. Navy to identify its cause generated a great deal of national controversy. Once the political storm subsided, a logistical issue remained: the Navy had no submarine rescue capability for depths below 1,300 feet. After the 1963 loss of the *Thresher*, the Navy had begun a research and development program aimed at producing deep-sea rescue vehicles. The loss of the *Scorpion* gave impetus to this program.

The Navy's first Deep Submergence Rescue Vehicle (DSRV), the DSRV-1, was launched in 1970. Shaped like a torpedo, with a fiberglass hull, this fifty-foot vessel could operate at depths of up to 3,500 feet. The DSRV-1 could link to the submarine's escape hatch and take as many as twenty-four men onboard to carry to the surface. The DSRV-2, built by Lockheed, was able to

breakdown

operate at up to 5,000 feet. Both submersibles could be transported by air or water or carried on a nuclear submarine, which could launch and recover them without surfacing.

The Navy also built an experimental rescue craft called the NR-1. About 136 feet long, with an operating depth of up to 3,000 feet, the NR-1 resembled a small submarine. The vessel had room for a crew of seven, and was powered by a small pressurized-water reactor. Its two propellers and tunnel thrusters made it highly maneuverable. Other special features included sonar to navigate and locate sea-floor objects, and a large recovery device.

Although none of these rescue submersibles have been required to aid sunken submarines, they have been used for comparable missions. In 1976, for example, the NR-1 helped in the rescue of an F-14 fighter that rolled off a Navy aircraft carrier and was submerged in 1,960 feet of water.

The possibility of nuclear contamination from the *Scorpion*'s reactor raises a final issue. The submarine's debris is scattered over a large area. Since the hull was compressed at both ends during the disaster, it is not possible to assess the condition of the reactor compartment. However, the seabed around the wreckage of the *Scorpion* has been investigated three times to date. Samples show minor amounts of cobalt-60, an indication that the primary reactor system experienced leakage. In March 1975, Admiral Hyman G. Rickover reported to Congress that while the cause of the *Scorpion* disaster remained undetermined, there was still "no evidence that it was due to a problem with the nuclear reactors." Twenty years later, the *Scorpion's* nuclear reactor still sits abandoned on the ocean floor.

Twenty years later, the *Scorpion*'s nuclear reactor still sits abandoned on the ocean floor.

Where to Learn More

Eriksen, Viking O. *Sunken Nuclear Submarines: A Threat to the Environment?* Norwegian University Press, 1990.

Middleton, Drew. *Submarine, the Ultimate Naval Weapon: Its Past, Present & Future.* Playboy Press, 1976.

"Presumed Lost." *Newsweek*, June 17, 1968, p. 74.

"Finding the *Scorpion*." *Newsweek*, November 18, 1968, p. 104.

"Loss of *Scorpion* Baffles Inquiry." *New York Times*, February 1, 1969, p. 1.

"Sub Found—But Mystery Remains." *U.S. News & World Report*, November 11, 1968, p. 12.

Ocean Ranger oil-drilling rig sinking

A broken window on an offshore oil-drilling rig precipitated a catastrophic chain of events that caused the sinking of the rig and the death of all 84 people on board.

Background

On February 15, 1982, a small broken window in the control room of the *Ocean Ranger*, a mobile offshore drilling rig, triggered a series of events that eventually caused the ocean vessel to capsize, resulting in the death of all 84 crew members. The broken window, a seemingly minor problem, launched a terrible sequence in which a number of factors on the rig—improperly trained operators, inadequate lifeboats, substandard emergency protective clothing, freezing temperatures, and a fierce storm—combined to doom the *Ocean Ranger's* crew.

The cause of the broken window remains a mystery. Perhaps heavy winds or high waves smashed the glass; perhaps it was a result of drilling operations that took place earlier that day. In any case, the shattered window allowed ocean water to drench several of the *Ocean Ranger's* control panels. The water caused a short-circuit in the ballast control panel, a development that destabilized the rig and caused it to lean precariously forward in the frigid North Atlantic waters. As subsequent events unfolded, crew members desperately scrambled about the rig. But they were ultimately unable to save the *Ocean Ranger* or themselves.

Built in 1976 in Hiroshima, Japan, the *Ocean Ranger* was a semisubmersible oil-drilling rig. Owned by the New Orleans-based Ocean Drilling & Exploration Company (ODECO), the *Ocean Ranger* was an odd-looking structure. The working platform was supported on eight columns, a style that made the oil-drilling rig look like an eight-legged table. The eight legs were supported in two groups of four on top of multicompartment tanks called ballast tanks. The four-hundred-foot-long ballast tanks could be filled with air to keep the structure floating or water to help the rig maintain its stability. If heavy loads were placed on the front of the ship, for instance, the weight would cause listing in the front. The ballast tanks would be adjusted accordingly so that water allowed into the rear ballast tanks would level the rig. When the load was removed, the ballast tanks would subsequently be pumped out to avoid listing at the rear. An experienced control room operator was generally assigned to operate the ballast system since it was such a crucial part of the oil rig's stability.

The ballast control panel was designed specifically for the *Ocean Ranger*. The panel consisted of an abundance of electrically operated switches that opened and closed valves on the ballast tanks. In the event power was lost, the switches could be operated by the use of a manual control rod. The ultimate value of this back-up methodology was questionable, though. Without power the rig's gauges would not work, making it impossible to determine the position of the valves. This shortcoming proved to be a significant one.

Details of the Disaster

The weather on February 14, 1982, was relatively calm during the day. The *Ocean Ranger* and two other mobile offshore drilling rigs were drilling for oil 160 miles off the coast of Newfoundland, Canada. These drilling rigs which ranged from three hundred to four hundred feet in length, were operating in waters over 250 feet deep. Due to the potential instability of the drilling rig and other potential hazards, each drilling rig was required to be accompanied by a rescue ship. The accompanying rescue ship typically doubled as the supply boat and drifted within two miles of the drilling rig. In the aftermath of the *Ocean Ranger* disaster, which left no survivors, investigators were forced to reconstruct the sequence of mishaps from radio transmissions received by the other mobile rigs and the three rescue ships in the area.

The unfortunate chain of events began at dinnertime on February 14. Internal communication was overheard that indicated that the crew was mopping up water and cleaning up broken glass in the control room, a clean-up process that was hindered by electrical shocks that several crew members received from a control panel. The investigation into the rig's demise later revealed that the window that broke in the control room was directly to the side of the ballast control panel. The incoming water short-circuited the panel, which meant the system could only be operated by manual controls. In all likelihood, not a single person on the *Ocean Ranger* knew how to operate the ballast control panel manually. Even if an operator was experienced with the manual controls, the system was not realistically operable since all information gauges were also shorted out. The erratic behavior of the ballast control board, which eventually caused the ballast tanks in the front of the rig to fill with water, was thus exceedingly difficult to reverse.

As the evening passed, the weather turned fierce. The drilling rigs were pummeled by fifty-five-foot-high waves, eighty-mile-per-hour winds, and subzero temperatures. Conversations throughout the evening between the *Ocean Ranger* and the other ships conveyed no cause for alarm until around 9:00 P.M. At that time, an internal transmission on the *Ocean Ranger* requested that an electrical technician report to the control room; valves used to stabilize the drilling rig were opening and closing on their own.

Shortly after midnight, the *Ocean Ranger* radio operator sent out a distress message. The message, which was repeated ten to twenty times in a half hour, transmitted that the drilling rig was suffering from a severe list of ten to fifteen degrees forward in rough seas and required immediate assistance. While this angle of tilt would normally not be a significant problem, the tall waves were flooding holes in the drilling rig where the anchor chains were kept, dramatically increasing the list.

Less than two hours later, the crew of the *Ocean Ranger* proceeded to life raft stations to abandon ship. The listing of the oil rig had reached the point of no return. As the crew boarded the lifeboats, they may well have thought that they would yet be delivered from harm. Unfortunately, the lifeboats offered the crew members little chance of survival.

The lifeboats the crew boarded in the early morning were not designed for the fierce environment they were about to battle. The launch of the boats required a seventy-foot drop into the ocean. This drop, coupled with high winds, made the safe use of these emergency boats an impossibility. Some investigators of the tragedy have even concluded that a number of the lifeboats experienced extensive damage from bouncing off the side of the Ocean Ranger during launching.

Evidence indicates that probably only one of the lifeboats successfully survived the launch and had a chance for rescue. The rescue ships only saw one manned lifeboat upon reaching the scene. This lifeboat, though,

Conversations throughout the evening between the *Ocean Ranger* and the other ships conveyed no cause for alarm until around 9:00 P.M. At that time, an internal transmission on the *Ocean Ranger* requested that an electrical technician report to the control room; valves used to stabilize the drilling rig were opening and closing on their own.

breakdown

sustained damage to the bow during the launch and the crew on board was forced to frantically bail out the water that gushed through the wound in the bow's side. Still, the boat remained afloat. Moreover, its occupants had life jackets, the boat's motor was operating, and the rescue boats were approaching. Armed with these factors in their favor, the men in the lifeboat might have been saved had the rescue ships possessed adequate life saving equipment.

The *Seaforth Highlander*, the rescue ship assigned to the *Ocean Ranger*, had moved toward the beleaguered rig as soon as it heard the distress signal. But while rescue ships typically stay within a mile or two of their assigned ship, the storm had pushed the *Seaforth Highlander* eight miles away from the *Ocean Ranger*. Fighting through the turbulent sea, the rescue vessel was unable to reach the rig until an hour after the distress signal first sounded.

HIGHLANDER'S **RESCUE ATTEMPT FAILS.** The crews on the rescue ships for the other two mobile offshore oil-drilling rigs had been monitoring the *Ocean Ranger* situation as well. Within one to two hours, both rescue ships were in the vicinity of the sinking oil rig, but the *Seaforth Highlander* was the only rescue team that saw any living members of the *Ocean Ranger* crew. Just before 2:00 A.M., the crew of the *Highlander* saw distress flares abruptly materialize out of the dark night. As the *Highlander* crew approached the flares, they spotted a single lifeboat with a hole in it churning in their direction.

The lifeboat and the rescue ship maneuvered in the roiling waves in an attempt to get side by side. The rescue ship tossed lifelines to the lifeboat. The lifeboat was fastened to the rescue ship with one of these lines, but the rough sea violently tossed the two boats, making every step of the rescue effort a treacherous one. With the lifeboat lashed to the *Highlander*, several men from the rig exited the covered part of the lifeboat to board the rescue ship. The boat suddenly capsized, throwing the men from the *Ocean Ranger* into the freezing North Atlantic sea. The crew of the *Seaforth Highlander* threw inflatable life rafts to the men below, who were buffeted about by the surging waves. Although the life rafts were thrown over within minutes and landed right next to the men, they made no effort to grab for them. The bitterly cold water had practically paralyzed the men. The *Seaforth Highlander* made several attempts to pull the crew out of the ocean, but it could do little else since the ship was not equipped with baskets to scoop people out of the water. Finally, with the unfortunate men from the lifeboat lost to the ocean, the rescue ship was forced to move on in search of other potential survivors. But none could be found.

The search for survivors continued for a week after the disaster, by air and sea. Drift plots were calculated to estimate the farthest distance that an object could drift from its original position under existing weather conditions. The search within the drift plot boundaries located several lifeboats and

Just before 2:00 A.M., the crew of the *Highlander* saw distress flares abruptly materialize out of the dark night. As the *Highlander* crew approached the flares, they spotted a single lifeboat with a hole in it churning in their direction.

Eighty-four crew members perished when the Ocean Ranger's ballast control panel short-circuited, causing a dangerous list of the rig.

bodies, some more than forty miles away from the capsizing. The search was called off on March 1, 1982. Eighty-four people were killed on the *Ocean Ranger*. Only twenty-two of the bodies were ever recovered.

Impact

Regulatory changes in the wake of the *Ocean Ranger* tragedy were numerous. One of the most disturbing aspects of the *Ocean Ranger* disaster was that the damage could have been limited to only the loss of property. All crew members probably reached the lifeboats safely. Unfortunately, the lifeboats were not designed to withstand the severe pounding of the seventy-foot drop from the rig into the ocean. In addition, while many crew members were able to shrug into lifejackets equipped with emergency lights that could easily be spotted by rescuers, the lifejackets provided no protection against the cold water. Without such protection, the jackets merely kept dead bodies afloat. Those who successfully kept their lifeboat afloat did not fare any better, for the rescue boats proved to be inadequately prepared for the harsh storm conditions as well.

As a result of the capsizing of the *Ocean Ranger*, the National Transportation Safety Board instructed the United States Coast Guard to require that:

1. An operating manual be provided for semisubmersible mobile offshore units that includes guidance for countering accidental flooding of ballast tanks, as well as guidelines for preventing flooding into the anchor chain compartments;

2. Control room operators be licensed in ballasting procedures for mobile offshore drilling units;

3. Exposure suits to protect those in the ocean be provided for 150 percent of the persons on offshore drilling rigs where water temperatures may go below sixty degrees;

4. Rescue vessels assigned to the mobile offshore drilling rigs be outfitted to retrieve disabled persons from the water under adverse conditions;

5. The suitability of approved lifeboats, life rafts, and lifesaving equipment be evaluated.

breakdown

To the families who lost fathers, sons, and brothers in the tragedy, such corrective measures provided little comfort. One month after the disaster, the families of the victims brought a $1.7 billion lawsuit against ODECO and Mobile Canada, the owners and operators of the *Ocean Ranger*, respectively. By mid-1984, all but a handful of the families had reached out-of-court settlements with the companies involved.

Where to Learn More

"Capsized Rig's Design O.K." *Engineering News Record*, February 25, 1982, p. 12.

Clugston, Michael. "An Aftermath of Sorrow and Anger." *Maclean's*, March 1, 1982, pp. 28–31.

—. "The Search of the *Ocean Ranger*." *Maclean's*, May 3, 1982, pp. 17–18.

—. "How the *Ocean Ranger* Sank." *Maclean's*, February 21, 1983, p. 14.

—. "A Preventable Tragedy." *Maclean's*, August 27, 1984, p. 45.

Giniger, Henry. "Hope Fades for 84 on Rig; 18 on Soviet Freighter Die." *New York Times*, Wednesday, February 17, 1982, p. 3.

Joyce, Randolph, "The Cruel Sea." *Maclean's*, March 1, 1982, pp. 26–27.

—. "The *Ocean Ranger*'s Mystery Deepens." *Maclean's*, March 8, 1982, pp. 24–25.

LeMoyne, James, et al. "The *Ocean Ranger*'s Night of Death," *Newsweek*, March 1, 1982, p. 48.

National Transportation Safety Board. *Capsizing and Sinking of the U.S. Mobile Offshore Drilling Unit Ocean Ranger,* February 15, 1983, Report no. NTSB–March 83–2.

"Wreck of the *Ocean Ranger*." *Time*, March 1, 1982, p. 29.

"Sea Extracts Its Price in Hunt for Oil." *U.S. News and World Report*, March 1, 1982, p. 6.

Exxon Valdez oil spill

Prince William Sound, Alaska **1989**

by Sally Van Duyne

An oil tanker ran aground in Prince William Sound, Alaska, resulting in a catastrophic oil spill that killed many thousands of birds, fish, and sea otters.

Background

In the early morning of March 23, 1989, the tanker Exxon *Valdez* ran aground on Bligh Reef in Alaska, spilling 10.8 million gallons of crude oil into Prince William Sound. It was the worst oil spill in U.S. history to date. More than 1,500 miles of shoreline were polluted, and many thousands of birds, fish, and sea otters were killed. Although the immediate cause of the grounding was human error, the accident can be seen in a larger context as a technological failure because oil is so integral to the functioning of our technology-based society, and because technology played an important role in attempts to prevent and minimize the damage of the spill.

Though the Exxon *Valdez* oil spill and a few others have been widely reported, many major spills have escaped public scrutiny. Between 1978 and 1990, there were 1,900 oil spills of more than ten thousand gallons worldwide. Of these, twenty-six were of more than ten million gallons, including the *Valdez* spill toward the low end of this group. The Exxon *Valdez* spill became so widely known partly because it was the largest spill ever in the United States and in North American waters, and partly because it did so much damage in the enclosed waters of Prince William Sound, where the oil could not disperse and break down as easily as it could have on the high seas. Before the spill, the Prince William Sound area—with its snow-capped mountains, many islands, and abundant wildlife—was a place of rare pristine beauty.

The oil carried by the *Valdez* had traveled 800 miles via the Trans-Alaska Pipeline (TAP) from Prudhoe Bay to the port of Valdez. Alyeska, a consortium of oil companies that included Exxon, had applied to Congress in 1970 for a permit to build a pipeline to transport the 9.6 billion barrels of oil that lay below the frozen ground of Alaska's North Slope. In 1973, Middle Eastern countries temporarily cut off oil supplies to the West, and that same year Congress voted to authorize the pipeline. Construction of the TAP began in 1974 and was completed in 1977. Two million gallons of oil now travel through the pipeline every day, filling the bellies of up to 75 giant tankers that leave the port of Valdez every month.

The federal government and the oil industry made many promises in order to appease environmentalists and the citizens of Alaska who opposed the building of the TAP, fearing that a catastrophic oil spill would be inevitable. Many of these promises were not upheld. For example, in the early 1970s the federal government promised to require double bottoms on tankers, and the oil industry promised to comply. This technological upgrade became a key factor in Congress's subsequent approval of the TAP route to Valdez. But when the oil industry encountered hard times in the 1980s, double bottoms were for the most part forgotten. In addition, when the TAP permit was issued, oil industry and federal officials also assured the public that ice conditions in Prince William Sound would be carefully monitored with state-of-the-art equipment to minimize the chances that a tanker would collide with an iceberg. This monitoring never occurred.

Safety standards also declined over the years. In 1977 the average tanker sailing out of Valdez carried about forty crew members, but by 1989 the 1,000-foot, 280,000-ton tankers carried only about twenty crew, while exhausting twelve- to fourteen-hour workdays had become a normal mode of operation. Furthermore, in the first years of the pipeline, Alyeska had a spill-readiness team that worked around the clock running drills and maintaining equipment. But by 1982, when public watchfulness had slackened, these team members had been assigned to other duties, equipment maintenance had been postponed, and an emergency response could not be as quickly assembled. Finally, as a result of Coast Guard cutbacks in the 1980s, fewer people were assigned to the Valdez Coast Guard station, and tankers were no longer inspected when they left the terminal. The radar at the Valdez station was replaced by a less powerful unit, which meant that tankers could no longer be tracked as far as Bligh Reef. Unfortunately, the tanker crews had not been

"Seconds before the tanker struck Bligh Reef, (the third mate) called Captain Joseph J. Hazelwood and told him the tanker was 'getting into serious trouble.'"—*New York Times,* Feb. 14, 1990.

informed about the limitations of the new radar system. If the old system had still been in use, the Coast Guard might have been able to warn the Exxon *Valdez* to turn sooner to avoid Bligh Reef.

Details of the Spill

The Exxon *Valdez* left the dock at Valdez at 9:12 P.M. on March 22, 1989, to embark on its five-day run to Long Beach, California. There had been a report of a heavy flow of Columbia Glacier ice into Prince William Sound, and this ice soon showed up on the ship's radar. A couple of hours into the voyage, the *Valdez* notified the Coast Guard station at Valdez that it was crossing into the lane for inbound vessels in an attempt to avoid the ice. However, the *Valdez* went farther out of its way than it had reported, crossing first the 2,000-yard zone separating freighter traffic, then the 1,500-yard inbound lane, which also appeared to be full of ice, and continuing straight without making a right turn. Bligh Reef lay six miles ahead, and there appeared to be a gap of only nine-tenths of a mile between the edge of the ice and Bligh Reef. The ship headed for the opening, knowing that a well-timed turn would be necessary. Since six-tenths of a mile would be needed to make the turn and the tanker was two-tenths of a mile long, the turn would have to start before the gap between the ice and the reef.

Before leaving the deck to go below to his cabin, Captain Joseph Hazelwood, who had nineteen years' experience with Exxon Shipping, told Third Mate Gregory Cousins to make a right turn when the vessel was across from Busby Island light and to skirt the edge of the ice, but failed to specify an exact course. Cousins was not licensed to pilot a ship in the sea channels approaching Valdez, but several crew members testified that it was nonetheless common practice to turn over command in this situation.

At 12:04 A.M. on March 23, 1989, the Exxon *Valdez* crashed aground on Bligh Reef, tearing open its bottom and spewing oil into the surrounding waters.

Perhaps because Cousins was looking at the radar screen, the tanker slipped past the light without starting to turn. When the ship's lookout sighted the buoy marking Bligh Reef, Cousins ordered an emergency course correction, but nothing happened because the ship had been placed on automatic pilot. At 12:04 A.M. on March 23, 1989, the Exxon *Valdez* crashed aground on Bligh Reef, tearing open its bottom and spewing oil into the surrounding waters. Although there is significant evidence that Hazelwood had been drinking before boarding the *Valdez* and may have been drinking during the voyage, a jury subsequently acquitted him of all charges except negligent discharge of oil.

Response to the spill, by all accounts, was slow and confused. Mobilizing the necessary equipment and materials was the first major challenge. Although Alyeska's stated purpose was to contain any spill within five hours, it took fourteen hours for the first barge to be loaded in Valdez and arrive on

breakdown

the scene with containment booms, which are intended to float on the water and keep the oil from spreading. A day and a half into the spill, only a small line of booms were visible from the air. In addition to being too late and too few, there were further problems with the booms. Some sank because of leakage or punctures in their buoyancy compartments, and some intended for use in protected harbors were mistakenly deployed in open seas. As a result, complete encirclement of the grounded tanker took a full 59 hours, and by that time the oil slick covered twelve square miles. However, about five days into the spill, after the effort to contain the great mass of the spill had failed, the booms were used successfully to protect a number of fish hatcheries.

Another fairly successful aspect of the cleanup was the lightering operation—or transferring the remaining oil from the Exxon *Valdez* into another tanker. By early Saturday morning, more than twenty-four hours into the spill, the Exxon *Baton Rouge* was tied up alongside and about four-fifths of the cargo of oil was recovered. Even so, by day four the prevailing currents had carried what had spilled 40 miles past islands and shoreline to the southwest; by day seven, 90 miles; by day eleven, 140 miles; and by day fifty-six, 470 miles. In the meantime, wave action churned the oil into a bubbly "mousse" mixture that quadrupled its volume and made collection by "skimmers"—vacuum equipment designed to siphon oil off the surface of water—impossible.

Because the long-term effects of two other remedies—chemical dispersants and bioremediation—are unknown, these were used only minimally. Rather than removing oil from the water, dispersants break oil into tiny droplets that descend from the surface into the water column and, through rapid release of hydrocarbons from the oil, cause a severe toxic hit on marine organisms for about six hours. In general, it is considered better not to use dispersants close to shore where marine life is densest, but a diversity of opinion exists. Three days into the spill the Coast Guard authorized Exxon to use dispersants, but by that time gale force winds made treatment impossible. Even if authorization had been secured earlier, there was not nearly enough dispersant available to treat a spill of this magnitude. By Monday morning, when a blizzard began producing twenty-five-foot waves, less than one percent of the spilled oil had been recovered.

In the other controversial process, bioremediation, fertilizer is sprayed onto beaches to stimulate growth of naturally occurring bacteria that degrade oil and change it to a harmless substance. Only seventy miles of shoreline were treated with this fertilizer, however, because of the uncertain long-term effects of the bacteria on other life forms.

After the failure to contain and recover the spilled oil, the operation devolved into one of cleaning shorelines. At the peak of operations, more than

At the peak of operations, more than 11,000 people, 14,000 vessels, and 85 aircraft were involved in the cleanup.

The first major challenge in cleaning up the area was mobilizing equipment and materials. Containment booms, such as that shown here, took fourteen hours to arrive at the spill.

11,000 people, 14,000 vessels, and 85 aircraft were involved in the cleanup. Some workers washed the rocks along shorelines with hot, pressurized absorbent towels, or simply with absorbent towels. Many other workers tried to save wildlife—by collecting dead animals so that the ingested oil would not get into the food chain, or by bringing sick ones in for treatment. More than 100 endangered bald eagles, 36,000 seabirds, and 7,000 sea otters were found dead. Many more are thought to have died but were never found.

Oil causes external damage to birds through loss of water-repellency and consequent loss of feathered insulation. The ingestion of oil lowers organisms' resistance to disease, reduces reproductive success, inhibits normal growth and development, and interrupts normal biochemical processes and behavioral patterns. About 627 birds and 200 otters were saved in the rescue effort, which had more value in terms of public relations than from a strictly biological viewpoint. Scientists do not know how long it will take for populations to restore themselves, but estimate that for many species five to twenty years will be necessary.

The management and cleanup of the spill were eventually taken over from Alyeska by Exxon, which in turn was monitored by the Department of Environmental Protection representing the state and the Coast Guard representing the federal government, as well as by special interest groups. When Exxon finished the bulk of its cleanup in September 1989, some of the shore-

breakdown

lines appeared to be clean, but a layer of tar still existed not far below the shore surface. In some places, the oil had penetrated four feet and threatened to penetrate deeper.

Impact

As a result of this catastrophic spill, Congress passed the Oil Pollution Act of 1990, requiring that all oil-carrying vessels operating in United States waters be equipped with double hulls by the year 2015. A Coast Guard study performed after the spill has shown that a double hull on the *Valdez* could have cut the amount of oil spilled by sixty percent. Another Coast Guard report showed that the cost of a double-hulled tanker, spread over its probable twenty-year lifetime, would be as low as three cents per barrel of oil carried.

Double-hulled tankers have advantages in a low-energy grounding, in which the outer hull might be punctured, but the inner hull, nestled six feet or more inside the outer, remains intact. In a high-energy grounding, however, a rock or reef might rip both hulls apart. Japanese shipbuilders are championing an intermediate-deck design that might be better in high-energy groundings. In this design, a deck divides the tanker into upper and lower compartments. The lower section is below the ocean surface. If the hull

More than 100 endangered bald eagles and 36,000 seabirds were found dead. Many more are thought to have died, but were never found.

The Oil Pollution Act of 1990 requires all oil-carrying vessels operating in U.S. waters to be equipped with double hulls by the year 2015. Such a hull on the Valdez *would have cut the spill by 60 percent.*

is punctured, water should run in instead of oil running out, except for a small amount of oil released as the hull rolls.

In another response to the spill, the petroleum industry contributed $7 million to create the Petroleum Industry Response Organization, which established five regional centers along the coasts of the United States for fighting oil spills. These are staffed twenty-four hours a day and increase the availability of equipment for removing and cleaning up oil spills.

The Alaska state legislature also acted to require all tanker captains leaving port to take a breath alcohol test no more than one hour before boarding. In addition, tankers now must keep two pilots on the bridge until after they have passed Bligh Reef, and tankers must be accompanied by two tugboats while still in Prince William Sound. Tanker pilots are no longer allowed to change lanes in the traffic separation scheme.

The litigation that followed revolved around two questions: who had been at fault and whether there was negligence regarding the attempted cleanup. The state sued Exxon, Alyeska, and all the other consortium companies, and Exxon countersued, charging that the state should pay much of the cleanup cost because it had interfered with the use of dispersants. The most significant settlement has required that Exxon set up a $900 million restitution fund.

Where to Learn More

Cahill, Richard A. *Disasters at Sea: Titanic to Exxon Valdez*. London: Century, 1990.

Davidson, Art. *In the Wake of the Exxon Valdez: The Devastating Impact of the Alaska Oil Spill*. Sierra Club Books, 1990.

Keeble, John. *Out of the Channel: The Exxon Valdez Oil Spill in Prince William Sound*. Harper-Collins, 1991.

National Research Council. Committee on Tank Vessel Design. *Tanker Spills: Prevention by Design*. National Academy Press, 1991.

Skerrett, P. J. "Designing Better Tankers." *Technology Review*, September 1992, p. 8.

U.S. Coast Guard, American Petroleum Institute, U.S. Environmental Protection Agency (sponsors). *Proceedings of the 1991 International Oil Spill Conference*. San Diego, California: American Petroleum Institute, March 4–7, 1991.

Automobile Failures

Ford Pinto rear-impact defect (1971–1976) 109

Firestone 500 steel-belted tire failure (1972–1978) 117

Audi 5000 sudden acceleration (1978–1986) 124

Ford Pinto rear-impact defect

1971-1976

A flawed automobile design gave rear-impact collisions the potential to set the entire car aflame and led to the deaths of at least fifty-nine people. A comprehensive recall and prolonged negative publicity and legal entanglements ensued for Ford.

Background

Soon after its debut in 1971, the Ford Pinto became the hottest subcompact on the market. Over the Pinto's 1971–1980 lifespan, more than three million of the vehicles were sold. By the middle of the decade, however, reports surfaced that the Pinto tended to catch fire after rear-impact collisions. *Mother Jones* magazine and the Center for Auto Safety maintained that design flaws in the vehicle made the model's fuel tank system vulnerable and hazardous. Ford Motors began to feel pressure from the National Highway Traffic Safety Administration (NHTSA). In 1978 Ford recalled 1.4 million 1971–1976 Pintos for safety modifications. By the mid-1980s, though, at least fifty-nine people had burned to death in Pinto accidents, resulting in more than one hundred lawsuits against Ford.

The initial sales figures for the Pinto heartened Ford executive Lee Iacocca, who spearheaded the development of the vehicle as an "import-fighter."

by James M. Flammang

Iacocca's goal was a sensible "econocar" priced under $2,000 and weighing less than two thousand pounds. Ford and Iacocca basked in the Pinto's success until the Center for Auto Safety—a consumer group run by disciples of Ralph Nader—began to receive a substantial volume of disturbing complaints about the Pinto. The Pinto fuel tanks, it was alleged, were easily punctured in rear-impact crashes. Such a development had the potential to set off a blaze of fire that could kill or seriously burn the occupants of the car.

The Center for Auto Safety demanded government action, and in the fall of 1977 the National Highway Traffic Safety Administration initiated a "defects investigation" of the Pinto. The Pinto wasn't the first Ford vehicle to be singled out as a possible fire hazard. The Illinois Supreme Court had ruled the flange-mounted gas tanks in the 1966 Fairlane 500 unsafe, and Ford was criticized at the time for withholding reports that revealed it had been aware of the risk.

Because the Pinto was Ford's first significant entry into the small-car market, it had been rushed into production. The typical forty-three month development phase for a new automobile was abbreviated to as few as twenty-five months (thirty-seven months in one historian's estimate). Tooling came early in the schedule, and $200 million in tooling was installed before the quality assurance process was completed. The amount already spent would have almost certainly discouraged any modifications of the design.

Although Ford had been a safety pioneer in the mid-1950s, offering such innovations as seatbelts, it retreated from those standards for the subcompact Pinto. "Safety doesn't sell" was a common attitude in Detroit, and the product objectives for the Pinto, as reported by the Society of Automotive Engineers, did not include vehicle safety. A 1969 memo suggested that a safer over-the-axle gas tank design had been rejected because it would slash luggage space in the vehicle. Charges were also levelled against Ford that it had employed a series of delaying tactics to fight a proposed safety rule—Federal Motor Vehicle Safety Standard 301—that could have compelled a redesign of the Pinto.

Details of the Controversy

In the fall of 1977, *Mother Jones*, a San Francisco-based investigative magazine, unleased a bombshell against Ford. A lengthy article demonstrated that the development phase for the Pinto had been accelerated and pinpointed flaws in the vehicle's fuel-tank structure and its placement in the vehicle. More damaging than the technical details, though, was the article's assertion, based upon previously-concealed corporate documents, that Ford executives knew from their own tests that Pintos were prone to catch fire after rear-end collisions. Ford executives did not correct the problem, the article contended, because doing so—at an estimated $10 to $15 per car—would cost the company more than what Ford estimated it would pay out in accident-related lawsuits.

Three design details bore the brunt of criticism in the devastating *Mother Jones* article. The magazine argued that the tank sat too far to the rear, barely six inches ahead of the bumper. It further charged that the fuel filler tube was likely to separate and create spillage. In addition, the article pointed out that four bolts protruding backward from the differential housing could easily puncture the tank, which was only three inches away, in the event of a rear-end collision. Several other under-chassis components were identified as capable of piercing the fuel tank as well. Finally, the *Mother Jones* article charged that the Pinto's floor pan could separate, allowing a fuel tank fire to spread into the passenger compartment, and that the vehicle's front doors tended to jam shut in a crash and prevent escape. Other critics of the Pinto noted its flimsy bumpers and generally fragile construction. Pinto was the first modern American Ford, said one, to lack rear subframe members (a steel skeleton), a cost-control and weight-saving measure.

When hit at thirty-plus miles per hour, the *Mother Jones* article claimed, a Pinto's rear end "would buckle like an accordion, right up to the back seat. The tube leading to the gas-tank cap would be ripped away from the tank itself, and gas would immediately begin sloshing onto the road." The buckled tank would jam against the differential housing, with its protruding bolts. Add a random spark, and both cars "would be engulfed in flames." Safety expert Byron Bloch (whose credentials would be caustically questioned by Ford) insisted that the company was "irresponsible" to put "such a weak tank in such a ridiculous location in such a soft rear end."

Mother Jones continued its damning examination of the company's performance. Ford documents revealed that early Pintos had been tested more than forty times. Engineers reported that in a twenty-one and a half miles per hour test, the "fuel filler pipe pulled out of the fuel tank and the fluid discharged through the outlet. Additional leakage occurred through a puncture . . . ." Unless the car had been structurally modified, claimed *Mother Jones*, "every test at twenty-five miles per hour or more ... resulted in a ruptured fuel tank." Ford's testing continued after the Pinto began production. A report on fuel tank integrity of 1971–1972 Pintos concluded that the rear-end structure was unsatisfactory for a twenty-mile-per-hour crash. The report contended that major revision would be necessary to enable the Pinto to withstand a thirty-mile-per-hour collision.

Ford documents also revealed proposals to improve the Pinto's rear-end safety. These proposals included repositioning the tank, moving the filler pipe, shielding the protrusions, and installing a bladder in the tank. The most effective of the solutions might have been the adoption of a design wherein the fuel tank rides above the rear axle and differential. Ironically, Ford held a patent on that type of tank and used it on the European-built Capri, which was imported into the United States. Soon after the Pinto's debut, the Capri passed the equivalent of a forty-five-mile-per-hour rear-end crash test. British ads even boasted of the Capri tank's safety.

Ford vigorously defended the Pinto, arguing that its fuel system presented no unreasonable risk. Ford officials insisted that, in addition to meeting all applicable government-mandated safety requirements, the Pinto was as safe as other vehicles of its size and type. Indeed, the Pinto did meet federal standards, but until 1977 those standards did not include a requirement that cars withstand a specified rear-end collision force.

Despite Ford's defense of the Pinto, a series of recalls followed. In October 1976, the NHTSA ordered 372,584 Pinto, Bobcat, and Mustang II models recalled because of potential fuel leaks from the engines. A few 1977 Pintos were recalled because Ford admitted that the rear-bumper nuts installed on the vehicle had the potential to puncture the fuel tank. The 1976 Pintos were recalled after testing revealed that a head-on collision at thirty miles per hour could lead to fuel leakage.

NHTSA announced in May 1978 that its own investigations "demonstrate that low-to-moderate-speed rear-end collisions of Pintos produce massive fuel tank leaks due to puncture or tearing of the fuel tank and separation of the filler pipe from the tank." In the "presence of external ignition sources," the NHTSA determined, such fuel leaks could "result in fire." A dozen tests of rear-end collision at thirty-five mile per hour yielded two fires from fuel spillage. Moreover, government experts knew of thirty-eight cases of Pinto fuel-tank damage that resulted in numerous fires and twenty-six fatalities.

On June 15, 1978, shortly before a public hearing that probably would have forced a recall, Ford announced a "voluntary" recall of 1.4 million Pintos from model years 1971 to 1976 and 30,000 Mercury Bobcats from 1975 and 1976 of similar make. Incredibly, Ford still refused to admit to the existence of a defect. Instead, they agreed to make changes to "end public concern"—a $30 to $40 million public relations gesture. Among the modifications performed for the recall, Ford agreed to install two high-density polyethylene shields around the car's fuel tank.

Consumer advocate Ralph Nader called Ford's planned remedy "an inadequate technical fix; the cheapest way out." Nader demanded that Ford install double-walled tanks such as the ones in use on bigger Ford vehicles. Retired Chrysler auto-safety director Roy Haeusler warned that many Pinto motorists were "sitting in virtual time bombs" due to unsafe tank designs.

Ford doubtlessly hoped the Pinto controversy would fade after the recall, but Ford remained beleaguered in the law courts. Among the lawsuits filed against Ford was a sensational Indiana case that soon would focus national attention on the Pinto. In August 1978, three teenage girls died when their 1973 Pinto burst into flames after being struck in the rear by a van. As the Indiana case opened, Ford faced more than fifty civil suits and at least two class-action suits. Courts had already awarded plaintiffs as much as $6 million in damages. As the gavel that opened the Indiana trial fell in early 1980, Ford earned the dubious distinction of being the first corporation charged with a criminal offense—"reckless homicide." Although in this case Ford only faced a maximum fine of $30,000, attorneys for both the prosecution and the defense knew a guilty verdict could affect twenty-three other civil suits pending at the time.

Rather than concentrating on accumulating proof of a design flaw in the Pinto, Indiana prosecutor Michael Cosentino centered his arguments on a narrower issue: that Ford had allowed the Pinto "to remain on Indiana highways, knowing full well its defects." Employing the legal talents of former Watergate prosecutor James F. Neal, Ford pleaded not guilty, and was ultimately acquitted of all charges. In this lawsuit, the novel principle that manufacturers of a product could be criminally responsible for injuries resulting from its use was

As the gavel that opened the Indiana Trial fell in early 1980, Ford earned the dubious distinction of being the first corporation charged with a criminal offense—"reckless homicide."

not upheld. Presiding Judge Harold Staffeldt found "a revolt against technology" implicit in the case, and refused to establish the legal precedent.

Despite Ford's acquittal, the negative publicity surrounding the Indiana case remained extremely damaging, and many consumer advocates continued to lobby against the car. The Pinto soon faded out of the marketplace, to be replaced in 1981 by the Ford Escort.

Impact

Had Ford executives and engineers been wholly unaware of the Pinto's potential to catch fire in rear-end collisions, the alleged defect would not have created such a public furor. After the emergence of seemingly incriminating documents, Ford officials denied that crash-tests of early Pintos had taken place, and insisted that the vehicle had no inherent safety problems. Ford executives noted that their own family members drove Pintos. Ford's corporate credibility, however, was suspect; in 1974, the company had pleaded guilty to cheating on emissions tests, paying a $3.5 million fine.

The controversy surrounding the Pinto created widespread public distrust of the American automotive industry in general and Ford in particular.

For the furor had raised a compelling and horrifying allegation that Ford Motors had in cold-blooded fashion put dollars ahead of lives. *Mother Jones* declared that Ford executives decided not to modify the Pinto for safety after a " 'cost-benefit analysis,' *which places a dollar value on human life*, said it wasn't profitable to make the changes" [italics in original]. After the enactment of the National Traffic and Motor Vehicle Safety Act in 1966, it was noted, Ford secured an agreement from federal policymakers that such a "cost-benefit" principle would be acceptable.

A Ford analysis to determine the desirability of installing a fuel valve in certain vehicles to help prevent fires during rollovers illustrates the nature of the "cost-benefit" principle. Analysts estimated that unless changes were made, 2,100 vehicles would eventually burn, causing 180 deaths and another 180 serious injuries. By placing monetary values at $200,000 per death, $67,000 per injury, and $700 per vehicle, Ford estimated that not modifying the vehicles would cost the company $49.5 million in lawsuit payments. Conversely, the analysis noted that modifying the vehicles would cost $137 million. By forgoing the safety modification, the analysis estimated that Ford could save $87.5 million.

Allegations that American-made vehicles represent fire and safety hazards did not end with the Ford Pinto. In the early 1990s, the Center for Auto Safety charged that almost five million General Motors pickup trucks from the model years 1983 to 1987 were fire-prone in side-impact collisions because of the "sidesaddle" placement of their fuel tanks. Civil lawsuits, class-action suits, regulatory threats, and various GM-initiated responses designed to neutralize the furor ensued. General Motors finally reached an agreement in 1994 with the U.S. government wherein government recall threats would cease in return for a contribution by GM of millions of dollars toward various safety programs. General Motors and its supporters trumpeted the agreement as a fair and measured response to the controversy, while outraged critics charged that the company had in effect bribed the government to get off its back. Even with this agreement, though, General Motors still has to face the numerous civil lawsuits that loom.

Where to Learn More

Dowie, Mark. "Pinto Madness." *Mother Jones*, September–October 1977, pp. 18–32.

"Car Safety: Who's for Burning?" *The Economist*, January 12, 1980, pp. 30–1.

Everett, David. "GM Settles Truck Suit with Coupons." *Detroit Free Press*, July 29, 1993, pp. A1, A4.

Lacey, Robert. *Ford: The Men and the Machine*. Little, Brown, 1986.

"Domestic Safety Defect Recall Campaigns." National Highway Traffic Safety Administration. 1976 ed., p. 21; 1977 ed., p. 16; 1978 ed., pp. 12–14.

Panztur, Andy. "Pinto Criminal Trial of Ford Motor Co. Opens Up Broad Issues." *New York Times*, January 4, 1980, pp. 1, 23.

Rowand, Roger. "An All-New Ball Game for Engineers." *Automotive News*, January 21, 1980, p. 48.

Stuart, Reginald. "U.S. Agency Suggests Ford Pintos Have a Fuel System Safety Defect." *New York Times*, May 9, 1978, p. 22.

"Pinto Ruling." *Time*, February 12, 1979, p. 87.

Firestone 500 steel-belted tire failure

Seven-and-a-half million Firestone-built tires were recalled when it was discovered that their treads were likely to separate from the main structure, especially when driven underinflated. Forty-one highway deaths may have resulted in part from the defective tire model.

by James M. Flammang

Background

After a promising send-off in 1972, Firestone's new "500" steel-belted radial tires became a cause for concern. Customers began to return failed tires in unusually high numbers, while tragic accidents were attributed to blown-out Firestone 500s. Most common of the complaints was that the outer tread—the portion of the tire that hits the road—was inclined to slither apart from the rubber carcass or main body of the tire. Over time, charges were made that forty-one deaths on the nation's highways were due in part to the defective Firestone tire model.

Through the early decades of motoring, tire technology lagged behind other automotive developments. Not until the mid-1950s did the first tubeless tires arrive. Then came the fiberglass-belted tire, a development that added strength to the tire carcass. Domestic cars soon borrowed the radial belt pattern from European automakers. The radial design elbowed aside the bias-belted styles. Radial tires have their plies or inner core material running at right angles to the beads or sides of a tire, thus providing the vehicle with superior strength, traction, and fuel economy.

By the 1970s, the new steel-belted radials seemed to promise the best of all possible worlds, mixing the strength of steel with the stability and longevity of the radial belt pattern. Industry sales began to sag by 1974, in part because radials lasted longer, dampening demand for replacement rubber.

In October 1973 *Consumer Reports* rated the Firestone 500 steel-belted radial in the top two of tire models, a significant endorsement. Neither the 500 nor any other tire showed damage in a 325-mile test at ninety miles per hour, so the magazine based its evaluation on tread life, not safety factors. No one seemed to suspect that anything within the tire might cause trouble as it aged.

Actually, though, someone within the Firestone organization who was familiar with the new tire feared trouble almost from the beginning of the tire's production. In September 1973 (a year after production began), Director of Development Thomas A. Robertson sent a memo to top management warning, "We are making an inferior quality radial tire which will subject us to belt-edge separation at high mileage." Nevertheless, Firestone made more than 23 million such radials over the ensuing five years. The company insisted that the tire had no safety defects.

The 1973 memo was not the first expression of unhappiness with Firestone that Robertson had made. In 1972 Robertson had expressed concern about Firestone's relationship with automakers that installed equivalent tires (made by Firestone, virtually identical to the 500s, but lacking the Firestone label) as original equipment on new cars. "We are badly in need of an improvement in belt separation performance," he warned, "particularly at General Motors, where we are in danger of being cut off by Chevrolet because of separation failures."

While Firestone continued production of the radial tire, however, several tragic accidents took place in which the company's tires quickly came under suspicion. In one of these incidents, the Louis Neal family was decimated in an accident that occurred near Las Vegas in June 1974. When one of its Firestone 500 steel-belted radials blew out, their car went out of control and crashed. The parents were killed and one child was severely crippled. Firestone settled out of court for $1.4 million.

Between 1973 and May 1978, when the House Subcommittee on Oversight and Investigations opened hearings, fifteen deaths were reported in which such blowouts were cited as a major cause or main contributing factor. By mid-1979 the number of deaths in which the tire allegedly was a factor had reached forty-one. The federal government counted fourteen thousand complaints from consumers.

breakdown

Consumer advocates knew about the Firestone problem by 1976, having received numerous complaints about tread separations and resultant blowouts. In 1977 the Center for Auto Safety—a watchdog group operated by activists who had worked with consumer advocate Ralph Nader—pushed for government investigation. The Center noted that half of the complaints it studied involved Firestone, so Clarence M. Ditlow, head of the center, wrote to Firestone president Mario A. Di Federico in November 1977. Rather facetiously, he suggested the "company should shift half of its advertising budget into quality control."

Acting upon data supplied by the Center for Auto Safety, the National Highway Traffic Safety Administration (NHTSA) surveyed 87,000 owners of new cars with questions about their radial tires. Of the 2,226 owners of Firestone tires who returned a questionnaire, 46 percent reported problems. Conversely, the problem rate for Goodrich was only 33 percent, while Goodyear and Uniroyal complaints were registered on 32 percent of the questionnaires. Despite a court order obtained by Firestone's vice president and general counsel, John F. Floberg, the figures were "inadvertently" released, according to the agency. The publicity surrounding the court order thus insured widespread coverage of the released information. Firestone chairman Richard A. Riley, meanwhile, continued to insist the 500s were safe, and that the company had "been completely aboveboard."

During ten months of debate, noted *Business Week*, "additional revelations about the tires hardened NHTSA's position, as well as public opinion." Firestone's prior knowledge of the "unusually high volume of its customers' complaints" became evident, while the company "repeatedly tried to thwart investigation." *Fortune* magazine charged that in its defense, Firestone had "used tactics that worsened the ordeal" and concluded that the company's response "may well become a classic."

Even before the large-scale 1978 recall, Firestone 500 steel-belted radials had been subject to four smaller recalls for manufacturing defects. Approximately 410,000 tires were recalled as a result. But Firestone still opposed a full recall. The company instead blamed a careless public, charging that drivers failed to keep tires properly inflated, bumped them against curbs, overloaded their cars, and drove too fast.

Critics charged that even if underinflation were actually the cause of failures, the company was negligent in failing to warn owners of the danger. Underinflation causes a tire to flex far more than normal. In addition to increased mechanical stress on the rubber, it can cause a tire to run hotter. Firestone's critics contended that if motorists were aware that a tire inflated to appreciably less than the recommended volume would trigger eventual tread separation, they would likely keep closer watch on tire pressures.

Firestone's prior knowledge of the "unusually high volume of its customers' complaints" became evident, while the company "repeatedly tried to thwart investigation."

The NHTSA investigated for seven months, studying 6,000 consumer reports. In July 1978 the agency made an "initial determination" of a safety-related defect. On December 5, 1978, Firestone and NHTSA agreed to a recall of the affected tires, built from September 1, 1975, to the end of 1976 (for five-rib tires) or through April 1976 (for the seven-rib style). "Failure," said the NHTSA announcement, "can result in a loss of air with a possible loss of control of the vehicle which may result in vehicle crash." The official decree covered 14.5 million tires, but only an estimated 7.5 million that remained on the road wound up entitled to free replacement. Approximately six million tires manufactured earlier than September 1, 1975, could be exchanged at half price. Production of the 500 continued into April 1978, but the recall did not apply to tires made after the cutoff dates, because internal construction had changed by then. Neither did it apply to nonradial (bias-belted) 500s.

Not all of the affected tires wore a "Firestone 500" label. A dozen others were included as part of the recall, including the Firestone TPC (used on GM cars); Montgomery Ward Grappler; Seiberling RT 78; Atlas Goldenaire II; Caravelle Supreme; Shell Steel Radial; K-Mart Steel Radial 400; and Zenith Supreme.

In a departure from customary practice, the federal government listed no specific engineering cause for the flaw and recall. Instead, NHTSA based its decision upon the simple fact that, based on the number and nature of complaints from consumers, an excessive number of these tires had been demonstrated to be defective. Thus, a pattern of failure was deemed sufficient to prompt the recall.

Details of the Defect

Like other belted tires of the 1970s, the Firestone 500 radials carried a set of reinforcing belts beneath the tread. Whether made of fiberglass or steel, these belts encircled the tire's carcass, enhancing the rigidity of its structure. In the case of the Firestone-built radials, heat buildup within the tire appeared to cause the tread to separate from the steel-belted inner layer. When such separation occurred, the ultimate result could be a blowout.

Prior recalls of some 500s suggested that a serious problem lay waiting. In March 1976, a small number of Firestone 500s were recalled because of a possibility that they were "undervulcanized, which could lead to separation in lower sidewall area." (Vulcanization is a process wherein heat and pressure are applied to harden the rubber.) A year later came a record-size recall of 400,000 tires of a model that exhibited "distortion or separation in tread area" in a high-speed indoor test. Firestone cited a temporary production problem as the reason for the defect.

NHTSA failed to specify the precise nature of the Firestone defect when it announced the major recall. But no other conclusive evidence regarding the

tire's performance has been presented from other quarters, either, so any analysis of the nature of the tire defect is somewhat speculative. One such scenario, however, based upon investigation by a Georgia newspaper, was presented in *Consumer Reports*.

After examining internal Firestone documents and considering basic manufacturing processes, the *Atlanta Beacon Journal* determined that time was a significant factor in tread separation. Most such tires failed later in life. While the tire might operate in a trouble-free manner for thousands of miles, a foundation for failure may have existed from the tire's first mile on the road.

One technical detail is certain: steel does not bond readily to rubber. Even when coated with brass, the twisted steel wires that form a tire's belt pattern resist becoming one with the carcass. As a result, all domestic tire makers encountered trouble producing their first radial tires.

To help overcome the fact that the brass-coated steel belts don't bond easily to the tire's rubber carcass, the belts were first coated with a rubber compound. This created a better base; but if that compound absorbed moisture from the air, it could set the stage for possible disaster. When the tire was vulcanized, ammonia formed in the base rubber. Mixed with the internal moisture, this created a corrosive substance. Over time, that substance tended to corrode the brass coating of the steel wires, weakening their bond with the surrounding rubber.

A Firestone document from mid-September 1975 appeared to affirm that diagnosis. As part of a company investigation of "dezincification" of belts and the effects of ammonia and moisture, employee P.F. Murray wrote that degraded adhesion resulted from "corrosion of the brass caused by ammonia from compounding ingredients combined with moisture."

Firestone and its defenders continued to dismiss the charge of an inherent defect. Malcolm Lovell, chairman of the Tire Industry Safety Council, concurred with Firestone that the problem stemmed from underinflation. Corporate records turned over to NHTSA, however, suggested that Firestone was hardly unaware that trouble was brewing. In addition to the Robertson correspondence, a 1973 letter from Atlas Tire—one of the companies that marketed a Firestone-built radial under its own name—stated that "Firestone is coming apart at the seams and drastic action is required." In 1976, representatives of Shell indicated they were ready to stop marketing their private-brand tire because of the rate of customer returns. Montgomery Ward warned that returns of its Grappler 8000 had reached "epidemic proportions," which "amplifies the fact we were given a bad product."

No other radial-tire line had a failure record anywhere near that of the 500 series. Firestone's claimed 7.4 percent "adjustment rate" (the number of tires returned for refund, divided by the total number sold) was twice the figure for competitors. Goodyear, Firestone's top rival, rated 2.9 percent. When Representative Al Gore questioned that rate during congressional hearings, Firestone's counsel insisted that 500s were their most expensive tire, so customers would be more likely to complain. Further investigation of Firestone return rates, though, revealed that in reality an industry record of 17.5 percent (not 7.4 percent) of these tires were returned to dealers.

Impact

Even if Firestone was not culpable for flawed manufacturing processes, the company's angry denials of responsibility and refusal to admit of any flaw in their product drew fire in the press. The integrity of the company's leadership was further questioned when, upon learning that a recall was imminent, Firestone decided to sell off the final 500s in southeastern states at clearance-sale prices. *Business Week* described this last-ditch maneuver as a "desperate effort to unload damaged goods."

Firestone finally capitulated. In recognition of the damage the controversy had wreaked, the company decided to discontinue production of the tire. At congressional hearings in May 1978, Firestone argued that the controversial tire had been discontinued eighteen months earlier, to be replaced by a new 721 series (also steel-belted radials). But while the phaseout had indeed begun by 1977, and significant design changes were instituted between 1976 and 1977, final 500s were coming out of the factory as late as April 1978.

breakdown

Analysts predicted that the wave of negative publicity surrounding the tire would skim two to three percent from Firestone's usual 25 percent share of the replacement-tire market. Meanwhile, the company prepared to spend $230 million for the recall. By mid-1979, about three million Firestone 500s had been replaced, but NHTSA chief Joan Claybrook and other critics expressed disappointment with the pace of the recall.

Firestone still faced a series of lawsuits charging property damage and loss of life, in addition to a $1.7-billion class action suit. By the time of the recall, about 250 such suits had been filed. Nine verdicts had gone against Firestone, twenty-two ruled in the company's favor, and sixty-four had been settled out of court. Firestone also faced an inquiry by the Securities and Exchange Commission, which questioned if the company had adequately informed its shareholders about the tire safety issue. Although the SEC apparently took no action against Firestone, in 1979 a group of about 4,000 shareholders filed a class-action suit against the company that accused it of concealing information about the product defect. Firestone settled with this group for $3.2 million in 1983 without admitting any fault or liability.

Although some critics compared the Firestone 500 debacle to President Nixon's Watergate crisis, the company's woes turned out to be relatively short-lived. To help bolster its tarnished image, Firestone enlisted folksy actor Jimmy Stewart to help promote the new 721 series. They also offered a then-radical two-year warranty. Firestone quickly rebounded on the strength of such moves and returned to its former stature in the industry. Memories of the company's actions and attitude at the height of the Firestone Radial 500 controversy evidently faded from the public consciousness.

Where to Learn More

"The Big Firestone 500 Recall." *Consumer Reports*, April 1979, pp. 199–200.

"The Case for Firestone." *Forbes*, November 13, 1978, p. 106.

"Firestone 500: Blow Out." *The Economist*, October 14, 1978, pp. 121–122.

Feldstein, Stuart A. "How Not to React to a Safety Controversy." *Business Week*, November 6, 1978, p. 65.

"Forewarnings of Fatal Flaws." *Time*, June 25, 1979, pp. 58, 61.

Gray, Ralph. "Firestone Adds Batch of New Entries in Recall Wake." *Advertising Age*, February 5, 1979, p. 4.

Hinsberg, Patricia. "Analysts Assess Firestone Recall." *Automotive News*, October 30, 1978, p. 2.

Kahn, Helen. "Secret Documents Hint at Firestone Coverup." *Automotive News*, January 1, 1979, pp. 1, 23.

Louis, Arthur M. "Lessons from the Firestone Fracas." *Fortune*, August 28, 1978, pp. 45–48.

Audi 5000 sudden acceleration

1978-1986

by Greg Janicki

Beginning in the late 1970s, Audi received more than 1,400 reports of accidents—which injured 330 people and killed seven—that resulted from sudden acceleration. The allegations led to the development of the automatic shift lock.

Background

On March 7, 1989, the National Highway Traffic Safety Administration (NHTSA), the government agency responsible for overseeing safety issues in the motor vehicle industry, released the results of its research on motor vehicle "sudden acceleration"—defined as unintended and unexpected high-power acceleration from a stationary position or very low initial speed, accompanied by apparent braking ineffectiveness. The NHTSA announced in a press release that an "exhaustive, independent study of the sudden acceleration phenomena in cars concluded that pedal misapplications that may be aggravated by vehicle design are the most probable explanation for most reports of sudden acceleration." These NHTSA test results were of particular interest to two groups: Volkswagen of America, the corporate parent of Audi; and former and current owners of Audi 5000 vehicles, as the investigation was a direct result of much-publicized allegations of sudden acceleration in Audi 5000 sedans, model years 1978 to 1986, equipped with automatic transmissions. Audi received more than 1,400 reports of accidents—which injured 330 people and killed seven—that resulted from sudden acceleration.

Victims of the Audi's alleged sudden acceleration reacted to the NHTSA findings with disbelief. To these owners of runaway cars, the Audi 5000 was capable of becoming a "possessed" vehicle that could not be stopped by any driver action. In their view, the NHTSA's use of the term "pedal misapplication," which implied that drivers mistook the gas pedal for the brake pedal, deflected the blame away from the party that was responsible: Audi. Audi accident victims stated in no uncertain terms that their foot was on the brake pedal, not the gas.

Audi stood by the NHTSA's claim that the sudden acceleration problem was the result of driver error, to which poor pedal design may have contributed. This view was supported by Audi's post-accident examinations of the vehicles at issue. These examinations revealed no mechanical defect that would account for the complete brake failure described by most accident victims.

The allegations of sudden vehicle acceleration were not restricted to Audi, although a disproportionate share of the cases involved the Audi 5000. Nor was the issue new when, in the early 1980s, Audi found itself at the center of controversy. As early as 1967, the NHTSA was researching cases of "unwanted power," as the phenomena was initially termed. Since that time, the NHTSA has conducted over one hundred investigations—involving twenty vehicle manufacturers—of the sudden acceleration problem. These manufacturers include General Motors, Ford, Chrysler, AMC, Toyota, Nissan, Honda, Subaru, Volkswagen, Mercedes-Benz, Saab, and Volvo.

The NHTSA's examinations focused on very specific vehicle components that could malfunction in the manner described by the victims of sudden acceleration. Among the more commonly investigated components were: cruise control systems that might cause the throttle (which controls the air flow to the engine and thus engine speed) to stick open; computer-controlled fuel injection systems (which regulate the amount of fuel sprayed into the engine cylinders) that might affect engine performance; and electronic idle-speed control systems that could malfunction and lead to sudden engine surges.

This series of investigations prompted twenty-six government-mandated safety recalls and influenced seventy-five voluntary recalls, in which the manufacturer modified the vehicles without government intervention. In some cases (Nissan, Volvo, and General Motors), the recalls addressed a mechanical defect thought to be responsible for the sudden acceleration. For example, a loose engine mount (the device that holds the engine to the vehicle frame) caused the engines in some General Motors vehicles produced in the 1970s to

To these owners of runaway cars, the Audi 5000 was capable of becoming a "possessed" vehicle that could not be stopped by any driver action.

twist in the engine bay, affect the throttle, and generate unwanted acceleration. Generally, however, no specific mechanical defect was discovered, and the NHTSA's final ruling in the majority of its investigations identified driver error as the apparent cause of the sudden acceleration accidents.

Details of the Controversy

The Audi 5000 sudden acceleration controversy was different from allegations involving other vehicles in two respects: the rate of reported occurrence, and the amount of publicity generated. Reported incidents of sudden acceleration in the Audi reached 645 per 100,000 vehicles, nearly five times the rate of occurrence for any other manufacturer's vehicle. A larger difference, however, may have been in the press coverage of the allegations against Audi. Since no correlation exists between design and engineering changes in the Audi 5000 and the increased number of acceleration problems reported, one argument holds that the increase in reported "cases" stemmed from the level of negative publicity that the Audi 5000 received.

Publicity over the acceleration issue primarily arose from three groups: Audi itself; the Center for Auto Safety (CAS), a consumer advocacy group founded by Ralph Nader; and the NHTSA. The publicity peaked on November 11, 1986, when CBS's *Sixty Minutes* made the Audi controversy its lead story. The controversy actually began in 1982, however, long before the *Sixty Minutes* cameras rolled, when Audi responded to a preliminary NHTSA investigation of public complaints about the Audi 5000 tending to accelerate unexpectedly. Audi engineers claimed at that time that floormat interference (the floormat sliding under the pedals and interfering with braking and acceleration) was the apparent cause of the problem, and recalled the vehicles to install a metal stud that would keep the floormats in place.

Incidents of sudden acceleration continued to be reported, however, and Audi initiated a second recall in September 1983. In this recall, Audi placed a spacer atop the brake pedal to further differentiate the brake pedal from the accelerator pedal and thus lessen the chance for pedal confusion. This second recall indicates the stance Audi continues to take regarding allegations of sudden acceleration: the occurrence is primarily due to driver error. These two recalls were voluntary, and the NHTSA, determining that Audi's recalls had addressed the problem, ruled that no further action was necessary and closed its investigation.

It was at this point that the media attention escalated. On March 19, 1986, Robert Adams, the Attorney General of New York, held a press conference to demand an Audi recall. Two months later, on May 28, Neil Hartigan, the Attorney General of Illinois, made the same demand, claiming that an

Breakdown

Audi recall was necessary "to ensure the public safety and welfare of the citizens of Illinois and our sister states."

On this same day, the Audi Victims Network (AVN), a group founded in February 1986 and comprised of forty drivers who claimed to be victims of Audi sudden acceleration, held a meeting with Audi representatives. And Audi itself chose this day to announce a third recall, in which it would increase the distance between the brake and accelerator pedals. This recall was consistent with Audi's policy of attributing the blame for sudden acceleration to driver error. To support its position, Audi produced statistics revealing that a relatively large percentage (thirty-six percent) of sudden acceleration incidents were reported of vehicles that had been driven less than four thousand miles. Audi's argument was that a driver unaccustomed to the vehicle and its pedals easily might apply the gas pedal by mistake. It is worth noting, however, that the positioning of the Audi pedals was not unusual. In fact, the distance between brake and accelerator pedals before the recall, 2.4 inches, was well within the typical range of 2.3 to 2.6 inches.

In June 1986, shortly after the pedal adjustment recall, Audi initiated its fourth service recall on the 5000, this time to install an automatic shift lock (ASL) device. In January 1987, Audi undertook a government-mandated recall to install the ASL on all 1978–1986 Audi 5000s with automatic transmissions. The ASL device required a driver to depress the brake pedal before shifting out of park. The reasoning behind the ASL installation was that even if the vehicle surged once the transmission was engaged, the vehicle's brakes held the car against full depression of the accelerator pedal, a brake characteristic common to all motor vehicles. Throughout these recalls, Audi strove to present itself as a company responsive to its customers' needs. This representation was hotly disputed by the AVN and the Center for Auto Safety, who viewed the sudden acceleration as a deadly engineering defect that Audi was not addressing.

A fifth Audi recall was initiated in tandem with the ASL installation to replace a faulty idle stabilizer valve, a device that controls the engine speed under varying load conditions (such as towing or extreme temperatures) when the car is at idle. The stated purpose of this last recall was to eliminate the potential for engine fires, but some critics perceived it as a method of covertly fixing the sudden acceleration problem. In the letter issued to all Audi 5000 owners regarding the fifth recall, Audi indicated merely that "irregular engine idle might cause unsatisfactory car performance." Dan Howell of the CAS, however, alleged that the process amounted to a "secret recall," since Audi would not have replaced the valve unless it affected the safety of the vehicle.

The controversy over the Audi also pitted the CAS against the NHTSA. In pubic statements, the CAS encouraged Audi owners not to settle for the ASL recall as a solution to the sudden acceleration problem. The CAS had received reports that the ASL devices were ineffective against sudden acceleration. Moreover, since accident victims claimed to have had the brake pedal depressed before the occurrences of sudden acceleration, CAS Executive Director Clarence Ditlow maintained that the recall "flies in the face of the facts of virtually every runaway Audi accident ever reported." Diane Steed, the NHTSA Administrator, countered that the CAS should have encouraged Audi owners to take advantage of the recall, since "your organization has not provided any other credible explanation (or solutions)."

The general report that the NHTSA released in 1989, which concluded that there were no mechanical defects to account for the occurrences of sudden acceleration, ended the federal government's investigation of the phenomena, even if it did little to appease those Audi 5000 owners who had experienced the problem. By this point, the NHTSA and Volkswagen of America had received more than 1,400 reports of sudden acceleration—resulting in 330 injuries and seven deaths—regarding the 250,000 Audi 5000 vehicles sold in model years 1978 to 1986.

Impact

In June 1988, the Circuit Court of Cook County, Illinois, proposed a class action settlement against Audi. The settlement offered what amounted to a rebate on the future purchase or lease of an Audi vehicle to owners of 1978–1986 automatic transmission Audi 5000s who had suffered property damage from sudden acceleration. Under the terms of this offer, victims would receive a certificate valued from $300 to $2,000, depending on the model year of the affected vehicle. This paradoxical measure would benefit plaintiffs only if they continued to purchase Audi vehicles—thereby stimulating sales of the very vehicles in question. Needless to say, the CAS advised owners not to accept the settlement and thereby forfeit their right to further compensation. Audi owners, however, were never offered any other settlement.

Due to the sudden acceleration controversy, Audi's sales dropped thirty percent in one year. The vehicle was redesigned and the 5000 nomenclature dropped, but the damage had been done, and most experts agree that the Audi 5000 was a financial disaster. Even though no proof was uncovered of defective design, Audi's "Art of Engineering" reputation was tarnished—a bleak prospect for a seller of high-tech and upmarket gadgetry.

The most widespread result of the Audi controversy, nonetheless, is evident in most vehicles equipped with automatic transmissions: the automatic shift lock. Although not required by federal law, the device at least partially protects drivers from sudden acceleration and shields auto manufacturers from the public relations disaster experienced by Audi.

breakdown

Where to Learn More

Center for Auto Safety. *Audi 5000 Sudden Acceleration 1992*. 1992.

—. "NHTSA Requests Audi Recall." *Impact*, Vol. 12, No. 2.

—. "NHTSA's Acceleration Report Leaves Questions Unanswered." *Impact*, Vol. 14, No. 4.

Csaba, Csere. "Audi Agonistes." *Car and Driver*, June 1987, pp. 51–57.

An Examination of Sudden Acceleration. Report DOT-HS-807–376, U.S. Department of Transportation, January 1989.

"NHTSA Announces Results of 'Sudden Acceleration' Study." *DOT News*, March 1989.

"The Riddle of Unintended Acceleration." *Road and Track Special Report*, 1987.

Windscale reactor complex fire (1957) 133

Three Mile Island accident (1979) 140

Tsuruga radioactive waste spill (1981) 147

Ginna power plant radioactive release (1982) 153

Bhopal toxic vapor leak (1984) 159

Institute, West Virginia, toxic vapor leak (1985) 166

Chernobyl accident (1986) 173

Chemical and Nuclear Disasters

Windscale reactor complex fire

England **1957**

The world's first major commercial nuclear power plant disaster took place in 1957 at Great Britain's lone plutonium-making facility. A report twenty-six years later estimated that thirteen people died of thyroid cancer that was caused by the Windscale accident, while others suggested long-term damage to the populace surrounding the reactor.

Background

On Thursday evening, October 10, 1957, a fire erupted in Unit 1 at the Windscale nuclear reactor complex on the coast of Cumberland in northwest England. The fire burned for more than twelve hours and released large quantities of radiation to the surrounding countryside. Although authorities found dangerous levels of radiation in milk produced by cows in the area, it was not until years later that the consequences of the fire began to be fully known. A 1983 report estimated that thirteen people died of thyroid cancer that was caused by the Windscale accident, while others pointed to statistics that indicated possible long-term damage to the populace surrounding the reactor.

The years immediately after the conclusion of World War II were difficult ones for British nuclear scientists. On the one hand, they were under considerable pressure from government officials to build a nuclear weapon. The

by David E. Newton

efforts of the United States and the Soviet Union made British government officials uneasy about lagging behind. On the other hand, the British had no access to weapons technology information from the Americans, alongside whom they had fought in World War II. The United States Atomic Energy Act of 1946 prohibited the export of such information from the United States to any foreign nation, including its longtime ally, Great Britain.

British nuclear scientists responded to the challenge with remarkable speed. In 1947 they began construction at Windscale of a pair of nuclear reactors for the production of plutonium. By the end of the 1940s, both Windscale units were in operation. Their enormous four hundred-foot-high exhaust stacks were familiar sights in the neighborhood, although residents of the area were never informed of the activities undertaken at the plants.

The Windscale reactors were of a somewhat uncommon design. They consisted of huge honeycombed graphite blocks, fifty feet high and twenty-five feet deep. Running horizontally through the blocks were twenty thousand channels, each containing a long, thin fuel rod filled with uranium. When the reactor was in operation, neutrons bombarded the uranium, producing heat through fission (splitting) reactions. Plutonium was created as a by-product of this process. The plutonium was eventually extracted from the fuel rods at a chemical processing plant that was also located at the Windscale complex.

The graphite blocks were cooled by air. Huge fans at one end of each block blew a blast of air down each fuel channel, carrying away heat from the fission reaction and out the exhaust stacks. Large rectangular blocks at the top of each stack trapped radioactive materials carried on the heated air.

The British nuclear effort proved extraordinarily effective. On October 3, 1952, their first atomic bomb was detonated at Monte Bello Island off the coast of Australia. The decision was also made to expand the Windscale complex; construction was begun on two more reactors. The two new plants were constructed at Calder Hall, adjacent to the older plants. While the heat created by the operations at the old plants was simply vented into the atmosphere, the heat generated at the new facilities was used to generate electricity. With considerable ceremony, Queen Elizabeth II opened the Calder Hall facility in October 1956.

Details of the Disaster

The glow of success on that day would be replaced almost exactly a year later, however, by a much different and more sinister kind of glow: the fire at Windscale's Unit 1. The accident came about as the result of a somewhat unusual physical phenomenon known as the Wigner effect. The phenomenon is named for the Hungarian-American physicist, Eugene Wigner, who first predicted its occurrence.

The Wigner effect occurs in graphite reactors that have been in use for some period of time. Some of the energy released by fission in the reactor moves carbon atoms in the graphite block out of position. The longer the reactor is in use, therefore, the more distorted the block becomes. If nothing is done about this phenomenon, the reactor may eventually release its stored up energy all at once, causing a possibly dangerous overheating of the graphite block. The solution to this problem is relatively simple. If the reactor is simply allowed to heat up to about 200 degrees Celsius, carbon atoms in the graphite block become more mobile and return to their normal positions, and the stored-up energy in the block is released safely.

Although American scientists were familiar with the Wigner effect, their British counterparts at Windscale apparently were not. The latter learned about the phenomenon firsthand in September 1952 when they observed the release of Wigner energy after the reactor spontaneously overheated. After that near-accident, operators devised an empirical, rule-of-thumb procedure for dealing with the Wigner phenomenon. They allowed the reactor to overheat about once every twenty thousand megawatt days of operation.

The policy appeared to work well until production pressures increased the length of time between implementations, first to once every thirty thousand megawatt days and then to once every forty thousand megawatt days. As these periods between energy release increased, so did the potential risk of a reactor accident. Still, by October 1957, operators had performed the operation successfully and without incident on eight separate occasions.

WINDSCALE OPERATIONS GO AWRY. The ninth operation, begun on Monday, October 7, 1957, would have a different result. Historians believe that plant operators may have been under unusual pressure on this occasion. To perform the Wigner release, the reactor has to be shut down for a few days. But the British government was pushing forward aggressively on its weapons program. A bomb test originally scheduled for June 1958 had recently been moved forward by seven months, to November 1957. The pressure to generate plutonium was intense. Experts believe that such pressures may have caused Windscale operators to delay the Wigner release too long or carry out the procedure in a careless fashion.

In any case, the October 7 disaster erupted as a result of the same complex mixture of mechanical failures and human errors characteristic of most nuclear reactor accidents. The operation began normally enough on Monday as cooling fans were turned down, a step that allowed the reactor to heat up of its own accord. By Tuesday morning the procedure seemed to be going normally. Wigner heat was being released in the reactor as anticipated. Operators turned the cooling fans back on as part of the procedure to return the reactor to normal operation while the release of Wigner energy continued.

The British government was pushing forward aggressively with its weapons program. A bomb test originally scheduled for June 1958 had recently been moved forward by seven months, to November 1957. The pressure to generate plutonium was intense.

By midday Tuesday, however, strange readings were observed. The temperature of the reactor appeared to be falling, although it should have remained constant during the loss of Wigner energy. Operators decided to resume heating of the reactor, although such an action had never been attempted in a similar operation before. The reactor had already reached its maximum permissible temperature of 250 degrees Celsius during the earlier heating.

Nonetheless, cooling fans were again turned off and temperatures again began to rise. Within a matter of hours, the temperature reached 300 degrees Celsius. By Wednesday evening, increasingly uneasy operators were no longer certain of the conditions in the graphite block. Wigner energy was still being released, but temperatures in the block had now reached a dangerous 350 degrees Celsius and, in one region, more than 400 degrees Celsius.

One of the problems facing facility personnel at this point was technical in nature. Thermocouples—which use metal wires, not liquid, to measure temperature—were built into the block at various locations to monitor temperatures in the reactor. Later examination, however, revealed that the placement of these thermocouples was such that regions of the block could give readings as much as 40 percent higher than readings given by the nearest thermocouple. Thus, a 400-degree Celsius reading observed by an operator might not

breakdown

reflect a temperature at least 100 degrees Celsius higher in a full channel only a few meters away.

As temperatures in the block continued to rise, alarmed operators switched the cooling fans back on. The fans had little effect, however. On Thursday morning, already worried operators made a particularly grim discovery. Monitoring instruments in the caps on top of the exhaust stack indicated that high levels of radiation were escaping from the reactor.

Such readings would normally indicate that one or more of the fuel rods in the block had broken apart. Normally, operators would be able to find out if that kind of accident had, in fact, occurred. Scanners placed at various positions in the block had been designed to monitor the integrity of all fuel rods. Heat released in the block over the preceding two days, however, had damaged the scanners so that they could no longer be used to trace possible fuel breakdowns in the reactor.

By Thursday evening, October 10, operators were sufficiently concerned about circumstances to take an extraordinary step. They decided to remove external sections of the block and look directly into the heart of the reactor. The procedure was an enormously dangerous, last-ditch effort to find out what was going on in the machine. To their horror, they saw a glow of white heat. Some of the fuel rods had obviously burst open, uranium metal was glowing, and the surrounding graphite was on fire. A major disaster was clearly at hand.

Workers first tried a brute force approach in the efforts to rein in the growing danger. But attempts to force the damaged fuel rods out of the reactor were unsuccessful because the warped rods proved impossible to budge. Operators then attempted to push out rods surrounding the damaged section in an effort to contain the damaged area of the block. This step proved successful.

The raging fire within the block continued to be a problem, however. Unless it could be put out, it would certainly spread throughout the graphite block and engulf the whole reactor. The frantic operators tried to smother the flames with huge volumes of carbon dioxide pumped in from nearby tanks. When this failed, operators decided to try flooding the reactor with water.

Operators knew that pouring water on the fire in Unit 1 at Windscale was a serious step. Graphite absorbs water and does not dry out well. In putting out the fire at the reactor, they were also condemning it to its death. More significantly, however, a possibility existed that the water would turn to steam and blow the reactor apart. Fortunately, that did not occur. When the first stream of water hit the graphite block at 8:55 A.M. on Friday, it hissed and turned to steam—but no explosion took place. In fact, two hours later,

To their horror, they saw a glow of white heat. Some of the fuel rods had obviously burst open, uranium metal was glowing, and the surrounding graphite was on fire. A major disaster was clearly at hand.

operators were convinced that the fire had been extinguished. As a safety precaution, however, they continued the flow of water for another twenty-eight hours. Unit 1 was dead; it was never returned to operation.

Meanwhile, terrible evidence of the accident began to appear in the area around the plant. Monitoring teams from the United Kingdom's Atomic Energy Authority (AEA) detected four radioactive isotopes—cesium 137, strontium 89, strontium 90, and iodine 131—in the surrounding countryside. Of these, only the last was present in concentrations high enough to be deemed a matter of concern. Experts knew that iodine 131 collects on grass, which is eaten by cows. The isotope then becomes part of the milk the cows produce. As a cautionary step, therefore, authorities destroyed all milk produced from an area of two hundred square miles surrounding the damaged plant.

Impact

While Unit 1 had been rendered inoperable, plans were made to continue the operation of Unit 2. Those plans were soon changed, however, when the decision was made to close down the undamaged reactor in order to see if it could provide information about the accident at Unit 1. Unit 2 was never reopened.

British nuclear industry officials claim that they learned a great deal as a result of the disaster. In 1988 John Collier, chairman of the AEA, said, "A new safety culture was born out of the Windscale fire which highlighted faults that have been corrected, making nuclear power operations safe and effective. We have learned important lessons from the 1957 fire, and these have been taken up by the industry worldwide."

For many years, the health effects of the Windscale accident were thought to be minimal. A 1983 report by the U.K. National Radiological Protection Board estimated that thirteen people died as a result of thyroid cancer caused by iodine 131 released during the accident. The Cumbria Area Health Authority reported that deaths from leukemia were "not significantly altered from the national rate."

But other health authorities were not so sure. Historian Margaret Gowing pointed out a possible factor to which little attention had previously been given. The isotope polonium 210, used as a trigger in atomic bombs, was also being produced in Windscale's Unit 1 reactor. Its release during the accident was little noted or studied, according to Gowing. But there is evidence to support the view that the isotope may have been responsible for a significantly higher leukemia death rate in the Copeland and South Lakeland areas downwind of Windscale. A 1983 article in the journal *New Scientist* suggested that the polonium factor may have made the Windscale accident "the

breakdown

worst environmental disaster that Western Europe has known [to date] this century."

Where to Learn More

Dickson, David. "Doctored Report Revives Debate on 1957 Mishap." *Science*, February 5, 1988, pp. 556–57.

Herbert, Roy. "The Day the Reactor Caught Fire." *New Scientist*, October 14, 1982, pp. 84–87.

Howe, Hartley. "World's First Atomic Alarm." *Popular Science*, October 1958, pp. 92ff.

Pearce, Fred. "Penney's Windscale Thoughts." *New Scientist*, January 7, 1988, pp. 34–35.

Urquhart, John. "Polonium: Windscale's Most Lethal Legacy." *New Scientist*, March 31, 1983, pp. 873–75.

Williams, Gurney, III. "Radioactive Accidents." *Science Digest*, August 1971, pp. 10–14.

Three Mile Island accident

Middletown, Pennsylvania **1979**

by David E. Newton

The worst accident in the history of American commercial nuclear power generation caused a partial meltdown of the reactor core. No one was killed or injured, but expert opinion remains divided about possible future health problems that might result from the accident.

Background

On March 28, 1979, a partial meltdown occurred at Unit 2 of the Three Mile Island nuclear power plant (TMI-2) in Middletown, near Harrisburg, Pennsylvania. A valve in a pipe carrying cooling water that was supposed to be closed accidentally remained stuck in the "open" position, allowing cooling water to flow out of the reactor. Heat built up within the reactor core, causing some fuel elements to melt and releasing radioactive gas and water to the surrounding environment. A number of operator mistakes contributed to the accident. No one was killed or injured, but expert opinion remains divided about possible future health problems that might result from the accident. The accident became a critical factor in the dramatic retreat from nuclear power in the United States that has occurred since 1979.

The two units that make up the Three Mile Island nuclear power plant sit on a small island in the middle of the Susquehanna River in south-central Pennsylvania. Unit 1 was put into operation in September 1974. Construction on Unit 2 began in 1968 and was completed ten years later. Unit 2 was formally declared open on December 30, 1978.

Both units at Three Mile Island were built by Babcock & Wilcox, a giant construction company that specializes in nuclear power plant components. The Three Mile Island complex is owned by a consortium of power companies consisting of Pennsylvania Electric Company and Jersey Central Power and Light Company, each of which holds twenty-five percent of its stock, and Metropolitan Edison, which holds the remaining fifty percent of its stock.

The Three Mile Island units are pressurized-water reactors (PWR). Heat is generated in the core of such reactors when neutrons bombard uranium atoms in fuel rods, causing fission (splitting the atoms and releasing energy) to occur. The TMI-2 plant had 36,816 fuel rods, each filled with hundreds of pellets of enriched uranium metal about the size and shape of a small checker.

Heat produced by the fission reaction is removed by cooling water that is pumped through the reactor core. The cooling water is then pumped out of the core to a heat exchanger, where it is used to boil water in a secondary system. Steam produced in the secondary system is used to drive turbines that turn electric generators. At their peak capacity, the Three Mile Island plants produced 880 megawatts of electricity, enough to meet the needs of 346,000 residents of surrounding Berks, Lebanon, and York Counties. Pressurized-water reactors of this design are among the most common of all reactors in use in the United States today.

Like all nuclear power plants, the Three Mile Island reactors contained a complex safety system with many backup components. The core itself is enclosed in a steel casing almost nine inches thick. The core and cooling system, in turn, are enclosed within a large containment dome, 190 feet high and 140 feet in diameter. Walls of the dome are four feet thick and made of reinforced concrete. The purpose of the containment dome is to capture any gases, radiation, or other materials released during a leak or accident in the core or cooling system.

PROBLEMS PLAGUED REACTOR FROM DAY 1. As carefully designed as TMI-2 was, it experienced a number of problems almost from the day it was licensed in February of 1978. During the test period, valves opened and closed when they were not supposed to and remained stuck in the wrong position, seals broke, recording instruments failed to work properly, and other "glitches" developed.

The situation did not improve even after the plant officially went online in December 1978. It had operated only two weeks when two safety valves

The plant seemed jinxed by one mishap after another.

failed, causing the plant to shut down for two more weeks. During February, additional problems with valves, seals, pumps, and instruments developed. The plant seemed jinxed by one mishap after another.

The existence of problems such as these was not entirely a surprise. More than a year earlier, a nuclear safety expert for the Tennessee Valley Authority, Carl Michelson, had discovered safety problems with Babcock & Wilson reactors. Michelson reported his findings to the Nuclear Regulatory Commission (NRC), whose job it is to monitor the safety of nuclear power plants in the United States. For whatever reason, the NRC did not act on Michelson's report and did not request any modifications in Babcock & Wilson reactors.

Details of the Failure

The accident at TMI-2 that began at 4:00 A.M. lasted for more than five hours. During that time, more than forty distinct events occurred, some caused by mechanical error and some caused by human error. The series of events began with a routine maintenance operation—changing the water in a system of pipes. During the operation, air accidentally got into a pipe, cutting off the flow of cooling water to the reactor core.

Under normal circumstances, monitoring instruments would have detected this problem and automatically switched over to a backup cooling

breakdown

system. However, the pumps used in the backup system were also undergoing routine maintenance and so could not deliver water to the pipes. To make the situation even more complicated and dangerous, tags attached to the pumps indicating that they were undergoing maintenance hung down in such a way that they hid the warning lights. Even though the system correctly indicated that a problem existed, operators could not see the indicator lights.

Without its cooling water, the reactor core began to heat up rapidly. Its temperature eventually reached more than 5,000 degrees Fahrenheit, and fuel rods began to melt. As they melted, they burned through the steel casing of the core and reached the floor of the containment vessel itself. Had the molten fuel melted through that barrier, a total meltdown could have occurred—perhaps resulting in an explosion that would have breached the containment barrier and released huge levels of radioactive material into the air.

During the meltdown, other components of the plant continued to fail. Water in the cooling system started to boil, and an emergency relief valve opened automatically to allow it to escape into the containment dome. But the valve then failed to close, and even more water was lost from the cooling system. All the while, operators were either reading gauges that were not working properly or reading working gauges and then taking the wrong actions.

Under the circumstances, the meltdown of the fuel rods was to be expected. What was unexpected was the development of a huge bubble of steam and hydrogen gas that formed inside the containment dome. The steam came, of course, from cooling water boiled out of the core. But where did the hydrogen come from? Scientists had not realized before the TMI-2 accident that cooling water would not only boil, but would also decompose to oxygen and hydrogen in contact with radiation and heat released in the meltdown. Hydrogen is a special source of concern because it is explosive. It would have been possible—although it did not happen in this case—for the hydrogen to explode, releasing radioactive materials over hundreds of square miles surrounding the plant.

As it was, radioactive material did escape from the reactor in other ways. Some contaminated coolant water was automatically pumped out of the containment dome into a nearby holding building. From there, it was eventually dumped into the Susquehanna River. Radioactive gases from the core also escaped though vents in the containment dome. The level of radiation was so high in these gases that it damaged the instruments designed to monitor them.

REACTIONS TO ACCIDENT WERE SLOW AND CAUTIOUS. The immediate reaction to the TMI-2 incident by scientists and politicians appeared to be uncertainty and confusion. Two hours after the backup pumps first failed, the plant's chief engineer was told that a "minor snafu" had occurred at the plant.

To make the situation even more complicated and dangerous, tags attached to the pumps indicating that they were undergoing maintenance hung down in such a way that they hid the warning lights. Even though the system correctly indicated that a problem existed, operators could not see the indicator lights.

It would have been possible—although it did not happen in this case—for the hydrogen to explode, releasing radioactive materials over hundreds of square miles surrounding the plant.

An hour and a half later, the situation had escalated into a "general emergency" for Unit 2. And by 8:15 A.M., plant managers had set up a direct telephone line to NRC offices in Washington, D.C. In their early press conferences, plant officials said that less than one percent of the core's fuel rods were damaged and that the internal temperature of the reactor was only 2,000 degrees Fahrenheit. Later they had to revise those figures to at least fifty percent loss of fuel rods and a temperature of 5,000 degrees Fahrenheit.

Everyone involved seemed to be concerned about causing unnecessary panic. Pennsylvania Governor Richard Thornburgh first considered calling for a general evacuation of the area, but then decided more modest precautions would be sufficient. He advised people to stay in their homes with their windows closed.

Radiation measurements taken the day of the accident showed levels ranging from thirty millirems immediately above the containment dome to five millirems three miles downwind from the plant. The problem is that experts still disagree about the health effects of low-level radiation. A person receives about twenty millirems of radiation from a typical chest x-ray, so the levels measured at TMI-2 seem reasonably safe. But some authorities believe that each additional dose of radiation, no matter how small, increases a person's chance of contracting cancer later in life. Exactly how much of the threat the TMI-2 accident was to long-term human health is still, therefore, a matter of some conjecture.

Cleanup efforts on the damaged reactor began almost immediately. The most important source of concern was the steam-hydrogen bubble in the containment dome. Engineers vented part of the gas into the atmosphere through filters that removed its radioactivity. They also were able to transfer some of the steam-hydrogen mixture to an outside building, where the hydrogen was combined chemically with oxygen to make water. Cleanup crews were able to remove 20,000 gallons of radioactive water that had flowed into the auxiliary building by transferring it to holding tanks. Finally, a variety of methods were used to cool down the hot reactor core itself and prevent any further meltdown.

The total lifetime cost of the structure will reach close to $2 billion, and it never produced any significant amount of electricity.

The long-term cleanup of TMI-2 was a slow, dangerous, and complex process that took eleven years. Eventually 150 metric tons of damaged fuel rods and other reactor components were shipped to the Idaho National Engineering Laboratory for storage and analysis. The total cost of the cleanup process was $973 million.

There are no plans to repair TMI-2. Safety experts will continue to observe and monitor the plant until early into the next century. At that point,

breakdown

it will be decommissioned along with its companion reactor, TMI-1. The total lifetime cost of the structure will reach close to $2 billion, and it never produced any significant amount of electricity.

Impact

The TMI-2 accident has had both short-term local, and long-term national and international effects. In the immediate area surrounding the Three Mile Island complex, residents became—and have remained—concerned about the possible effects of the accident on their health. Given the nature of short-term radiation, it is possible that increased rates of cancer or birth defects may not show up for years.

A reflection of these concerns is the more than 2,200 lawsuits that have been filed by area residents because of the accident. To date, 280 claims have been settled at a total cost of about $14 million. Operations at TMI-1 were significantly affected by the events at the neighboring reactor: more than one hundred modifications were made in the older plant at a cost of $95 million. To complete the necessary renovations, the plant was shut down for six years. During that time, an improved and expanded training program for TMI-1 personnel was developed and implemented. Much of the training at the plant is now done in an $18 million full-scale replica of the TMI-1 control room.

The top portion of the TMI-1 reactor, which is still in operation. The similarly designed TMI-2 reactor was the site of the 1979 accident.

The TMI-2 accident became the subject of a number of investigations and studies by both governmental bodies and industry groups. Probably the two most important of these were an NRC study, whose results became generally known as the Rogovin Report, and a study commissioned by President Jimmy Carter, eventually known as the Kemeny Report. As a result of these studies, the NRC issued new regulations in 1980 requiring modifications of existing plants and new safety features to be included in future plants.

The nuclear power industry also became more interested in safety issues after the TMI-2 accident. Companies established the Institute of Nuclear Power Operations (INPO), whose purpose it is to review, evaluate, and recommend ways of improving nuclear power plant performance.

Probably the greatest single result of the TMI-2 accident was its impact on the future of nuclear power in the United States. Orders for nuclear power plants had already begun to decline in the year preceding the TMI-2 event. But the accident seemed to mark a real turning point in the public's attitude about nuclear power. Activists around the nation finally had an almost-worst-case scenario for what might happen in a nuclear accident. They began to speak out against plants under development and to work to defeat plans for new plants. Those efforts have been largely successful. Since 1979, no new nuclear plants have been ordered and fifty-nine planned reactors have been canceled. Seventeen new plants have been opened, but all were in final stages of planning or construction at the time of the accident.

Where to Learn More

Adams, John. A. "TMI Plus 5: Part I—A Slow Comeback." *IEEE Spectrum*, April 1984, pp. 27–33.

Burnham, David. "Nuclear Experts Reportedly Knew of Flaw in Some Reactors in 1977." *New York Times*, May 25, 1979, p. 18.

Eisenhunt, Darrell. G. "TMI Plus 5: Part II—NRC as Referee." *IEEE Spectrum*, April 1984, 33-9.

Fischetti, Mark. A. "TMI Plus 5: Part III—Band-aids and Better." *IEEE Spectrum*, April 1984, pp. 39–43.

Ford, Daniel. "Three Mile Island, 2—the Paper Trail." *New Yorker*, April 13, 1981, 46-7.

Franklin, Ben A. "Files Show Many Prior Problems at Three Mile Island." *New York Times*, April 19, 1979, p. 18.

Gray, Mike, and Ira Rosen. *The Warning: Accident at Three Mile Island*. Norton, 1982.

Kemeny, John G., chairman. *Report of the U.S. President's Commission on the Accident at Three Mile Island: The Need for Change; The Legacy of Three Mile Island*. Government Printing Office, 1979.

Levine, Joe, Mary Hickey, and Denise Laffan. "Cleansing the Atom." *Time*, March 1989, pp. 18–24.

Matthews, Tom, et al. "Nuclear Accident: Three Mile Island Plant, Pa." *Newsweek*, April 9, 1979, pp. 24–30+.

Moss, Thomas H., and David L. Sills, eds. *The Three Mile Island Nuclear Accident: Lessons and Implications*. New York Academy of Sciences, 1981.

Rogovin, Mitchell, and George T. Frampton, Jr. *Three Mile Island: A Report to the Commissioners and the Public*, vols. 1 and 2. Nuclear Regulatory Commission Special Inquiry Group, January 1980.

Tsuruga radioactive waste spill

Tsuruga, Japan **1981**

Due to human error, nearly four thousand gallons of radioactive wastes escaped from a nuclear power plant in Japan. Although officials attempted to hide the accident from public notice, the subterfuge was discovered six weeks later during a routine study of seaweed in the area.

Background

On March 8, 1981, the negligence of a single worker at the Tsuruga Nuclear Power Plant in Fukui prefecture in Japan triggered a spill of radioactive waste of disquieting proportions. The employee, who cleaned out a pipe in the building where radioactive wastes were treated, neglected to close a valve in the pipe, allowing the holding tank to overflow. Radioactive waste covered the floor of the waste treatment plant, leaked into an adjacent building, seeped into the ground, and eventually worked its way into the Sea of Japan. Officials at the plant attempted to hide the accident from public notice, but the subterfuge was discovered six weeks later during a routine study of seaweed in the area.

Japanese economic development since the end of World War II has amazed the world. Only a few short decades after the bombing of Hiroshima and Nagasaki and surrender to Allied forces, the nation had established itself as a world economic power. The one Achilles' heel of the "Japanese miracle,"

by David E. Newton

however, is the nation's lack of natural resources. The Japanese do not have sufficient reserves of coal, oil, or natural gas to maintain their recent pace of economic development. As recently as 1978, the nation imported 90 percent of the energy resources it used; 75 percent of that total was petroleum.

The OPEC (Organization of Petroleum Exporting Countries) oil embargo of 1973 made it abundantly clear to the Japanese how vulnerable they were to the rest of the world in this regard. Sobered by the helplessness it felt during that period, the government decided to place a renewed emphasis on the development of nuclear power to establish energy independence for the nation.

Nuclear power in Japan, however, has had a troubled history. The nation that experienced the devastation of the world's first two atomic explosions has long grappled with a fundamental concern about the use of nuclear energy, even for peaceful purposes. When the Japanese government finally decided to permit and sponsor nuclear research in 1955, it adopted a law that contained many safeguards for citizens and guaranteed that the nation's nuclear research would never by used for military purposes.

Progress on the development of commercial nuclear power was rapid after passage of the 1955 Basic Law on Atomic Energy. The first research reactor was opened in 1957 at Tokaimura in Ibaraki Prefecture, and the first commercial plant came online eight years later.

The government's original goal was to open more than thirty nuclear power plants by the year 1990, reducing the nation's dependence on foreign oil from 75 percent to 50 percent. That timetable proved overly optimistic, but progress was rapid nonetheless. By 1986 the Japanese had opened thirty-one commercial reactors that were producing almost twenty-four megawatts of electricity. Atomic energy had emerged as the largest single source of power in the nation, accounting for 26 percent of the nation's energy supplies.

The nuclear power plant at Tsuruga, the nation's second oldest, was opened in 1970. It was constructed by General Electric (GE) based on designs provided by Ebasco Services of New York State. The plant was operated by Japan Atomic Power Company (JAPC), the company in charge of all Japanese reactors. JAPC's activities were, in turn, monitored by two government agencies, the Agency of Natural Resources and Energy (ANRE) and the Ministry of International Trade and Technology. After the March 8 accident, GE pointed out that the spill took place in a part of the treatment plant built by the Japanese, not by the American company.

Details of the Accident

One of the routine operations that takes place in a nuclear waste treatment plant is the flushing out of pipes from time to time. On March 8, 1981, a worker at the Tsuruga plant was performing this operation. He neglected to notice, however, that a valve in one of the intake pipes had failed to close. As a result, radioactive wastes poured into a holding tank until it began to overflow.

A later investigation by ANRE found that the indicator light for the valve was not working properly. The light indicated that the valve was closed when, in fact, it was still open. The ANRE report concluded, however, that the operator "should have known that [the] indicator light was malfunctioning."

The series of events that followed was not revealed to the public until April 18. Amazingly, plant managers themselves did not know about the spill until two days after it had occurred. The story that eventually emerged was somewhat confused, and it changed with each new report.

Investigators eventually determined, however, that radioactive water from the unsealed pipe filled the holding tank until it overflowed. The radioactive waste then poured onto the floor of the waste treatment building, which was connected to the reactor building by pipes. The material then seeped into the laundry room next door. From there, it drained through cracks in the laundry room floor into the ground beneath. Eventually it diffused into a sewer line and worked its way into the nearby Bay of Urazoko, an inlet of the Sea of Japan. According to later estimates, anywhere from fifteen to forty tons of radioactive waste escaped from the holding tank, the worst spill in Japan's history. Authorities estimated that no more than one cubic meter of radioactive waste ever reached the bay, although such estimates are highly problematic. Moreover, the attempted cover-up cast a shadow over the veracity of all subsequent statements made by plant officials.

When plant officials learned of the accident, they ordered workers to clean up the radioactive waste by hand, using mops and buckets. The task was an enormous one; it took more than two weeks to complete and required that the facility hire fifty additional workers from outside the plant.

The plant managers concealed the accident, deciding not to announce the leak to the outside world. The contamination that resulted was discovered by chance when local health officials made a routine check of seaweed in Urazoko Bay. They found levels of radiation at least ten times greater than normal. The levels of some isotopes were even higher. The reading for cobalt 60, for example, was five thousand times greater than any previously recorded in the area. When workers traced the source of radiation, they were dumbstruck to find that it came from an outlet pipe for the sewer running underneath the nuclear power plant.

Confronted with this evidence, plant officials acknowledged on April 18 that the accident had taken place the previous month. They claimed that the accident posed no danger either to workers in the plant or to nearby residents.

According to later estimates, anywhere from fifteen to forty tons of radioactive waste escaped from the holding tank, the worst spill in Japan's history.

Those involved in the clean up, officials claimed, had been exposed to no more than 35 millirems of radiation, less than the level permitted under health regulations in both Japan and the United States. (The average annual radiation dose received by a person in the United States is thought to be about 180 millirems. Most of this exposure can be traced to natural radiation and medical and dental x-rays.) Plant executives admitted, however, that the workers' radiation-exposure badges were altered, so there was no firm evidence to support this claim.

Impact

In light of the Tsuruga accident and management's irresponsible reaction to it, the Japanese government returned to the plant's past history of safety violations. In the months following the March 8 spill, astonished JAPC officials gradually uncovered details of more than thirty accidents that had occurred in the plant's recent history. The most recent incident prior to the March 8 spill had taken place when repairs were made to a cracked pipe between January 24 and 28, 1981. During that event, more than forty workers might have been exposed to dangerous levels of radiation. Other disquieting chapters in the plant's history were discovered as well. On January 10, 1975, for instance, a spill similar to the March 8 accident released thirteen tons of radioactive

breakdown

material into the surrounding environment. On that occasion, thirty-seven workers were exposed to radiation during the cleanup process.

Officials of JAPC continually tried to reassure the general public that the Tsuruga accident was a minor event of no great significance. It was, they said, "nowhere near as serious as America's Three Mile Island" and they promised that there was never any "real damage" as a result of the spill. Skeptical local residents were not easily reassured. "How do we know what is the effect of fifteen tons in the bay?" asked one nearby resident.

National reaction to the company's belated April 18 announcement was also swift. Widespread outrage spurred the nation's second largest political party, the Socialists, to call for an end to Japan's nuclear power program and a shutdown of all existing plants. A grass-roots anti-nuclear movement found the nation's mood a fertile one for a membership drive and soon enrolled more than 45,000 members throughout the nation.

In response to these actions, JAPC's chairman, Tomiichiro Shirasawa, and president, Shunichi Suzuki, announced their resignations on May 13. They accepted full responsibility for the accidents and coverups at Tsuruga and called for a return to confidence in the role of nuclear power in Japan's future. The plant itself was closed down for repairs. Those repairs ultimately cost about $10 million and kept the plant out of operation for six months.

The long-term effects of the Tsuruga accident have been relatively modest. The role of nuclear power in Japan's energy equation has remained fairly constant. Japan's official policy is still one that hopes to wean itself from dependence on foreign oil. As a result, the development of nuclear power has continued at about the pace the nation set for itself two decades ago.

Where to Learn More

Firth, Suzanne. "Chilling Reminder of Things Past." *MacLean's*, May 4, 1981, pp. 32–33.

"Japan's Three-Mile Island." *Newsweek*, May 4, 1981, p. 42.

"Japanese Concede Errors in Nuclear Plant Mishap." *New York Times*, April 4, 1981, p. A6.

"Nuclear Contamination Found in Japanese Soil." *New York Times*, April 19, 1981, p. 7.

"Earlier Mishap Is Revealed at Japanese Nuclear Plant." *New York Times*, April 21, 1981, p. 5.

"Japan Says Nuclear Mishap Exposed 56 to Radiation." *New York Times*, April 22, 1981, p. 8.

"45 Workers Are Reported Exposed to Nuclear Radiation." *New York Times*, April 26, 1981, p. 6.

"Nuclear Executives in Japan Resign over Recent Mishaps." *New York Times*, May 14, 1981, p. 11.

"Repercussions Continue at Japan's Three Mile Island and at the Original." *Power*, July 1981, pp. 124–26.

Smith, R. Jeffrey. "Japanese Agitated by Nuclear Plant Spill." *Science*, June 5, 1981, p. 1124.

Stokes, Henry Scott. "For the Japanese, Sudden Misgivings about Nuclear Power." *New York Times*, May 16, 1981, p. 3.

Ginna power plant radioactive release

Ontario, New York **1982**

Failure of a pipe in a nuclear power plant caused shutdown of the reactor and release of radioactive gas into the atmosphere.

by David E. Newton

Background

On January 25, 1982, a small pipe in the steam generating system of the Robert E. Ginna nuclear power plant in Ontario, New York, ruptured. Hot water from the primary cooling system leaked into the secondary cooling system. In dealing with the problem, operators were forced to release cooling water contaminated with radioactivity into an emergency relief tank, which overflowed and dumped about seventeen hundred gallons of water onto the floor of the reactor building. At the same time, a small amount of radioactive steam was released through emergency safety valves in the top of the containment dome.

The Robert E. Ginna nuclear reactor, originally known as Brockwood, was opened in 1970 with a production capacity of 470 megawatts of electricity. It was built at Ontario, New York, about fifteen miles east of Rochester. The facility was constructed for the Rochester Gas & Electric Company (RG&E) by Westinghouse Electric Corporation, one of three United States companies making pressurized water reactors (PWR). In a PWR, heat produced by nuclear fission reactions in uranium fuel rods is absorbed and carried away by cooling water maintained under high pressure. The high pressure prevents the cooling water

1
5
3

from boiling although it reaches temperatures of more than three hundred degrees Celsius.

The heated cooling water from the primary system is then pumped into a secondary steam generating system. The secondary system consists of thousands of long, narrow tubes through which hot water from the primary system passes. The tubes are surrounded by cold water that is heated by the primary water until it boils and changes to steam. The steam is then used to turn turbines that operate electrical generators. The Ginna plant was equipped with two steam generating systems, known as A and B.

One of the critical design problems in a PWR system concerns the construction of the tubes in the secondary system. These tubes must be thin enough to allow the efficient transfer of heat from the hot primary water to the cold secondary water. But they must also be strong enough to withstand mechanical vibration, turbulence, and corrosion from the surrounding water. The standard design calls for tubes about a millimeter thick made of a nickel alloy called Inconel.

Damage to secondary tubes has long been recognized as a problem in PWRs. Over time, the tubes have a tendency to become dented, pitted, or corroded. There are instances on record in which tubes actually break up, permitting primary water to escape into the secondary system. Three different techniques are used for dealing with the problem of damaged tubes. When the tubes are easily accessible, they can simply be removed from the secondary system. Another approach is plugging, in which a tube is sealed up and essentially taken out of service. A third approach is sleeving, in which a tube of a smaller diameter than the damaged tube is inserted inside it. During a routine test of the secondary system at Ginna in May 1981, four tubes out of 3,260 in the B steam generator were plugged, three were pulled, and fifteen were sleeved. At the time, a total of 113 tubes had been plugged, while another twenty-one had been sleeved and seven others had been pulled.

Details of the Accident

The first indication of a problem at the Ginna plant came at 9:25 A.M. on January 25, 1982, when five different warning systems went off simultaneously. The warnings indicated that pressure in the primary cooling system was dropping rapidly, by more than one thousand pounds per square inch in less than five minutes. Three minutes later, the reactor's automatic safety system was triggered. Control rods dropped into the core and shut down the nuclear fission chain reactions in the fuel rods. At the same time, the emergency cooling system turned on and cold water flowed into the core.

At 9:40 A.M., a warning light indicated the cause of the problem. One of the 3,260 tubes in the B steam generating system had ruptured. Hot water

from the primary cooling system had begun to flow into the cold water of the secondary system. As the primary water escaped into the secondary system, some of it changed into steam and was vented automatically into the atmosphere. The automatic venting lasted for no more than two minutes and released a minimal amount of gas to the atmosphere. Operators declared an "alert," the lowest level of safety warning, at 9:40 A.M.

Operators at the facility were faced with several difficult decisions that had to be acted on quickly. They had to reduce pressure in the primary system to prevent any more hot water from escaping into the secondary system. At the same time, however, they had to maintain pressure in the primary system at a level high enough to keep water from boiling and forming a steam cap above the core. A delicate balance had to be struck.

The approach of the Ginna staff was to slowly equalize pressures in the primary and secondary systems by opening and closing a pressure relief valve in the primary system by hand. They did so successfully at 10:07 and 10:08 A.M., but during a third attempt at 10:09, the valve failed to close. Water flowed out of the primary system and pressure again started to drop rapidly. At 10:44 A.M., operators declared the next higher level of safety warning, a "site emergency."

The Ginna nuclear reactor, which was the site of a 1982 accident that shut down the reactor and caused the release of radioactive material. Despite the accident, the reactor was back in operation within six months.

The failure of the valve in the pressurizer to close created two new emergencies. First, the pressurizer tank began to overflow, dumping cooling water into a relief tank beneath the reactor. Eventually the tank became full and burst open (as it was designed to do), releasing radioactive water onto the reactor building floor and, from there, into the bay beneath the building. Workers quickly recognized this problem, however, and shut off a master valve that stopped the loss of cooling water from the pressurizer. A total of 1,690 gallons of contaminated water was eventually lost from the reactor.

At the same time, some of the pressurized water in the reactor began to boil, producing a bubble of steam above the core. The danger was that, as the steam bubble grew, it might force cooling water down until the fuel rods were exposed. If that were to happen, a meltdown like the one that had taken place at Three Mile Island three years before might occur.

Operators attempted to deal with this threat in two ways. They gradually added more water to the primary cooling system in a bid to cool and compress the steam bubble. In addition, they flooded the reactor core itself with cold water, trying to cool its metal structures as quickly as possible. The procedure worked, and by 11:15 A.M. the steam bubble had disappeared, to the considerable relief of the crew.

As workers grappled with the crisis in steam generating system B, they also began to shut down system A. At 11:29 A.M., they started venting steam from system A and pumping cooling water into that system. By 12:30 P.M., the temperature in the system was dropping at a rate of two degrees per hour. Two days later, at 4:30 P.M. on Wednesday, January 27, the reactor was declared to be in a cold shutdown condition. The emergency was over.

Follow-up studies of the Ginna incident focused on two major questions. What was it that caused the tubes in the B steam generating system to rupture? And what damage, if any, had been done to the reactor structure by flooding it with cold water during emergency procedures?

The first question was answered during the Nuclear Regulatory Commission's (NRC) study of the accident. Investigators found a number of pieces of scrap metal in both steam generating systems. These included long pieces and fragments of tubing from the steam generating systems, a piece of wire, and several strips of steel. The NRC suggested that some of the debris may have resulted from sloppy workmanship. During routine repairs, the NRC speculated, workers may have allowed bits and pieces of scrap metal—and, perhaps, even parts of their tools—to fall into the steam generating systems. These materials may have been tossed around by cooling water in the reactor, colliding with tubes and eventually causing one of them to break open.

The question of thermal shock to the reactor vessel required longer study. It is not possible in most cases to determine visually if metal has been damaged as a result of exposure to rapid temperature changes. By mid-May, however, the NRC had conducted detailed tests and determined that the reactor vessel had not been damaged. It gave RG&E permission to restart the reactor, and on May 27, the plant was once again restored to full power.

Impact

The situation that developed at Ginna was inevitably compared to the far more serious incident at Three Mile Island of 1979. News reports recalled the earlier disaster and described the Ginna event as "one more setback for the nuclear power industry." Yet, in many ways, the two incidents were very different. As a spokesman for RG&E said, "This accident [at Ginna] didn't come within a country mile of Three Mile Island." Although the valve that stuck open at Ginna was the same kind of valve that caused the Three Mile Island problem, the Ginna failure had less serious repercussions because of a couple of factors. The equipment in place at Ginna had been improved as a result of lessons learned at Three Mile Island. More important, however, was the performance of plant operators at Ginna. They knew what to do as the emergency developed, and they followed the correct steps to keep the reactor under control. As a result, the plant was back in operation less than six months later. In comparison, the accident at Three Mile Island so badly damaged the facility that it will never again reopen.

As with other incidents at nuclear power plants, a great deal was learned about the operation and handling of reactors. A study by the Institute of Nuclear Power Operations (INPO), for example, praised Ginna's operators for their performance during the emergency. But they noted a number of improvements that could still be made in plant manuals and training. They found that actions other than those taken by operators would have resolved the crisis even more quickly.

A study by the Institute of Nuclear Power Operations, praised Ginna's operators for their performance during the emergency.

The events at the Ginna plant also increased already sizable concerns about the safety of the tubes in the steam generating system of PWRs such as the one that failed. Every PWR contains thousands of such tubes, and engineers have long realized that they may be the weakest point in the whole plant. Procedures to deal with long-term corrosion and damage, described above, have long been known and used. But the lesson of Ginna is that tubes can also fail quickly as the result of violent impact or other still-unknown factors. As one report on the Ginna accident observed, tube failures had become "an expensive and complicated problem for utilities to solve."

Where to Learn More

Blake, E. Michael. "Ginna—A Special Case." *Nuclear News*, December 1982, pp. 52–53.

"Pipe Failure Closes New York Nuclear Plant." *Chemical & Engineering News*, February 1, 1982, p. 5.

Marbach, William D. "Again a Nuclear Mishap." *Newsweek*, February 8, 1982, pp. 63–65.

Marshall, Eliot. "Corrosion May Not Be Prime Culprit at Ginna." *Science*, March 5, 1982, p. 1215.

—. "NRC Reports on Ginna Nuclear Accident." *Science*, April 30, 1982, pp. 498–99.

—. "Reactor Mishap Raises Broad Questions." *Science*, February 12, 1982, pp. 877–78.

"Ginna Tube Burst Investigated." *Nuclear Engineering International*, March 1982, pp. 10–11.

"NRC Holds Off Restart in Wake of Tube Break." *Nuclear News*, March 1982, pp. 45–47.

"The NRC Task Force on Ginna Praised the Operators...." *Nuclear News*, May 1982, p. 21.

"Unit Restarted: Generators To Be Inspected in September." *Nuclear News*, July 1982, p. 43.

"Hindsight on Ginna." *Nuclear News*, February 1983, p. 50.

Peterson, Ivar. "Ginna Atomic Plant Scrapped by Steel?" *Science News*, April 24, 1982, p. 277.

—. "The Ginna Problem: Isolated or Generic?" *Science News*, January 30, 1982, p. 68.

—. "Nuclear Shutdowns: Tubular Woes." *Science News*, February 13, 1982, p. 105.

Bhopal toxic vapor leak

Bhopal, India **1984**

A toxic vapor leak that released fifty thousand pounds of deadly gas over the Indian countryside resulted in massive loss of life and widespread injury.

Background

by Lamont Ingalls

On the morning of December 3, 1984, a poisonous cloud of methyl isocyanate (MIC) gas, an element in the pesticide produced by the Union Carbide plant in Bhopal, India, escaped from the facility and drifted over the city. Investigators later determined that water had been incorrectly added to tank 610, a receptacle for methyl isocyanate. The introduction of the water triggered a reaction with the methyl isocyanate that caused an increase in pressure. The ensuing explosion allowed fifty thousand pounds of deadly gas to escape over the Indian countryside. The deadly cloud cut a wide swath of death and destruction through the populace of Bhopal. Thousands of people were killed and many more badly injured as the gas attacked their nervous systems. The horror at Bhopal prompted harsh public scrutiny of all chemical plants on a worldwide basis, and the courts began the long process of litigation over damage claims.

The Union Carbide site at Bhopal was first developed in 1969 as a mixing and packaging plant for pesticides imported from the United States. Over time a shantytown of local residents developed around the plant. In 1980 the facility was expanded to manufacture the carbamate pesticides Sevin and Temik. One chemical used in large quantities in the production process was methyl isocyanate (MIC), a highly reactive, volatile, and toxic compound. Methyl isocyanate was stored on-site in large underground storage tanks. The Bhopal methyl isocyanate storage tanks had capacities of approximately fifteen thousand gallons, over three times the size of methyl isocyanate storage tanks at any other chemical manufacturing facility.

The dangerous toxicity of methyl isocyanate is clearly evident in the warnings issued by the chemical industry and regulatory agencies. The threshold limit value (TLV) of methyl isocyanate established under United States Occupational Safety and Health Act (OSHA) standards is exposure to 0.02 parts per million of methyl isocyanate in an eight-hour period. Exposure beyond this limit is considered deleterious to a worker's health, for as scientists have noted, methyl isocyanate causes irritation of the eyes, nose, and throat at two parts per million. Exposure at the twenty-one parts per million level is tortuous. The TLV of methyl isocyanate is one-tenth that of phosgene, the chemical used in World War I as the warfare agent mustard gas.

Shoddy management and negligence manifested itself in one of the most horrible ways imaginable.

Given its deadly properties, it is very important that stored methyl isocyanate be protected from overheating, from escaping into the atmosphere, and from the introduction of contaminants, including water, with which it might react. Methyl isocyanate is also highly reactive with such common metals as iron, copper, tin, and zinc. Any contamination of methyl isocyanate by a metal, water, or any other substance with which it reacts creates chemical reactions that have the potential to escalate into a runaway reaction. A runaway reaction, or a chemical chain reaction, occurs when the heat of reaction is not mitigated by surroundings that conduct the heat of reaction. Under these conditions, the heat of reaction rapidly builds to an explosive level. During bulk storage methyl isocyanate is often protected and cooled by a blanket of dry nitrogen. To prevent or slow reactivity, the temperature of bulk-stored methyl isocyanate is maintained at 0 degrees Celsius or below.

The exact operative mechanisms of the Bhopal release are still subject to debate. In accidents and releases that occur in most modern processing plants, investigators have access to an extensive database of operator logs; electronic sensors and recording devices linked to computer control, monitoring, and data storage systems; and computer models of cause-and-effect scenarios. At the Union Carbide plant in Bhopal, however, the array of gauging, monitoring, and recording systems typical of a modern processing plant were either not in place, out-of-service, or not set properly prior to the explosion. Thus, only a most-probable-cause scenario can be postulated.

breakdown

Details of the Disaster

For six weeks prior to the accident, the Bhopal plant's methyl isocyanate production unit had been shut down due to the abundance of Sevin and Temik already on site. As is usual during downtime, workers had been repairing, cleaning, and performing maintenance on the unit. A standard item of maintenance involved cleaning the filters in the four lines that carried methyl isocyanate from the storage tank into the processing unit. These four lines were connected to the pipeline for the relief valve vent header (RVVH). This RVVH configuration was designed to carry toxic vapors from the methyl isocyanate storage tanks to the vent gas scrubber (VGS) unit should pressure build up in the storage tanks. The VGS was designed to "scrub" any toxic release with caustic soda to neutralize the methyl isocyanate and then route the scrubbed gas to a flare tower, where it would be burned.

To prevent water from traveling toward the methyl isocyanate tank via the RVVH piping during the cleaning process, a maintenance worker closed a valve to isolate the filter pipelines from the RVVH. The worker, however, did not insert a slip blind—a metal disc—into the valve to seal it, as is usually done when filters are washed. In addition, two of the four bleeder valves that allowed water to flow out of the lines during the washing process were completely clogged; the flow rate from the other two indicated a partial blockage.

This was noted, and the washing process was temporarily halted, but the filter washing procedure soon resumed.

As noted in an inspection earlier in the year, many of the valves in the plant were leaky. The filter isolation valve was no exception. Thus, water pressure increased in the partially clogged filter washing system and water began flowing past the isolation valve and into the RVVH.

The piping between the RVVH and the methyl isocyanate storage tank contained a number of closed valves which, under as-designed configurations, would prevent the entry of water into the storage tank via the RVVH. There was also a one-way rupture disc designed to break in the event of increased pressure from methyl isocyanate vapor and allow the toxic vapor to flow into the RVVH. The two substances—the water and the methyl isocyanate—could thus be kept separated. However, a jumper line had recently been installed between the RVVH and the process vent header (PVH). This header was designed as a route for venting gases released during movement of methyl isocyanate to the production unit. Any gases released from the tank would thus vent to the scrubber. The jumper line—a less expensive alternative to adding a backup line for the process vent headers—allowed gases from the storage tank to vent to the scrubber through the headers of either the PVH or the RVVH should one of the header units be down for repairs.

The jumper line, which had been installed in May 1984, was opened on December 2 to allow repairs on the PVH. This open line allowed the water backing up the line from the filter washing process to enter the PVH instead of the RVVH. From the PVH, the water was able to enter tank 610 because of leaking valves in the piping connecting the PVH to the storage tank.

Employees at the plant were aware that the valves designed to seal the tank from the PVH were leaking. Recent efforts to pressurize tank 610 with liquid nitrogen so that the methyl isocyanate could be transferred to a Sevin production unit, when needed, had been unsuccessful. The difficulty was traced to the valves. But while the pressurization efforts continued for a week, nothing was done to locate and correct the faulty valve, or valves.

There were several other conditions that contributed to the explosive tank failure and subsequent toxic release. In addition to the leaking water—which reacted with the methyl isocyanate to create intense heat—tank 610 was 75 to 87 percent full, well above the 50 to 60 percent recommended in Union Carbide safety standards. Tank 619, which had been designated a back-up tank for any potential overflow, should have been empty. Instead, it contained approximately twelve tons of methyl isocyanate. In addition, the methyl isocyanate in tank 610 was contaminated by chloroform—a substance that reacts both with methyl isocyanate and with the stainless steel walls of the storage tank—at a level much higher than that recommended in Carbide's safety standards. Finally, the plant had neglected to address the temperature

Tank 619, which had been designated a back-up tank for any potential overflow, should have been empty. Instead, it contained approximately twelve tons of methyl isocyanate.

breakdown

of the methyl isocyanate in the storage tank. The methyl isocyanate was between fifteen and twenty degrees Celsius. Standard safe storage procedures specify a temperature of zero to five degrees Celsius, preferably lower.

In short, a number of factors combined to cause the most deadly toxic leak in history. When the operators on duty noted a sudden rise in the pressure in tank 610, from two to thirty to fifty-five pounds per square inch, there was nothing that could be done to prevent, or even slow down, the runaway reaction. The operators hurriedly investigated ways to slow or neutralize the chemical reaction, but their options were limited.

The vent gas scrubber was on standby status, and could not be turned on in time to neutralize some of the escaping gases. The flare tower was not available to burn any of the release because the piping linking the methyl isocyanate tank to the vent gas scrubber, and subsequently to the flare tower, had been removed. In addition, the operators feared that moving the reacting methyl isocyanate into the overflow tank, which had twelve tons of methyl isocyanate in it, would only create additional dangers. A desperate attempt to douse the leaking toxic vapors rushing from a stack on the relief valve vent header failed as well, for while the stack was 120 feet high, the spray reached only 100 feet.

Plant operators watched helplessly as shoddy management and negligence manifested itself in one of the most horrible ways imaginable. Approximately twenty-seven tons of methyl isocyanate vapor and fourteen tons of reaction products were released into the atmosphere as a result of the explosion of tank 610. The release of this searing cloud of toxic vapor occurred over a period of approximately ninety minutes and affected an area of fifteen square miles.

The toxic contents of tank 610 and associated reaction products spread into the slums downwind of the plant. The narrow streets and flimsy dwellings of this area became a charnel house of human beings and animals staggering about and gasping for breath amid a heavy white vapor that boiled from the plant and filled the low-lying areas. The gas proved immediately deadly and killed people up to five miles away from the site. A neighborhood where the greatest loss of life occurred was four miles from the plant.

The Indian Supreme Court eventually estimated that about 3,000 people were killed by the toxic vapor. Other investigators put the loss at 2,500 to 5,000, while medical personnel who directly treated the victims in Bhopal have stated that up to 12,000 unfortunate victims died as a direct result of the leak. The victims died immediately from either asphyxiation or suffocation caused by pulmonary edema (fluid in the lungs), or in subsequent days from causes directly attributable to exposure to the effects of the toxic vapor.

Those injured by the release of methyl isocyanate and its reaction products suffered from a range of terrible ailments. Acute respiratory distress, eye

Approximately twenty-seven tons of methyl isocyanate vapor and fourteen tons of reaction products were released into the atmosphere as a result of the explosion of tank 610. The release of this searing cloud of toxic vapor occurred over a period of approximately ninety minutes and affected an area of fifteen square miles.

irritation, and problems of the circulatory, gastrointestinal, and central nervous systems were all reported. Long-term effects included chronic lesions of the eyes, permanent scarring of the lungs, and injuries to the liver, brain, heart, kidneys, and immune system. An epidemiological study of the yearly rate of spontaneous abortions and infant deaths in the years after the accident found the rate in Bhopal to be three to four times the regional rate.

An Indian government commission estimate of those injured by exposure to the vapor included 30,000 with permanent injuries, 20,000 with temporary injuries, and 150,000 with minor injuries. This figure is disputed by victims' rights organizations who say that this estimate is much too low.

Impact

The magnitude and implications of this event created a great sense of uneasiness in the industry and in the general public, leading to questions about the principles of plant operations and the nature of the chemical industry in general. The manner in which Union Carbide operated the plant in India came under a barrage of outraged criticism as well. All aspects of the Bhopal plant, from operational readiness to industry and site-specific safety design configurations, came under close scrutiny.

The tragedy at the Union Carbide facility in Bhopal became the subject of an intense inquiry into the causes of the release on the site and the potential for accidents at other processing facilities using and storing methyl isocyanate. These inquiries were concerned with such issues as tank construction and monitoring; site safety warning and containment systems; the potential for failures caused by operator error; identification of site configurations that undermine the safety inherent in the original design of the methyl isocyanate storage tank and production unit; and storage system safety maintenance and emergency response procedures.

In addition to these vital safety considerations, however, other issues concerning the management of the Bhopal plant were brought up as well. How could the operators of the plant permit conditions to deteriorate in such a way? Why did they allow a shantytown to develop around the plant without an appropriate measure of emergency planning? Industry management and interest groups and regulatory agencies must address these issues to similar preconditions for a disaster are not permitted to evolve.

The questions of criminal prosecution for negligence and fiscal compensation to the victims have been the subject of intense debate and litigation in the government chambers and court systems of India. Initially, Indian prosecutors brought charges of criminal negligence against the Indian and American management of Union Carbide. Some months after the accident, Union Carbide stated that an angry employee sabotaged the plant by deliberately allowing water to enter the methyl isocyanate storage tank. No one associated with the Bhopal plant has been directly charged with this sabotage.

After several years of negotiations, Union Carbide agreed to a settlement of $470 million with the government of Rajiv Ghandi. The dropping of all criminal charges against Carbide officials initially charged was part of this settlement. The amount was challenged on legal grounds, but was upheld as constitutional by the Indian Supreme Court in 1991. Union Carbide has been unable to completely close this ugly chapter in their existence, however. The present Indian government regards the initial settlement as unacceptable. The original claim against Union Carbide was for $3.3 billion, an amount the present government feels is more representative of the damage the company's plant did to the nation of India. Government officials also expressed interest in pursuing criminal charges against Carbide management. Union Carbide India has paid, as ordered, $190 million in interim compensation, which the Indian government is to distribute among the survivors of the tragedy pending the final outcome of the settlement.

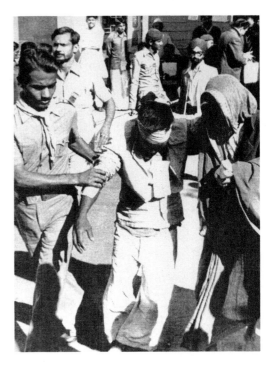

The toxic fumes leaking from the plant were immediately deadly, killing persons up to five miles away. Eventually, thousands were evacuated from their homes.

Presently, under the authority of the Bhopal Claims Act, the Indian government is giving survivors 200 rupees a month (approximately U.S. $10). These payments are to last as long as the Bhopal case remains unsettled in the courts and governing bureaus. It is likely that litigation and the debate over responsibility and compensation will continue for several more years.

Where to Learn More

"Union Carbide's Bhopal Bill." *Business Week*, February 27, 1989, p. 40.

Everest, L. *Behind the Poison Cloud*. Banner Press, 1985.

"Bhopal Tragedy's Health Effects." *Journal of the American Medical Association*, December 5, 1990, p. 2781.

"Public Health Lessons from the Bhopal Chemical Disaster." *Journal of the American Medical Association*, December 5, 1990, p. 2795.

Kurzman, D. *A Killing Wind: Inside Union Carbide and the Bhopal Disaster*. McGraw-Hill, 1987.

Lepowski, W. "Lessons from Bhopal," *Chemical & Engineering News*, November 17, 1986, pp. 39–45.

—. "Indian Activists Press Bhopal Accident Issues in U.S. Visit." *Chemical & Engineering News*, May 13, 1991, pp. 22–3.

Institute, West Virginia, toxic vapor leak

An explosive failure of a temporary storage tank containing an aldicarb oxime mixture caused a toxic vapor leak that injured 135 people.

by Lamont Ingalls

Background

Immediately following the tragic methyl isocyanite gas leak at Bhopal, India, on December 3, 1984, which killed 2,500 or more people and injured at least 200,000 more, the Union Carbide chemical plant at Institute, West Virginia, was shut down. This facility was the only chemical plant in the United States that manufactured and used methyl isocyanate (MIC). Yet when the plant reopened with new safety regulations in place, an accident still occurred, a leak of toxic materials that injured 135 people.

In the Bhopal incident, a cloud of methyl isocyanate had spread rapidly from a Union Carbide facility into a heavily populated area, where it killed and maimed thousands. The incident in India triggered intense concern among Union Carbide management and the residents of Institute about the potential for a similar incident there. Methyl isocyanate manufactured at the Institute facility at that time was shipped to a plant in Georgia, where it was combined with aldicarb oxime, another toxic substance, to form aldicarb, a component of the pesticide Temik.

Methyl isocyanate is highly corrosive, toxic, and unstable, and its manufacture and storage must take place under stringent conditions of isolation and control. The Institute facility had not always been successful in maintaining those conditions. From 1980 to 1984 twenty-eight methyl isocyanate leaks were documented at the Institute plant. Although the leaks had been confined to the site, the safety of the plant was in some doubt. The nightmarish developments in Bhopal convinced Union Carbide officials to close the West Virginia facility for a safety review.

During this period of closedown for inspection and analysis of plant process design, Union Carbide installed several additional safety features. One of these was a computerized air-monitoring system designed to detect and identify any releases of hazardous vapors in the plant. The system could also predict the movements and the toxicity or explosive levels of a vapor release. Such predictive modeling would enable safety personnel to act using real-time information, making it possible for them to warn off-site emergency response teams and nearby residents if the vapor cloud appeared to be spreading beyond plant boundaries.

Other changes were made to alleviate the possibility of a release of methyl isocyanate or associated toxic substances. Safety devices with primary and redundant systems to control methyl isocyanate were installed, and the on-site storage of methyl isocyanate was reduced.

In addition to the internal review undertaken during the months of the shutdown, the Institute plant was subject to a close safety review by federal officials who audited the site for violations of Occupational Safety and Health Administration (OSHA) regulations. In February 1985, OSHA officials declared that a Bhopal-scale accident was a very remote possibility in the United States and that the Institute plant could safely return to operation.

Prior to the Bhopal incident, methyl isocyanate was shipped to Georgia in unmixed form. These shipments were discontinued and were not resumed following the restart of the plant on May 4, 1985. Instead, plant processes were reconfigured so that the procedure wherein methyl isocyanate reacted with aldicarb oxime (AO) to produce aldicarb could take place at the Institute facility. The aldicarb was then shipped to the Georgia plant for additional processing. Although not as toxic as methyl isocyanate, small amounts of AO were known to cause nausea, tremors, eye and lung irritation, and heart palpitations. Aldicarb oxime had also been found by the Environmental Protection Agency (EPA) to cause cancer in laboratory animals under certain conditions.

Details of the Accident

The conditions at the Union Carbide plant in Institute that led to the toxic leak built gradually over the course of nearly two weeks. While the storage tank and site safety systems ruptured quickly, victimized by excessive system vapor pressure, the root causes of the ruptures accumulated quietly during the first part of August 1985.

The buildup of pressure before the explosion was the product of a thermal runaway reaction. This type of chemical chain reaction occurs when more heat is released during the reaction than can be carried away by cooling or through absorption by the walls of the storage vessel.

The post-Bhopal process redesign called for installation of a storage tank and attendant support and safety systems. This configuration would be used to store aldicarb oxime prior to movement to the mixing vessel where the aldicarb oxime would react with methyl isocyanate. This storage area was to be a temporary facility, to be used only until a permanent storage tank could be constructed.

The storage tank had a capacity of five thousand gallons and normally contained a mixture of aldicarb oxime and methylene chloride, a common solvent used to enhance the methyl isocyanate-aldicarb oxime reactive process. The lower two-thirds of the storage tank was enclosed by a steam jacket. This jacket was used, as needed, to heat the mixture because methylene chloride becomes solid below seventy degrees Fahrenheit. The steam for the jacket was controlled by a motor-operated valve.

On August 1, 1985, an aldicarb oxime-methylene chloride mixture was pumped into the storage tank from a mixing tank. This mixture was excess from the aldicarb production process. From August 1 to August 7, a faulty gasket on the motor-operated valve allowed steam to leak into the heating jacket. This heat caused the methylene chloride to vaporize. The vapor condensed in other parts of the system, including a spare storage tank, the crystallizer, and the "knockout pot," a vessel that collects the gas prior to venting to a vapor scrubber (a vapor scrubber treats gases and renders them less harmful to the environment). This vaporization of the methylene chloride caused the aldicarb oxime to concentrate in the bottom of the storage tank, in turn creating conditions that allowed a chemical heat reaction to proceed more rapidly than in the standard aldicarb oxime mixture.

On August 7, operators started pumps to transfer the contents of the storage tank to the mixing tank. After two and a half hours, the pumps stopped functioning. The operators assumed the tank was empty. In fact, there were still about five hundred gallons of the concentrated aldicarb oxime mixture in the tank. No attempt was made to verify that the storage vessel was empty. The tank level gauge was broken near the top and remained out of service. No other efforts were made to gauge the contents.

From August 7 to August 11 the concentrated aldicarb oxime mixture in the tank continued to be heated by the steam that was leaking into the jacket. Plant operators remained oblivious to this growing danger because they had neglected to program the electronic sensing system to display the temperature and pressure of the tank.

At 9:25 A.M. on Sunday, August 11, a runaway thermal reaction began in the storage tank. The startled operators heard a deep rumbling noise in the tank. Within seconds, they noticed excess flow to the flare designed to burn escaping gases. This high pressure at the flare indicated that an automatic safety valve had opened in the scrubber.

Within thirty-five seconds, the rupture disk on the knock-out pot failed, launching the toxic vapor mixture directly into the atmosphere. This rupture was followed immediately by a blowout of the gaskets at the cleaning access holes on top of the storage tank. This gasket failure also released toxic vapor into the atmosphere.

The control room was rapidly engulfed in a thick, toxic cloud that prevented the operators from seeing their controls. One of the operators, though, was able to set off the toxic gas release warning. The six operators, trapped by the gas, huddled in the control room and passed two breathing apparatuses around the frightened circle.

Within seven minutes the release was complete. The vapor cloud drifted through the plant, scattering workers. Personnel monitoring the cloud through the computerized sensing system noted that the release did not appear to be heading off-site. But the toxic cloud continued to move, drifting into nearby populated areas.

The toxic vapor cloud—composed of aldicarb oxime, methylene chloride, and various breakdown products, including sulfur compounds—spread silently through the area immediately outside the plant. People in their homes and backyards, drivers on nearby roads, and golfers at an adjacent golf course were all stricken. The toxic cloud caused instantaneous nausea as well as immediate eye, throat, and lung irritation. Altogether, 135 people in the Institute area were seriously exposed. So many were impaired by the toxic cloud at the golf course that an emergency aid center was set up at one of the greens. Of the 135 people given emergency treatment, twenty-eight were admitted to area hospitals. Eight of those hospitalized were workers from the Institute plant.

Investigators descended on the area quickly. A poll of area residents in the vicinity of the plant found that most learned of the leak only from seeing the vapor cloud or feeling the effects of the gas. Few residents pointed to the emergency warning sirens designed to warn the populace of danger. Union Carbide management, however, insisted that the lag in warning time of twenty-one minutes initially reported on the computerized emergency

> Within thirty-five seconds, the rupture disk on the knock-out pot failed, launching the toxic vapor mixture directly into the atmosphere. This rupture was followed immediately by a blowout of the gaskets at the cleaning access holes on top of the storage tank. This gasket failure also released toxic vapor into the atmosphere.

response log was due to a computer problem. Union Carbide management contended that the actual time from detection to activation of the warning sirens was slightly over one minute.

Investigators noted that site safety staff operating the newly installed air-monitoring system reported that the system had erroneously predicted the cloud of toxic vapor would not drift outside plant boundaries. A subsequent inquiry revealed that Union Carbide had not purchased the software that would have enabled the system to predict the movements of vapors associated with the release of aldicarb oxime.

Problems with the release containment systems were also found. The piping and pressure gaskets were not designed to hold a flow of the magnitude caused by the runaway thermal reaction. Although earlier modeling indicated that design criteria were adequate, the phenomenon of two-phase release may have affected the system's vapor handling capacity. This type of release creates a mixture of vapor and liquid under pressure—like foam on a mug of beer. A two-phase release does not allow the proper release of pressure in systems designed for vapor-only pressure releases.

breakdown

Yet another concern was the escape of toxic vapor directly into the atmosphere from the knockout pot and storage tank after the failure of a rupture disk and gaskets. All systems in place to contain tank failure for toxic substances of this type are required to vent into a closed system; the Union Carbide system was in violation of site safety design and operations procedures. Another safety system—a water containment sprinkler—did not have enough volume to suppress a release of this magnitude.

Union Carbide's review of the operating history of this storage unit also disclosed several operator errors. These errors were numerous. A level gauge that would have shown that the tank still contained an aldicarb oxime-methylene chloride mixture had gone unrepaired. High-pressure alarms had been shut off or ignored. A broken high-temperature alarm had not been repaired. The operators had neglected to request information on the tank from the unit's sensing computer, although the computer had been recording the increases in pressure and temperature since the steam line first began to leak. The review of the performance of the plant operators, coupled with investigators' findings about the general condition of the plant, painted an appalling, damning portrait of a facility that had evidently learned nothing from the Bhopal disaster that had unfolded less than a year before.

Impact

After the August 11 toxic leakage, OSHA auditors made a thorough inspection of the plant. Union Carbide was cited for 221 violations of OSHA regulations. These violations included failure to follow plant safety operating procedures when transferring the aldicarb oxime mixture and improper safety systems to prevent air contamination in the event of a leak. As punishment for the violations, OSHA imposed a $1.4 million fine, the largest fine the organization had handed down in its sixteen-year history.

Coming as it did a few months after the tragedy at Bhopal, India, this accident further heightened alarm in the chemical industry and the general public about the quality of safety and design measures related to toxic release containment. Politicians and citizens alike called for site safety control through legislation and increased study and classification of toxic substances. The vapor release also heightened the industry-wide need to review safety backup systems, chemical reaction consequences, and the design of vessels for storing volatile toxic substances.

Where to Learn More

"Beyond Bhopal: Toward a Fail-Safe Chemical Industry." *High Technology*, April 1985, pp. 55–61.

"Carbide Springs Another Leak." *Chemistry and Industry*. August 19, 1985, p. 530.

Diamond, Stuart. "Carbide Asserts String of Errors Caused Gas Leak." *New York Times*, August 24, 1985, p. 1.

"—. "Carbide Blames a Faulty Design for Toxic Leak." *New York Times*, August 13, 1985, p. 1.

—. "Chemical Pipe Size Called Key Safety Factor." *New York Times*, August 14, 1985, p. 19.

"OSHA Cites Union Carbide for Leak." *Professional Safety*, November 1985, p. 8.

"Union Carbide: New Accidents Revive Safety Issues." *Chemical and Engineering News*, August 19, 1985, p. 4.

breakdown

Chernobyl accident

Ukraine **1986**

The world's worst nuclear power plant disaster eventually resulted in a level of fallout ten times that of the atomic bomb dropped on Hiroshima, Japan, during World War II. At least thirty-one workers and emergency personnel were killed immediately or died soon after the accident, some two hundred thousand residents of the area were evacuated, and clouds of radioactive material were carried over most of northern Europe.

Background

On April 26, 1986, two mammoth explosions blew apart Unit 4 of the Chernobyl nuclear power plant in the Ukrainian republic of the former USSR. The plant is located about seventy miles north of Kiev, the capital of the Ukraine. At least thirty-one workers and emergency personnel were killed immediately or died soon after the accident as a result of radiation sickness. Some two hundred thousand residents of the area were evacuated, and clouds of radioactive material were carried over most of northern Europe. Total fallout from the accident eventually reached a level ten times that of the atomic bomb dropped on Hiroshima, Japan, during World War II.

by David E. Newton

The Chernobyl complex consisted of four reactors constructed between 1977 and 1983. By 1986, the four units were operating nearly at capacity and generating four million kilowatts of electricity. All four reactors at Chernobyl were graphite-moderated, water-cooled boiling water reactors known as RBMKs. At the time of the accident, twenty-one reactors of this design were in operation in the Soviet Union. Energy supplied by nuclear power plants accounted for about fifteen percent of all the electricity generated in the nation during this period.

The RBMK design is uncommon, and plants of this kind are found almost exclusively in the countries that make up the former Soviet Union. They were built because of their ability to perform two quite different functions at the same time: generate electricity and produce plutonium. The decision to build these dual-purpose plants dates back to the 1950s. The Soviet government committed itself to a weapons-development program that would keep it on a par with the United States nuclear arsenal. In order to accomplish that objective, weapons developers needed a constant and dependable supply of plutonium, the raw material needed for atomic and hydrogen bombs. The RBMK design was selected, therefore, because it could meet both domestic needs for electricity and military demands for weapons-quality plutonium.

The core of the RBMK reactor consists of a huge pile of graphite blocks weighing about two thousand tons. The purpose of the graphite is to slow down neutrons produced by fission in the fuel rods, a function performed by coolant water in most other reactors. Imbedded in the block are about seventeen hundred fuel rods, each containing hundreds of disc-shaped pellets of uranium. The reactor also contains control rods, which dampen the nuclear reaction when lowered into the block.

The RBMK is cooled by water that is pumped through the graphite block, from bottom to top. The cooling water travels through channels in the block that also hold the fuel rods. As the water passes over the fuel rods, it picks up heat and begins to boil. Steam formed by the boiling water collects at the top of the reactor, where it is removed and delivered to the steam turbine that generates electricity.

The RBMK reactor contained a number of design characteristics that made it inherently risky to operate as a commercial power source. Western scientists had been warning Moscow for a decade before the Chernobyl accident about these dangers. But the Soviets remained confident about the safety of the RBMK reactors. This confidence was driven not only by the practical reality of military demands, but also by one important advantage of the RBMKs: They could be refueled without the extended downtime needed to refuel Western reactors. Ironically, it was this very advantage that led to the disaster of April 26, 1986.

One problem with the RBMK design is that it makes no provision for a containment shell, a precautionary feature that is part of all reactors used in the United States. A containment shell is a last line of defense designed to retain gases and radioactive materials released should an accident occur in the reactor core. The Three Mile Island accident in 1979, for instance, would have had immeasurably more serious repercussions if the products of the core meltdown had escaped into the atmosphere.

Another problem with the RBMK design is that a loss of cooling water increases the rate of fission (or nuclear splitting)—and hence heat production—in the core. The process is just the reverse of that in water-moderated reactors (such as those used in the United States), where loss of cooling water causes a decrease of power production in the core. This design flaw creates a peculiar dynamic wherein the reactor is most likely to spin out of control when operating at its lowest level of power.

Unit 4 of the Chernobyl nuclear complex, the site of world's worst nuclear accident to date.

Details of the Accident

At 1:24 A.M. on Saturday, April 26, Unit 4 of the Chernobyl Nuclear Power Plant was rocked by two enormous explosions. The roof of the plant blew apart and radioactive gasses and materials were hurled more than 1,100 meters (3,600 feet) into the atmosphere. Two workers were killed instantly and another dozen received levels of radiation that would result in their deaths during the course of the next two weeks. Meanwhile, an invisible but deadly cloud of radioactive material floated off on the early spring air.

As with most nuclear accidents on Soviet soil, government officials made no public announcement about the event. Not until monitoring instruments in Sweden detected a dramatic increase in wind-borne radiation did the Soviets finally acknowledge the disaster. The news was reported on April 28 in a short five-sentence report by Tass, the official Soviet news agency.

But the political situation in the Soviet Union in 1986 was not what it had been a decade earlier. On May 14, First Secretary Mikhail Gorbachev, acting in accordance with his new policy of *glasnost*, took to national television and provided the world with a detailed description of all that was known at the time about the explosions. Still, it would be many months before all the details of the accident were unraveled.

The key event that led to the cataclysmic explosion was apparently a decision by the plant crew to carry out an unauthorized experiment. Operators at the plant wanted to know what would happen if there was a power outage and steam stopped flowing to the turbines. Would the kinetic energy of the spinning turbine blades be sufficient to maintain the cooling pumps until the emergency diesel generators turned on? The way to find out, the crew reasoned, was to carry out a controlled test of this situation. As the plant crew set the experiment in motion, a series of blunders by workers quickly ensued. Any one error by itself would not have been fatal, but the combination proved to be a tragic one for the men and women sleeping peacefully in the surrounding countryside.

Investigators pointed to six principle errors in judgment by the crew at Chernobyl. Perhaps the most important of these six mistakes was the crew's decision to disable the reactor's emergency coolant system. At the outset of the test, the reactor began to lose power. Because the test could only be continued if the reactor remained in operation, the crew disabled the coolant system. The reactor continued to lose power, so the crew removed all the control rods from the core. This move dramatically increased the reaction rate of the reactor. Almost instantly, the fission rate became cause for concern.

As power in the core began to increase, the crew attempted to reinsert the control rods manually. But the channels into which the rods were supposed to fit had deformed because of heat in the core. The rods did not drop properly, and power release in the reactor surged out of control.

As steam vented from the reactors, water levels dropped dramatically in the core. Loss of water, in turn, increased power output from fission reactions. In less than a second, power output from the core increased a hundredfold. As temperatures increased to more than five thousand degrees Celsius, parts of the core melted. Molten metal reacted with the remaining cooling water, producing hydrogen gas and even more steam, until finally the top of the reactor blew off under the powerful onslaught—the first of the two explosions.

Details of the second explosion are less clear. Some authorities believe that it was largely a chemical and physical phenomenon, like the first explosion. They reason that it would take no more than a few seconds for the hydrogen gas initially produced to be ignited by heat released during the meltdown.

Other experts believe, however, that the second explosion may have been a pure nuclear reaction. Unlike most reactors in use today, an RBMK can at least theoretically explode like a nuclear (atomic) bomb. Some scientists believe that parts of the molten core may have achieved critical mass during meltdown. If that had occurred, then a true bomb-like explosion could have occurred, accounting for the second explosion.

breakdown

Impact

The Chernobyl accident has had both short-term and long-term effects on the local area, on the world as a whole, and on the further development of the nuclear power industry. In addition to the thirty-one people who died immediately or within two weeks of the accident, another 299 were injured. About 135,000 residents were evacuated from the area within eighteen miles of the damaged plant, and later another 200,000 from other areas. But these numbers do not begin to reflect the magnitude of the damage done to the health of human and other residents of that region over the next generation and beyond.

Plants and animals in the immediate area of Chernobyl and downwind of the plant were heavily contaminated by fallout. Crops could not be harvested and most farm animals were destroyed to prevent their use as food. Almost a decade after the accident, levels of radiation are still so high in some areas that no native food can be grown or consumed. Those people who remain in the region survive on food that is shipped in from safe areas.

The chief contaminants remaining in the soil are cesium 137 and strontium 90. These two radioactive isotopes have half lives of thirty and twenty-eight years, respectively. That means that they will constitute a hazard for many more decades if they are not removed. Yet decontamination and removal

The damaged reactor at Chernobyl is visible in the center of this photo, taken about two weeks after the 1986 accident. Eventually, workers built a steel-and-concrete tomb to isolate the reactor, but by 1992 the shell had cracked and begun to leak radioactive material into the environment.

of contaminated topsoil has not progressed very far. The result is that many residents of the area still face a constant and serious health risk from radioactive isotopes in the environment.

The fallout that covered the western Soviet Union spread to parts of Europe, raising concern about food supplies there also. On May 7, 1986, for example, Canadian customs officials announced that vegetables arriving from Italy were contaminated with radioactive iodine 31. At about the same time, member states of the European Community banned all fresh meat produced in Eastern Europe. As far away as Lapland, reindeer meat was so contaminated with radiation that it was declared unfit for human consumption.

And what of the reactor itself? Soviet engineers employed a wide array of techniques to extinguish the flames in the reactor, to cool it down, and to cover up the damaged facility. One of the first steps, for example, was to pump liquid nitrogen into the core to cool it down and to put out fires. Next, thousands of tons of sand, clay, lead, and boron were dumped on top of the plant from helicopters. These materials absorbed neutrons and helped put out fires. In the surrounding area, dikes were built to contain contaminated water, and several inches of soil were removed and transferred to a storage area.

Eventually, workers began to build a huge sarcophagus over the damaged plant. The steel-and-concrete tomb was designed to isolate the ruins of Unit 4 for the hundreds of years during which it would continue to emit dangerously high levels of radiation. The first shell proved faulty, however, to the considerable disgust of the rest of the world. By 1992, the shell had cracked. New radiation wafted out of the shell into the environment. The Ukrainian government found it necessary to make plans for a second shell, stronger than the first, to install on top of the original sarcophagus.

After a horrible catastrophe such as the one that occurred at Chernobyl, scientists always hope to learn new information that can be used to increase safety in the future. At first, officials of the former Soviet Union were reluctant to consider changes in reactor design of their RBMK plants; they felt that operator errors, not plant problems, had caused the accident. Eventually, however, they adopted a number of modifications to make the reactors safer to operate. For example, control rods that could not be removed completely from the reactor core were designed.

Scientists outside the Soviet Union, however, did not benefit significantly from events that occurred during the accident. They had long been leery of the RBMK design and had rejected the use of such plants in their own countries. As one American nuclear expert said, "Most of the lessons from Chernobyl have been learned already and applied in the United States."

The Chernobyl accident had a significant impact on the ongoing debate over the merits of nuclear power. That impact varied from country to country,

breakdown

though. In the United States, where memories of the 1979 Three Mile Island accident had not yet faded, Chernobyl merely confirmed the fears that many had voiced about the dangers of nuclear power. In France, Japan, Belgium, and other nations that depend heavily on nuclear power, the Chernobyl accident had less of an impact. And in a few nations, such as Great Britain, the accident for the first time opened up a heated debate about the role of nuclear power as a source of energy. Meanwhile, the people of the Ukraine and other contaminated areas try to go about their business and lead normal lives, mindful that the ultimate toll of the Chernobyl incident may not be known until many years have passed.

Where to Learn More

Barringer, F. "Four Years Later, Soviets Reveal Wider Scope to Chernobyl Horror." *New York Times*, April 28, 1990, p. A1.

—. "Chernobyl: Five Years Later, the Danger Persists." *New York Times Magazine*, April 14, 1991, p. 28.

Cooke, S. "Human Failures Led to Chernobyl." *Engineering News Record*, August 28, 1986, pp. 10–11.

Diamond, S. "Moscow Now Sees Chernobyl's Peril Lasting for Year: Big Area Stricken." *New York Times*, August 22, 1986, p. A1.

—. "Design Flaws, Known to Moscow, Called Major Factor at Chernobyl." *New York Times*, August 26, 1986, p. A1.

Flavin, C. *Reassessing Nuclear Power: The Fallout From Chernobyl*. Worldwatch Institute, 1987.

Jackson, J.O. "Nuclear Time Bombs." *Time*, December 7, 1992, pp. 44–45.

Medvedev, G. *The Truth about Chernobyl*, trans. Evelyn Rossiter. Basic Books, 1991.

Moore, T., and D. Dietrich. "Chernobyl and Its Legacy." *EPRI Journal*, June 1987, pp. 4–21.

Reinhardt, W. "Soviet Reactor Was Flawed." *Engineering News Record*, May 22, 1986, p. 16

Seneviratne, G. "Soviets Alter Nuclear Designs." *Engineering News Record*, September 4, 1986, p. 10.

Shaherhak, T. *Chernobyl: A Documentary Story*, trans. Tan Press. St. Martin's Press, 1989.

Sweet, W. "Chernobyl: What Really Happened." *Technology Review*, July 1989, pp. 42–52.

Toman, B. "Disaster's Impact on Health Won't Be Known for Years." *Wall Street Journal*, April 23, 1987, p. 28.

U.S. Council for Energy Awareness. *Chernobyl Briefing Book*. March 26, 1991.

U.S. Department of Energy. *Health and Environmental Consequences of the Chernobyl Nuclear Power Plant Accident*. 1987.

U.S. Nuclear Regulatory Commission. *Report on the Accident at the Chernobyl Nuclear Power Station*. The Commission, 1987.

Van Der Pligt, J. "Chernobyl: Four Years Later: Attitudes, Risk Management and Communication." *Journal of Environmental Psychology*, June 1, 1990, pp. 91–99.

Bridge, Building, and Other Structural Collapses

Molasses spill (1919) 183

Tacoma Narrows Bridge collapse (1940). 189

Ronan Point tower collapse (1968) 196

MGM Grand Hotel fire (1980). 202

Hyatt Regency Hotel walkways collapse (1981) 208

East Chicago, Indiana, highway ramp collapse (1982). . . . 216

Mianus River Bridge collapse (1983) 221

Stava Dam failure (1985) 228

Schoharie Creek Bridge collapse (1987). 234

L'Ambiance Plaza collapse (1987) 241

Molasses spill

Boston, Massachusetts **1919**

A giant, five-story-high steel tank suddenly fractured, releasing millions of gallons of deadly molasses that engulfed people, animals, and property.

Background

by Richard Weingardt

Boston's inner harbor was memorialized on January 15, 1919, by one of the most bizarre structural failures ever to occur anywhere. The disaster temporarily put the city's working-class North End in the national spotlight and made larger headlines than the Paris Peace Conference and events in revolution-torn Russia. On that mild winter day, a massive tidal wave of sweet, sticky death gushed from a fractured steel tank without warning, leaving twenty-one people dead, over one hundred and fifty injured, and many buildings crushed under nearly twelve thousand tons of thick, brown, sugary molasses.

The huge fifty-foot high, ninety-foot diameter steel tank that ruptured had been used by the U.S. Industrial Alcohol Company for storage of up to fifteen thousand tons of molasses. It loomed above and was sandwiched between several buildings—a freight depot, firehouse, stables, offices, and an elevated railway.

The tank was ordered from Hammond Iron Works in 1915 by the Purity Distilling Company on authorization of U.S. Industrial Alcohol. The treasurer of Purity ordered it without consulting an engineer, an oversight that would have serious consequences. The only requirement used in making the order was that the tank have a factor of safety of three for the storage of molasses weighing twelve pounds per gallon (a weight fifty percent heavier than water). The order called for construction of a tank larger than any that the Hammond company had previously built. Later, at the Massachusetts Superior Court hearings convened to investigate the disaster, the treasurer explained that the Hammond Iron Works were "experienced and reputable [tank] makers" and that he relied on their skill and experience when he made the order.

When the tank was completed, the sides of the circular structure consisted of seven rings of steel sheets, each about seven feet high, varying in thickness from .687 inch at the bottom to .312 inch at the top. The tank's flat bottom rested on a cement sand cushion, with a concrete slab foundation. The slab was supported on concrete piles. The tank's roof, conical in shape, was made up of curved steel sheets supported by framing (beam rafters).

All the steel sheets used in construction of the tank actually proved to be thinner than those shown on the Hammond drawings used to obtain the building permit. For instance, the bottom ring—the part of the structure that receives the most pressure from the contents contained within—was supposed to measure .687 inch of thickness. The finished ring, however, measured only .667 inch. The steel thickness of the other six rings were similarly five to ten percent less than the figures indicated on the permit plans. In addition, the bottom ring (ring one) had a twenty-one-inch diameter manhole opening cut out of it.

The steel sheets that made up the rings were spliced together in two ways. While the sheets in the bottom rings included butt joints and splice plates, the sheets in the other six rings were joined using lap joints. Both types of joints were riveted together with six rows of rivets—three on each side of the joints. The rings were connected to each other by a lap joint using a single row of rivets.

The tank was completed early in 1916, but the only testing that took place was a cursory one in which six inches of water were placed in the bottom of the receptacle. On a dozen occasions during the tank's three years of service it held as much as 1.9 million gallons (for periods of up to twenty-five days). On the day that the tank finally succumbed to the pressure within, the contents measured some 2.3 million gallons and had been housed there for four days. Months later, during the legal proceedings, several witnesses recalled that the seams of the tank were leaking molasses prior to the disaster, but the observation apparently did not provoke concern.

Months later, during the legal proceedings, several witnesses recalled that the seams of the tank were leaking molasses prior to the disaster, but the observation apparently did not provoke concern.

184 BRIDGE, BUILDING, AND OTHER STRUCTURAL COLLAPSES

Details of the Disaster

It was 12:40 P.M. in Boston, still lunch hour for the many pedestrians walking the city's streets, when the normal bustle was interrupted by sounds not unlike those of machine-gun fire. A torrent of molasses two stories high exploded out of the ruptured tank. Six children were immediately swallowed up.

Unable to withstand the pressure of its contents any longer, the tank had fractured, propelling a 2.5-ton section of the lower part of the tank onto a playground 182 feet away. Another section of the structure wrapped itself around and completely sheared off one column of an adjacent elevated railway. Traveling at about thirty-five miles per hour, the escaping molasses swept over and through everything in its path. At its most destructive moments, the gooey wave was 15 feet high and 160 feet wide.

Ralph Frye, a reporter for *The Boston American* who covered the event, recalled, "what looked like a moving wall of volcanic lava filled the street and was moving relentlessly toward me. Everything it overtook—horses, automobiles, people—disappeared. People and animals lost their lives either by drowning or by the impact of wreckage carried along by the tide. Occupied houses in the path of the wave were demolished, while the cellars of others were filled with molasses. Horse-drawn and motor vehicles were marooned or floated away. Rescue crews found one man and his wagon embedded in a mountain of molasses, man and horse both frozen in motion. Several other horses had to be shot to put an end to their misery.

By mid-afternoon the flood had settled. The molasses covered more than a two-block area and the general vicinity looked like it had been hit by a cyclone. Many buildings had been destroyed, bulldozed off their foundations, while rails from the elevated railway dangled in the air and the tank itself lay on the ground, a heap of crumpled junk metal. Police and firemen used huge hydraulic siphons around the clock to pump molasses out of flooded cellars. It was nearly a week before all the bodies of victims were recovered and months of effort expended before the area returned to a state resembling normalcy.

During the trial that followed, the Purity Distilling Company suggested several possible causes for the disaster. Possible explanations trotted out by company spokesmen included an explosion, vibrations from trains using the adjacent elevated track, or a runaway trolley freight car. The explosion theory got the most play, but all three explanations were easily dismissed.

Examination of the wreckage showed two principal fractures in the steel plate of the lowest or bottom ring. One was a vertical line that ran through the manhole and extended up into the second ring, part way up its lap joint, which was located directly over the manhole. Investigators pointed out that

What looked like a moving wall of volcanic lava filled the street and was moving relentlessly toward me. Everything it overtook— horses, automobiles, people—disappeared.

this design placed the weakest part of the second ring—a lap joint—right above the weakest part of the first ring: the manhole opening. The other major fracture was a diagonal break, again through solid metal, that began near the same lap joint (in the second ring).

The second ring was separated from rings one and three by a tear in the single-riveted lap joints which connected them. In addition, the vertical lap joint of the second ring—the one directly opposite from the manhole location—was completely fractured. In the rings that had vertical joint failures, the connections failed because rivets were sheared off and the steel plates between rivets ripped open. Some joints had a combination of both separations.

The tank originally thought to have a safety factor of three in reality had none. An ill-conceived design in many ways, its weakest elements were its connections, especially the lap joints of the second ring, and the inadequate reinforcement given the tank's bottom ring after the manhole opening was made. The use of thinner material than called for on the permit drawings did not help matters. All things considered, the tank was improperly designed, detailed, and constructed, and calculations were never checked by an experienced engineer. Its failure was due entirely to structural weakness.

breakdown

Impact of the Collapse

Immediately after the event, the Boston Building Department instituted a requirement that all calculations of designers be filed with their plans, and that stamped drawings be signed. The catastrophe also probably influenced the adoption of engineering certification laws in all states not having such legislation, as well as the requirement that all plans for major structures be sealed by a registered professional engineer before issuance of a building permit.

The Boston molasses disaster resulted in countless lawsuits, and litigation took nearly six years. Over three thousand witnesses—six million words of testimony filling 40,000 pages of court records—appeared before the Massachusetts Supreme Court rendered its opinion: the tank as built had been tragically flawed. The total settlement for 125 damage claims, small by today's standards, reportedly exceeded $1 million (in 1925 dollars).

The Boston molasses disaster heightened public and industry awareness of the potential repercussions of poorly designed projects. Certainly, the events of that day in Boston served to sharpen the engineering industry's attention to stress points and their possible impact on public safety if insufficiently addressed.

Where to Learn More

Bluthardt, Robert. "Wave of Death." *Firehouse*, June 1983, pp. 86–88, 136.

Brown, Burtis. "Details of the Failure of a 90-Foot Molasses Tank." *Engineering News-Record*, May 1919, pp. 974–76.

Frye, Ralph. "The Great Molasses Flood." *The Reader's Digest*, August 1955, pp. 63–67.

Harding, Priscilla. "The Great Boston Molasses Disaster of 1919." *The American Legion Magazine*, December 1968, pp. 12–15.

—. "Bursting of Boston Molasses Tank Found Due to Overstress." *Engineering News-Record*, January 1925, pp. 188–89.

Tacoma Narrows Bridge collapse

Washington State **1940**

The bridge failure that brought an abrupt end to efforts to create "a slender ribbon bridge deck" also introduced the importance of considering wind dynamics in bridge design.

Background

Although the newspapers were filled with important stories from throughout the world on Saturday, November 8, 1940—stories such as the RAF bombing of Berlin, the Luftwaffe bombing of London, and the return of Franklin D. Roosevelt to Washington, D.C., for an unprecedented third presidential term—the *New York Times* still made room on its front page for a single-column story, "Big Tacoma Bridge Crashes 190 Feet into Puget Sound."

At the time of its demise, the five-month-old Tacoma Narrows Bridge was the third largest suspension span bridge in the world. The center span measured 2,800 feet and stretched between two 425-feet-high towers, while the side spans of the bridge each measured 1,000 feet in length. The suspension cables hung from the towers and were anchored 1,000 feet from the shoreline on the riverbank. The designer, Leon Moisseiff, was one of the world's foremost bridge engineers. He and his partner Fred Lienhard had earlier developed the calculations for determining load and wind forces used by bridge designers

by Rita Robison

189

everywhere. But while impressive in scope and designed by noted engineers, the Tacoma Narrows Bridge quickly succumbed to the power of nature's winds.

Following the widespread design effort of the 1930s to "streamline" products of all shapes and sizes, from teakettles to locomotives to airplanes, Moisseiff sought to produce a very slender deck span arching gently between the tall towers. His design combined the principles of cable suspension with a girder design of steel plate stiffeners—running along the side of the roadway—that had been streamlined to measure only eight feet deep.

The $6.4 million bridge opened with much fanfare on July 1, celebrated as a defense measure to connect Seattle and Tacoma with the Puget Sound Navy Yard at Bremerton, Washington. Owned by the Washington State Toll Bridge Authority, the bridge had been financed by a Public Works Administration grant and a loan from the Reconstruction Finance Corporation and had been constructed in only nineteen months.

The bridge gained notoriety even before it opened, though. It acquired the nickname "Galloping Gertie" from people who experienced its strange behavior. Forced to endure wind-spawned undulations that pitched and rolled the deck, workmen complained of seasickness. After the opening, it became a challenging sporting event for motorists to cross even during light winds, and complaints about episodes of seasickness incurred while traversing the bridge became common.

Despite Moisseiff's reputation as a top-ranked engineering consultant, State and Toll Bridge Authority engineers grew increasingly nervous about the slender two-lane span. Only thirty-nine feet wide, the bridge's shallow depth in relation to the length of the span resulted in a ratio of 1:350, nearly three times the figure for the Golden Gate or George Washington bridges. Engineers tried several methods to stabilize, or dampen, the oscillations—the up-and-down waves of the deck.

The first method involved attaching heavy cables—called tie-down cables—from the girders and anchoring them with fifty-ton concrete blocks on shore. The cables soon snapped, and another set installed in a second attempt to leash the bridge lasted only until the early morning hours of November 7. Another measure, a pair of inclined stay cables that connected the main suspension cables to the deck at mid-span, remained in place but proved ineffectual. Engineers also installed a dynamic damper, a mechanism consisting of a piston in a cylinder, but this also proved futile as its seals were broken when the bridge was sandblasted prior to being painted.

Frustrated and worried, bridge engineers continued to examine the bridge. Measurements and movie camera films taken over several months provided them with additional information on the bridge' movements in the wind. They charted the oscillations and vibrations, and discovered the movements were peculiar. Rather than damping off quickly as they did in the Golden Gate and George Washington bridges, Galloping Gertie's vibrations seemed almost continuous. The puzzle, however, was that while only certain wind speeds seemed to set off the vibration, the engineers could find no correlation between the vibration and the wind speeds.

Led by Frederick B. Farquharson, professor at the University of Washington's engineering school, the study team applied actual measurements of the bridge movements to a scale model, hoping to find ways to stabilize it. They suggested installing additional stabilizing cables, attaching curved wind deflectors, and drilling holes in the girders to permit wind to pass through. Unfortunately, the report was issued only a week before the bridge collapsed.

Interest in the phenomenon rose with the onset of the brisk fall winds that push through the valley-like narrows that lie between the cities of Tacoma and Bremerton. The public as well as the engineers kept watch, for there seemed to be an understanding that the bridge was fundamentally crippled. When the bridge finally snapped, it became one of history's most documented disasters. Cameras—still and movie—recorded the collapse on film. A newspaper man was a mid-span survivor; he supplied a firsthand account of the disaster.

Details of the Collapse

Witnesses included Kenneth Arkin, chairman of the Toll Bridge Authority, and Professor Farquharson. As Arkin later recalled, that morning he had driven to the bridge at 7:30 to check the wind velocity. By 10:00 the wind had risen from thirty-eight to forty-two miles per hour while the deck rose and fell three feet thirty-eight times in one minute. He and Farquharson halted traffic, watching while the bridge, already waving up and down, began to sway from side to side as well. Then, remarkably, it began to literally twist in the wind.

Meanwhile, newspaperman Leonard Coatsworth abandoned his car in the middle of the bridge, unable to drive any further because of the undulations. He turned back briefly, remembering that his daughter's pet dog was in the car, but was thrown to his hands and knees by the bucking bridge. Other reporters described him, "hands and knees bloody and bruised," as he crawled five hundred yards while the bridge pitched at forty-five degree angles and concrete chunks fell "like popcorn." The driver and passenger of a logging truck told a similar tale of terror wherein they were forced to jump to the wildly careening deck and crawl to one of the towers, where they were helped by workmen.

By 10:30 the amplitude (distance from crest to valley) of the undulations was twenty-five feet deep and suspender ropes began to tear, breaking

He turned back briefly, remembering that his daughter's pet dog was in the car, but was thrown to his hands and knees by the bucking bridge.

the deck and hurling Coatsworth's car and the truck into the water. When the stiffening girder fell one hundred ninety feet into Puget Sound, it splashed a plume of water one hundred feet into the air. Within a half hour, the rest of the deck fell section by section until only the towers remained, leaning about twelve feet toward each shore. Overlooking the bridge was an insurance company billboard that bragged, "As safe as the Narrows Bridge." The slogan was covered up before the end of the day. The only casualty of the collapse was the dog.

Moisseiff's first public comment on the demise of the Tacoma Narrows Bridge reflected his utter dismay: "I'm completely at a loss to explain the collapse." Charles E. Andrew, chief engineer in charge of construction, said that the collapse was "probably due to the fact that flat, solid girders were used along the sides of the span." He wanted to make clear that his original plans called for open girders, but "another engineer changed them." He compared Galloping Gertie to New York's Whitestone Bridge, completed a year earlier, the only other large bridge designed with web-girder stiffening trusses, "and these caused the bridge to flutter, more or less as a leaf does, in the wind. That set up a vibration that built up until failure occurred."

The Whitestone, now known as the Bronx-Whitestone, was indeed very similar in some ways to the Tacoma Narrows. The Whitestone's 4,000-foot length, coupled with a 2,300-foot main span and 375-foot high towers, gave it a form reminiscent of the Tacoma Narrows. Indeed, its designer, Othmar Ammann, had consulted Moisseiff, as had the designers of such structures as the Golden Gate and the San Francisco-Oakland Bay bridges. However, the stiffening trusses of the Whitestone were twice as heavy and the deck twice as wide as on the Tacoma Bridge. It, too, had early oscillation problems, but they had been successfully damped with a device similar to the one tried on Galloping Gertie.

After the Tacoma failure, Ammann recognized the danger of the too-slender deck and insisted that a new steel truss be superimposed onto the deck. His redesign, which also added cable stays between the towers and deck to prevent twisting, stabilized the bridge. In 1990, a tuned mass damper (a fairly recent invention) was added to the deck during a rehabilitation.

The first investigations into the collapse of Tacoma Narrows detailed how the bridge had twisted apart. For months the motions of the thoroughfare, while disturbing, had been symmetrical and the roadway had remained flat. The lampposts on the sidewalks remained in the vertical plane of the suspension cables even as they rose, fell, and twisted. But on November 7, a cable band slipped out of place at midspan and the motions became asymmetrical, like an airplane banking in different directions. The twisting caused metal fatigue, and the hangers broke like paper clips bent once too often.

Impact

But what caused Galloping Gertie to twist so violently when other bridges had survived gale-force winds? Engineers looking into the phenomenon of the twisting bridge explained that winds do not hit the bridge at the same angle, with the same intensity, all the time. For instance, wind coming from below may lift one edge of the bridge while pushing down the opposite edge. The deck, trying to straighten itself, twists back. Repeated twists grow in amplitude, causing the bridge to oscillate in different directions.

The study of wind behavior grew into an entire engineering discipline called aerodynamics. This area of study quickly established itself as an integral part of the airplane industry. *Vortex shedding* and *flutter* were added to the vocabulary as a result. Eventually no bridge, building, or other exposed structure was designed without testing a model in a wind tunnel. With the development of graphic capabilities, some of this testing is now done on computers.

Dozens of papers are published each year about these subjects; nevertheless, misconceptions continue. In 1990, K. Yusuf Billah of Princeton University noticed that popular physics textbooks in use across the nation detailed an incorrect version of the cause of the Tacoma Narrows collapse. He enlisted the help of Robert H. Scanlan of Johns Hopkins University and the

Moisseiff's first public comment on the demise of the Tacoma Narrows Bridge reflected his utter dismay: "I'm completely at a loss to explain the collapse."

two scientists "set the record straight" in the February 1991 issue of the *American Journal of Physics*. The textbooks were claiming "forced resonance (periodic natural vortex shedding)" as the cause. Instead, Billah and Scanlan pointed out, "the aerodynamically induced condition of self-excitation [vibration] was an interactive one, fundamentally different from forced resonance."

Two years after the collapse, the remains of the Tacoma Narrows Bridge were scrapped. In 1950 the state opened a new $18 million bridge designed by Charles Andrew and tested in wind tunnels by Farquharson and other engineers. Its four-lane, sixty-foot-wide deck and stiffening trusses twenty-five-feet deep form a box design that resists torsional forces. Excitation is controlled by hydraulic dampers at the towers and at midspan.

The Tacoma Narrows Bridge collapse remains one of the most spectacular failures in the history of engineering. It is certainly one of the best known because of the movie film and widely-reproduced still photos that document the incident. While the details of the failure have become blurred over time, as Billah and Scanlan demonstrated, the basic lessons have been retained. The science of wind engineering, for instance, is now routinely applied to every type of structure.

This new bridge was opened in 1950. Its four-lane deck and stiffening trusses form a box design that resists torsional forces. Excitation is controlled by hydraulic dampers at the towers and at midspan.

Where to Learn More

Alexander, Delroy. "A Lesson Well Learnt." *Construction Today*, November 1990, p. 46.

Ammann, O.H., T. von Karman, and G. B. Woodruff. "The Failure of the Tacoma Narrows Bridge." Report to the Federal Works Agency, March 28, 1941.

Billah, K. Yusuf, and Robert H. Scanlan. "Resonance, Tacoma Narrows Bridge Failure, and Undergraduate Physics Textbooks." *American Journal of Physics*, February 1991, pp. 118–24.

Farquharson, Frederick B. "Collapse of the Tacoma Narrows Bridge." *Scientific Monthly*, December 1940, pp. 574–78.

Goller, Robert R. "Legacy of Galloping Gertie 25 Years After." *Civil Engineering*, October 1965, pp. 50–53.

Jackson, Donald C. *Great American Bridges and Dams*. Preservation Press, 1988, pp. 327–78.

"Big Tacoma Bridge Crashes 190 Feet into Puget Sound." *New York Times*, November 8, 1940, p. 1.

Peterson, Ivars. "Rock and Roll Bridge." *Science News*, 1990, pp. 244–46.

Petroski, Henry. "Still Twisting." *American Scientist*, September–October 1991, pp. 398–401.

Ronan Point tower collapse

London, England **1968**

by Loretta Hall

Inadequate connections between walls and floors caused the progressive collapse of one corner of a prefabricated high-rise apartment building. More than a dozen residents were injured, five fatally.

Background

At a quarter to six on the morning of May 16, 1968, the residents of the Ronan Point apartment building in London awoke to the sound of an explosion, followed by the cascading collapse of an entire corner of the twenty-four-story structure. Primarily living rooms were destroyed as the concrete panels fell, and fortunately most of the tenants were still in bed, out of the path of worst destruction. Even so, over a dozen residents were injured, five fatally. As a result of the Ronan Point collapse, the British government acted quickly to inspect and reinforce hundreds of similar prefabricated concrete high-rise apartment buildings and to restore public confidence in the construction technique, which was widely used to address the post–World War II housing shortage that still affected the country.

In the Ronan Point neighborhood, for example, over a fourth of the dwellings had been destroyed by enemy attacks during World War II. To address housing needs, an $11.5 million complex of nine identical apartment buildings was planned for the area. Ronan Point, which opened in spring of

1968, was the second to be completed. Its upper twenty-two stories provided 110 "flats," as the British refer to apartments.

In the quest to rebuild European cities as quickly as possible, a variety of systems had been developed to construct large buildings from concrete wall and floor panels that were mass produced at central locations and brought to the construction site for assembly. This prefabricated construction (also referred to as system building) was very efficient in terms of minimizing cost, labor force, and construction time.

The Borough of Newham selected Taylor-Woodrow-Anglian, a London contractor, to build its nine-tower complex using the Larsen and Nielsen prefabrication system, developed by Danish engineers. The system had been widely used throughout Western Europe, Turkey, and Hong Kong for fifteen years; Taylor-Woodrow had built 3,000 such apartment units in the British Commonwealth since 1962. In a decision that would later raise questions of conflict of interest, the contractor insisted that Philips Consultants be selected as the project's structural engineer. Philips was a wholly owned subsidiary of one of Taylor-Woodrow-Anglian's two parent companies.

As with other prefabrication systems, the Larsen and Nielsen method featured one-story-tall wall panels and room-size floor slabs, which were stacked and cemented together like a high-rise gingerbread house. In a typical interior joint, two floor panels would rest atop opposite edges of a wall panel. The gap would be filled with concrete, and another wall panel would be set directly above the lower wall. Exterior wall panels were formed with a lip that would extend past the end of the floor slab as it rested on half the width of the wall. The lips on the upper and lower walls were offset so they would overlap and could be bonded together with concrete.

What differentiated the various systems was primarily the design of the interpanel joints. A row of concrete teeth was cast into the edges of the Larsen and Nielsen floor panels to increase the surface area contacted by the concrete grouting used to bond the wall and floor sections together. Two strands of steel reinforcing bar were installed horizontally between the floor panel edges (in the case of an exterior wall, there would be only one floor panel and one reinforcing bar).

On a previous project, a government engineer concerned about insufficient connection between the walls and floors had required the addition of steel bolts running vertically through the wall panels. At a joint, the end of the bolt would extend through a tie plate in the lower edge of the upper wall; a nut atop the bolt could be tightened to press the tie plate firmly into contact with the concrete poured between the wall and floor panels. Apparently Philips Consultants was not convinced of the need for the bolts, which were

Apparently Philips Consultants was not convinced of the need for the bolts, which were also included in the Ronan Point design—a postcollapse inspection would reveal that the bolts were uniformly left untightened.

also included in the Ronan Point design—a postcollapse inspection would reveal that the bolts were uniformly left untightened.

Another difference of opinion between Philips Consultants and a government engineer involved the loads for which the building should be designed. The initial design called for the building to withstand an imposed floor loading of thirty pounds per square foot and a wind loading of seventeen pounds per square foot. Philips Consultants was told to increase the values to forty pounds per square foot imposed floor loading and twenty-four pounds per square foot wind loading.

After modifying the design to meet the borough's specifications, Philips Consultants submitted a document certifying the proposed building's structural stability. Perhaps out of a desire to save time, or simple complacency, that certification was accepted without an independent review of the design details and calculations. The tower was built, and 250 tenants moved into their new homes.

Details of the Collapse

Ivy Hodge was one of Ronan Point's new tenants. When she awoke on May 16, 1968, Hodge put on her robe and slippers and went to the kitchen to heat a kettle of water. Her friend Charley Pike had been kind enough to hook up her gas stove when she moved into her eighteenth-floor flat a month before. Since the local gas pressure sometimes dropped low enough to extinguish pilot lights, allowing gas to leak when the pressure returned, she had promptly taken the safety precaution of disconnecting the pilot.

Everything looked and smelled normal this morning as she filled the kettle and set it on the stove. But when she struck a match to light the burner, she was knocked to the floor by an explosion. She suffered only second degree burns on her face and arms, but her apartment sustained fatal damage.

Walls, floors, and furniture from above came crashing down into her living room. The resulting shock to the floor and supporting walls under her apartment exceeded their loading capacity. Floor by floor, the corner of the building crumbled to the ground.

Two exterior wall panels of her corner living room were blown outward and fell to the ground. The disappearance of those two wall sections left the six floors above her apartment without vital support for their weight. Walls, floors, and furniture from above came crashing down into her living room. The resulting shock to the floor and supporting walls under her apartment exceeded their loading capacity. Floor by floor, the corner of the building crumbled to the ground.

When the dust settled, all that remained of Ronan Point's southeast corner was twenty-one tiers of floor slab remnants—their two interior edges still connected to neighboring panels—dangling toward a pile of rubble below. The corner wall panels had disappeared completely. The building was designed so that the collapsed corner section consisted mainly of living rooms. Since most

breakdown

residents had been asleep in their bedrooms at the time of the collapse, the casualties were not as numerous as they might have been. Still, more than a dozen residents were injured, and five were killed.

The explosion was attributed to poor installation of Hodge's gas stove by Charley Pike, whose good intentions were not matched by knowledge or experience. He had connected the stove to the building's gas line with a brass nut that did not meet British Gas Board standards. He compounded the error by over-tightening the nut, which was weak enough to crack slightly. The result was a slow leak.

High-rise apartment buildings were relatively new fixtures in England in the late 1960s, and building codes had not been revised to reflect their characteristics—particularly with respect to wind loads, which logically have a greater effect on tall buildings than short ones. Although prefabricated construction was officially encouraged as a solution to the housing scarcity, building codes had not adapted to address system building specifically. Furthermore, since it was virtually unknown in frame or brick buildings, Britain's building codes did not take into account the possibility of progressive collapse (in which failure of one component triggers failures in adjacent components, allowing damage to spread through a structure rather than being contained to the area of the initial failure).

Recognizing the inadequacy of official guidance regarding the structural stability of a category of buildings that housed tens of thousands of people, the government moved quickly to avert public panic. Within days, the British home secretary appointed an inquiry committee consisting of a lawyer and two prominent engineers. The investigation was directed at Ronan Point specifically, but also at prefabricated high-rise buildings in general. In the specific case, the tribunal found that the design and construction of the joints between wall and floor panels were inadequate to allow the components to act as an integral system when subjected to an overload.

Following a gas explosion in one of the apartments, inadequate connections between walls and floors resulted in the progressive collapse of one corner of the prefabricated Ronan Point apartment building.

Impact

The impact of the Ronan Point tower collapse extended to more than the eighty families evacuated from that particular building. The investigative committee's interim report, released three months after the disaster, asserted that all prefabricated buildings employing load-bearing walls could be susceptible to progressive collapse. It went on to say that another Ronan Point-type disaster could be triggered by some event other than a gas explosion—such as ground settlement, accidental physical damage, or heat rising through a structure that was on fire.

Some 30,000 apartments in roughly 500 system-built structures over six stories high were suddenly suspect. Local authorities were advised to tell residents of all high-rise apartments whether their buildings were prefabricated, and to inspect such buildings for structurally sound joints between wall and floor panels. Gas supplies were to be cut off in any buildings failing inspection.

Examining that many buildings took time. On November 15, 1968, the *New York Times* reported that 1,400 families were being evacuated from twenty-nine apartment towers in London. The 6,000 evacuees were housed at government expense during a year-long, $2.4 million structural reinforcement program.

The tribunal's final report, issued in early November, found fault with specific individuals and actions involved with Ronan Point's design and construction. It also addressed broad criticism at architects and structural engineers, in general, for inadequate attention to the design of prefabricated buildings. Numerous members of the Institution of Structural Engineers responded with pointed rebuttals and objections to the report's recommendations.

In addition to its provisions for inspecting and reinforcing existing buildings, the report also recommended changes in the way future system structures would be designed. Specifically, it said the problem of progressive collapse should be addressed by designing structurally sound joints and by positioning load-bearing walls in such a way that there would be alternative paths for transferring loads (thus, if one wall section failed, the load above it could be borne by neighboring sections).

In an attempt to account for explosive forces within future buildings, the report recommended requiring them to withstand higher wind loads than current codes required. Critics argued that static and dynamic loads would affect a structure differently, and expressed doubt that designing a building to tolerate a constant pressure from a strong wind force would ensure that it could withstand the quick burst of pressure from an explosion.

FATE OF THE RONAN POINT TOWER. The events at Ronan Point influenced both design philosophy and building codes around the world. But in the Borough of Newham, a damaged building required attention. In the year following the disaster, the damaged corner was reconstructed, and brackets were added to reinforce the connections between floor slabs and exterior wall panels. Tenants moved back into the building. Within five years, however, ominous wall cracks began appearing and the building was evacuated again.

breakdown

Rehabilitating the building to meet new building codes would have been prohibitively expensive, so the building was condemned to destruction. A public-minded architect named Sam Webb, suspecting shoddy workmanship, convinced the government to disassemble Ronan Point rather than leveling it with explosives. The strategy paid off. The joints between walls and floors were found to be loosely filled with rubbish, not firmly packed with concrete. This frightening discovery raised further questions about the safety of similar buildings. Eventually, hundreds of such structures were condemned and demolished.

The Ronan Point collapse touched off wide-ranging debates about the stability of prefabricated construction, the adequacy of building codes, and the advisability of supplying high-rise apartments with gas for cooking. Ultimately, system building and gas fuel were sanctioned—provided the design of each structure accounted for the possibility of explosion and progressive collapse, and the craftsmanship was adequate.

Where to Learn More

"Anatomy of Collapse." *Engineering*, November 15, 1968, p. 707.

"Failure of a High-Rise System: How Safe Should the Structure Really Be?" *Architectural Record*, November 1968, pp. 169–170.

"Gas Turned Off: British Fear Explosions in High-Rise Prefab Buildings." *Engineering News-Record*, August 22, 1968.

"The Implications of the Report of the Inquiry into the Collapse of Flats at Ronan Point, Canning Town." *The Structural Engineer*, July 1969, pp. 255–84, and September 1969, pp. 387–89.

Levy, Matthys, and Mario Salvadori. *Why Buildings Fall Down*. Norton, 1992, pp. 76–83.

The joints between walls and floors were found to be loosely filled with rubbish, not firmly packed with concrete. This frightening discovery raised further questions about the safety of similar buildings. Eventually, hundreds of such structures were condemned and demolished.

MGM Grand Hotel fire

by David N. Ford

The second most deadly hotel fire in United States history led to the deaths of eighty-five people and the injury of more than 600 others, and resulted in a nationwide reevaluation of fire codes.

Background

One of America's deadliest hotel fires, the November 21, 1980, blaze that claimed the MGM Grand Hotel in Las Vegas, Nevada, was triggered by a lowly short-circuit in the hotel's deli area. Despite fire protection systems that met regulatory standards, the spreading fire soon engulfed the world's largest gambling hall in smoke and flames. Thick black smoke filled the air ducts and escape stairwells in the twenty-one floors of guest rooms. Scenes reminiscent of Hollywood disaster films became reality as guests were awakened by screams and smoke. Some raced to the roof or ran down smoke-filled stairwells. Others called for help or huddled by broken windows as smoke billowed into their rooms. By the time the fire had been extinguished, eighty-five people had died and over 600 others were injured. Many of the injured guests had been victimized by smoke inhalation rather than the fire itself. The disaster dramatically accelerated the updating of fire code regulations for both new and existing high-rise buildings.

The MGM Grand Hotel is an enormous facility that includes a casino, two 1,000-seat theaters, forty shops, five restaurants, 2,076 guest rooms, a jai alai facility, and a sports arena. A "T" shaped tower of guest rooms rises above two entertainment levels, each as large as twenty football fields. The fire and its impact were concentrated near the casino on the upper entertainment level and in the guest tower. Of the fire protection systems designed and built into the MGM Grand, the four most important during the fire were the building egress system, the fire suppression and alarm system, the system of fire zones, and the heating, ventilation and air conditioning (HVAC) system.

MGM'S FIRE PROTECTION SYSTEMS. Underneath all the glitter and the bustling gambling tables, the giant facility's frame reflected several efforts by the designers to anticipate future fires. The hotel's building egress system was intended to provide safe routes of passage out of the building to safety. People in the casino and adjacent spaces could exit the building directly onto the street through several large sets of doors. Hotel guests could exit through one of the two stairwells in each of the three branches of the T-shaped guest tower.

The fire suppression and alarm system was designed to detect and control a fire. The fire suppression system hinged on a bank of automatic water sprinklers located in selected portions of the building that activated when heat from a fire was detected. The minimum guidelines of the fire code in effect at the time of the hotel's design did not require that the entire facility be equipped with sprinklers. Thus, the casino, deli, most floors in the guest tower, and many other areas were not protected by sprinklers. An especially important area that was not protected was the casino's "eye in the sky," a network of walkways above the casino's ceiling that allowed security personnel to monitor gambling operations unnoticed. The MGM alarm system was designed to alert the hotel's security office of an outbreak of fire. The security office would then verify the alarm and use the building's alarms and public address systems to alert occupants to any danger.

A system of fire zones isolated distinct sections of the hotel and casino facility to prevent the spread of fire and smoke and to protect occupants and property. Fire zones are formed by enclosing parts of a building with fire-resistant construction. These enclosures must effectively seal off the many openings between building parts and any gaps between construction materials through which fire and smoke could pass. Important openings in fire zone enclosures at the hotel included access panels into elevator and air shafts, structural joints for building movement, and the junctures of structural steel and drywall.

The heating, ventilation, and air conditioning (HVAC) system at the hotel was designed to stop the flow of air into the building during a fire. Fire dampers—hinged louvers similar to those on attic exhaust fans in many residences—are fundamental to this strategy. The fire dampers in large HVAC systems are typically installed where air crosses fire zone enclosures and adjacent

The MGM Grand Hotel was a facility whose faulty and inadequate fire protection systems had been crippled by modifications.

to air distribution fans. Fire dampers are usually held open by a link designed to melt in the heat of a fire, thereby closing the louvers and stopping the flow of air. In this way, fire dampers allow the passage of air through the building under normal circumstances while maintaining the integrity of fire zone enclosures.

Several factors, however, crippled the fire protection systems at the MGM Grand Hotel, dramatically hampering their effectiveness during the November 21 fire. The original construction did not fulfill the intent of the designers. Potential smoke paths across fire zone enclosures were left open, or were covered with materials unable to resist fire or stop smoke. Moreover, materials with inadequate flame-spread and smoke ratings were used to build ceilings and attic areas, and the elevator shafts were not adequately vented.

Another contributor to the fire was the nature of the decorations, furnishings, and finishes on the casino level; all contained high amounts of synthetic materials. These materials were highly combustible and produced large amounts of smoke.

Physical and operational modifications made since the opening of the hotel reduced the effectiveness of its fire prevention systems as well. Some fire dampers had been bolted open or had their "melt-down" links replaced with metal wire, for instance, a modification that prevented the dampers from functioning as originally intended. Finally, in accordance with management wishes, several areas of the sprawling building that had been designed for 24-hour use—spaces where the fire code did not require sprinklers, on the assumption that any fire would be detected quickly—were in fact closed down during low-use periods. One such area was the delicatessen, where the fire started.

The MGM Grand Hotel was thus a facility whose faulty and inadequate fire protection systems had been crippled by modifications. Yet these modifications raised little or no protest from regulators. Despite the numerous flaws in its fire protection systems, the hotel was not in gross violation of the fire design and construction standards that prevailed at the time. The building underwent all required fire reviews and inspections before opening, and passed a fire inspection just six months before the disastrous fire.

Details of the Fire

About 7:10 A.M. on November 21, 1980, an MGM Grand Hotel employee noticed sparks coming out of a gaming board in the closed-down deli. A chef tried to extinguish the fire, but soon was forced to flee the area as the roaring flames soared higher. The fire fed on fresh air supplied by the HVAC system and the abundant combustible materials in the area, generating smoke that

breakdown

was laden with unburned fuels. These flammable gases collected in the "eye in the sky" above the casino, infiltrating the casino space itself as the fire department entered. Fire fighters later reported that they noticed a stratified layer of smoke six to eight feet from the ceiling upon entering. Suddenly the force of the fire blew apart the glass doors at the west end of the hotel and the dynamics of the situation grew immediately more dire. Within approximately twelve seconds, the thick cloud of smoke dropped to four feet above the floor while the fire, strengthened by the oxygen sucked in from the destroyed doorway, took on the appearance of a fire storm.

The decorations, furnishings, and finishes on the casino level contained high amounts of synthetic materials— materials that caught fire easily and produced large amounts of smoke.

The inadequacies in the hotel's fire protection systems aided the progress of the fire. The fire incapacitated the alarm system, preventing those in the tower from receiving any warning. The fire zone enclosures failed as well, allowing smoke to pour into the hotel's air ducts, elevator shafts, and stairways and migrate throughout the building. The eviscerated HVAC system, instead of depriving the fire of oxygen, actually provided it with additional fresh air. The chimney effect created by the vertical passageways and the HVAC system drew the smoke quickly up into the guest tower hallways and rooms. The building egress system, however, proved to be the most deadly factor. The only path of exit from the guest rooms was down the stairwells to the street. Once hotel guests entered these stairwells, self-locking doors prevented them from returning to the hallways. Thus, as smoke filled the stairwells, many guests became trapped. Only the automatic sprinkler system performed as designed. It prevented the fire from spreading into the guest tower or beyond the casino-level areas that were not equipped with sprinklers.

Most of the guests and employees on the casino level were able to flee out of the building ahead of the fire. Some guests in the hotel tower, rather than attempting to evacuate down the stairwells, escaped to the roof. Many other guests remained in their rooms and broke or opened windows to gain access to fresh air. The fire department was able to control the fire by around 8:30 A.M., and evacuated the majority of the survivors by 11:00 A.M., many of them whisked from the roof by helicopters.

Impact

The MGM Grand Hotel disaster spurred nationwide revision of local fire codes. The tragic blaze brought two issues to the forefront of fire code discussions: the danger of smoke over and above that of fire, and the failure of fire protection systems to evolve with fire protection capabilities.

Over ninety percent of those who died in the disaster were overcome by smoke rather than fire. Several communities thus increased the emphasis on smoke control in their fire protection regulations. In addition, smoke detectors that provide signals to a building' HVAC system became more commonplace. Such detectors instruct HVAC systems to exhaust air out of a fire area and pressurize the surrounding spaces to contain the circulation of the smoke. Although fire protection professionals are not in complete agreement over the feasibility of all smoke control methods, many cities now require smoke control systems for all high-rise buildings.

Outdated fire prevention systems also were examined with an increasingly critical eye following the MGM Grand Hotel conflagration. Fire-protection systems in long-standing buildings often fail to evolve with continuously improving fire protection technology. Fire codes can require existing buildings to be upgraded to comply with newly adopted guidelines, but such retroactive codes, while they increase safety, carry significant costs for building owners and communities. The regulatory environment of a city can thus prove a pivotal factor when a developer or business searches for a building site. This perpetual thirst for further development discouraged many cities from instituting retroactive fire code regulations. Since the MGM Grand fire, though, several cities have adopted retroactive codes. The legality of several of these fire code provisions has been challenged in court.

Nonetheless, the MGM Grand Hotel fire illustrates how a technological disaster can act as a catalyst for societal change. Such disasters often lead to a reevaluation of the relative values placed upon different aspects of the

community—human life, buildings and facilities, the prospect of economic expansion. The nation's second most deadly hotel fire provoked a flurry of discussion about alternative approaches to and priorities within fire protection. The fire code reforms that resulted point to the large-scale political significance of the MGM Grand Hotel disaster.

Helicopters were used to rescue nearly 1,000 people from the fast-moving MGM Grand Hotel fire.

Where to Learn More

Brannigan, Vincent M. "Record of Appellate Courts on Retrospective Fire Safety Codes." *Fire Journal*, November 1981, pp. 62–72.

"MGM Grand Hotel Victim of Old Code." *Engineering News Record*, November 27, 1980, pp. 10–11.

"MGM Fire Rekindles Smoke Debate." *Engineering News Record*, December 4, 1980, pp. 14–15.

"Compromised Codes Threaten Life Safety." *Engineering News Record*, January 29, 1981, pp. 26–30.

"MGM Fire: Short Circuit to Disaster." *Engineering News Record*, June 11, 1981, pp. 13–14.

"Cities Stiffen Fire Codes." *Engineering News Record*, January 14, 1982, pp. 16–7.

"Fire at the MGM Grand." *Fire Journal*, January 1982, pp. 19–32.

Hyatt Regency Hotel walkways collapse

Kansas City, Missouri **1981**

by Virginia
Kent Dorris

The collapse of two suspended walkways caused by a simple design change resulted in the worst structural failure to date in the United States, killing 114 people and injuring nearly 200 others.

Background

On the evening of July 17, 1981, some fifteen hundred people had gathered in the glass-walled, four-story atrium at the Kansas City Hyatt Regency Hotel for the hotel's weekly tea dance. As the Steve Miller Orchestra played swing music, some guests danced on the floor of the open lobby while others watched from three pedestrian walkways that crossed the space overhead. Just as the band struck up Duke Ellington's "Satin Doll," a jarring sound not unlike a clap of thunder rang out and two of the overhead walkways collapsed, showering glass, concrete, steel, and people down on the terrified dancers below. Frantic rescue personnel used heavy equipment to reach survivors, but the destruction was so great that the last victims buried under the debris were not found until twelve hours after the collapse occurred. The collapse, one of the greatest structural tragedies in the history of the United States, killed 114 people and injured nearly 200 others.

The Hyatt walkways collapse was especially disturbing because it was caused by the failure of a connection later described by engineers as of a sufficiently elementary nature to be used as a design problem in an under-graduate engineering school class. The connection that failed was not built as originally shown in architectural drawings, but instead was constructed according to shop drawings, prepared by the steel fabricator, that depicted an alternative design. Investigators blamed the failure on that design change, which effectively doubled the stress on the connection.

The tragedy focused new attention on the design of engineering details by fabricators and materials suppliers and raised questions about the respon-sibility of a project's engineer-of-record for the oversight of such details. Two engineers eventually lost their professional licenses as a result of the walkway collapse.

The Kansas City Hyatt Regency, designed by Patty Berkebile Nelson Dun-can Monroe Lefebvre Architects Planners and the structural engineering firm of Gillum Colaco Associates as a joint venture, opened about one year before the walkway collapse. The hotel included a forty-story guest-room tower and a four-story wing containing restaurants and meeting rooms; these structures were connected by a large, open atrium lobby. Dramatic atriums had become a trademark of Hyatt hotels during the preceding ten years, following a trend begun with the opening of architect John Portman's Atlanta Hyatt Regency, which contained a spectacular twenty-two-story-high open atrium.

The Kansas City Hyatt atrium contained three hanging walkways, each 120 feet long—consisting of four spans of 30 feet each—and slightly more than eight-and-a-half feet wide. The walkways spanned the atrium at the sec-ond-, third-, and fourth-floor levels. Each walkway was connected to balconies at either end. The walkways' box beams were welded to embedded plates to form a rigid joint on the south end while the north end connection was con-structed as an expansion joint; sliding bearings provided the beams with room to expand or contract in reaction to changes in temperature without causing stress or cracking.

The walkways were constructed of lightweight concrete on metal deck-ing. Each walkway was supported from underneath along its length by sixteen-inch-deep, wide-flange steel beams, and across its width by eight-inch-deep steel box beams, welded beneath the walkways at thirty-foot intervals. The hanging rods that suspended the walkways from the roof supports attached to both ends of the box beams at these seams. The box beams were made from pairs of eight-inch steel channels that were welded together at their open ends. The hanging rods, which were also made of steel, measured one and a quarter inches in diameter.

The fourth- and second-floor level walkways were constructed one above the other along the west wall of the atrium, while the third-floor level

The connection that failed was not built as originally shown in architectural drawings, but instead was constructed according to shop drawings that depicted an alternative design.

walkway was built about thirteen feet away toward the center of the room. To support the weight of the walkways, the ends of the hanging rods were passed through holes drilled through the welded box beams and secured from below by a washer and nut. No stiffeners, plates, or other reinforcements were used to further secure the connections. Each walkway was hung from three pairs of steel rods.

The design change that occurred between completion of the original design drawings and construction of the hotel concerned the way in which the walkways were connected to the steel hanging rods. The original drawings called for both the fourth- and second-floor level walkways to be hung from the same continuous steel rods. The rods, which would have been about forty-five feet long, would have been attached at the top to the atrium ceiling, passed through the box beams at the fourth-floor level walkway, and continued down to pass through the box beams at the second-floor level walkway. The weight of each walkway would have been supported by the nut-and-washer connection under the box beams at each level.

Instead of using continuous rods, however, contractors hung the walkways from two separate sets of rods. As constructed, each transverse box beam of the upper walkway had two holes drilled through either end of it: one hole two inches from the end and another hole six inches from the end. One set of rods passed through the outside holes, suspending the fourth-floor bridge from the atrium ceiling and supporting its weight with only a nut and washer underneath each beam. Another set of beams passed through the inner holes, held in place by a nut and washer connection above the fourth-floor beams, and supported the second-floor walkway from the bottom by another nut and washer connection. This change in design diverted the weight of the second-floor walkway from the ceiling supports to the connections of the rods and beams above it.

Henry Petroski, a civil engineering professor at Duke University who studied the failure, suggested that the situation could be compared to one in which two men hang separately by their hands from the same rope. If their hands were strong enough to support their own weight, the men would not be in danger of falling. But if instead of grasping the rope, the man at the bottom held onto the legs of the man hanging above, the man at the top would suddenly be supporting twice his weight. If the person at the top was just barely strong enough to support the double load, any small weight addition would be enough to make him lose his grip.

The design was probably changed because the use of such a long steel rod in the detail would have been somewhat tricky, perhaps involving casting a long rod in which the lower half was threaded like a screw so that a bolt could be twisted almost halfway up its length to support the upper walkway.

breakdown

Engineers later suggested that the best way to accomplish the original design would have been to use a sleeve nut, a device that could connect two separate threaded rods below the fourth-level walkway to form one continuous rod.

Details of the Collapse

Initial speculation about the tragedy focused on the possibility that such a large crowd of people had congregated on the walkways to watch the dance contest that the weight capacity was exceeded. Others theorized that people dancing on the walkway had set in motion a vibration that caused the collapse.

Investigations into the collapse were launched by several groups, including Failure Analysis Associates of Palo Alto, California, Packer Engineering Associates of Chicago, Lee Lowery, a professor at Texas A&M University, and Rex Paulsen of Fay Engineering Company in Denver. Probably the most prominent investigation was undertaken by the National Bureau of Standards (NBS), which simulated the conditions of the collapse in the laboratory and tested the original materials from the collapsed walkways as they became available.

The report produced by NBS investigators, led by Edward O. Pfrang, the chief of the agency's structures division, was released in February 1982. NBS blamed the change in the design detail for the catastrophe and concluded that as built, the walkways could support only 27 percent of the combined dead load—the weight of the materials of the bridge—and live load—the weight of the people standing on it—that they should have been designed to carry under the Kansas City building code. Using video footage shot by a local television crew filming the tea dance, investigators were able to estimate that only sixty-three people were standing on the second- and fourth-level walkways at the time of the collapse, a number that would have created a live load of less than ten percent of what the walkway should have been designed to support. Each of the hanging rods should have been able to support 68,000 pounds to meet the design load requirements, but the box beam connections collapsed under a load of just 18,600 pounds.

Each of the hanging rods should have been able to support 68,000 pounds to meet the design load requirements, but the box beam connections collapsed under a load of just 18,600 pounds.

NBS found that the collapse of the walkways began when the welding of one of the fourth-floor box beams split apart, and the nut and washer supporting the bottom of that walkway slipped through the hole. The load of both walkways was then transferred to the remainder of the fourth-level walkway connections and these box beams, too, fractured, unable to sustain the weight. The fourth-floor walkway collapsed onto the one below it, plummeting both walkways down onto the lobby floor.

Although the report concluded that the connections as originally designed would have withstood the forces that caused the collapse, it found

The third walkway of the Hyatt Regency remained intact, while two other suspended walkways collapsed primarily due to a change in the design of the suspension rods.

that design lacking as well. The original hanging rod design would have supported only about 60 percent of the design load requirement under the building code, the investigators charged. The report also mentioned minor reservations about the quality of the welding of the channels that comprised the steel box girders, but indicated that materials and workmanship did not play a significant role in the disaster.

Impact

Despite objections from investigating engineers and lawyers representing victims of the catastrophe, the hotel's owners, Crown Center Redevelopment Corporation, removed the only remaining atrium walkway within days of the collapse. A later inspection of that structure, however, uncovered evidence that box beams for that walkway were also deformed near the rod-to-box-beam connections, an indication that the third walkway was probably overstressed as well. The hotel's owners replaced that walkway with a new seventeen-foot-wide causeway at the second-floor level, supported on ten columns built up from below. The hotel remained closed for eleven weeks; it reopened in the fall of 1981. Following the collapse, the owners of nearly sixty other Hyatt hotels with atriums of various designs inspected their structures for safety.

At least 150 lawsuits were filed in circuit court after the collapse seeking total compensatory damages of $1 billion and punitive damages of about $500 million. Virtually all of the suits were eventually settled out of court. In 1983 a grand jury in Kansas City cited a lack of evidence in deciding not to issue indictments against the parties involved for criminal negligence.

In February 1984, however, the Missouri Board for Architects, Professional Engineers and Land Surveyors filed a complaint against the building's chief structural engineer, Jack K. Gillum, and the project engineer, Daniel M. Duncan, both then officers with St. Louis-based GCE International. The complaint accused the two engineers of gross negligence in the design and analysis of the walkways. The complaint launched a protracted investigation and hearing during which 450 exhibits were examined and 5,000 pages of transcript were produced.

During the hearing, which was closely watched by the engineering community, Gillum and Duncan argued that the failed connection was designed by the project's steel erector and fabricator, Havens Steel Company of Kansas City. The engineers' attorney affirmed that it had become common practice

within the construction industry to delegate the task of designing steel connections to the steel fabricator because the fabricator could best select the most economical way of building such details. An engineer for Havens, in turn, testified that the detailing on the Hyatt project had been subcontracted to WRW Engineering of Kansas City. None of the parties admitted changing the connection design, and each blamed the other for the alteration. However, the shop drawings submitted by Havens were stamped and initialed by the architectural joint venture, the structural engineer, and the contractor.

Much testimony at the hearing centered on an incident that preceded the walkway tragedy. In 1979, during the construction of the hotel, part of the atrium's roof had collapsed. Although no one was hurt in the incident, it prompted the building's owners to ask for a review of the structure, essentially giving the engineers a second chance to review their initial calculations. Evidence presented showed that Duncan submitted a report at that time indicating that he had checked the suspended bridges, and that Gillum told the project's construction manager that every connection in the atrium had been reviewed.

In November 1985 Gillum and Duncan were found guilty of negligence for having failed to review the steel shop drawings. Missouri administrative law judge James B. Deutsch, who presided at the hearing, said he found

Firefighters (upper right) continue rescue efforts as others look on. The collapse of the walkways killed 114 people and injured nearly 200 others.

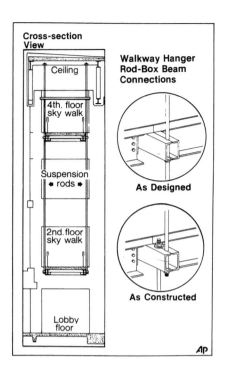

Cross-section View

Ceiling

4th. floor sky walk

Walkway Hanger Rod-Box Beam Connections

As Designed

Suspension rods

2nd. floor sky walk

As Constructed

Lobby floor

AP

This cross-section of the Hyatt walkways shows the faulty design that was a primary factor in the tragic collapse.

evidence of deliberate fraud on the part of the engineers for not thoroughly checking the connections when the roof collapsed in 1979. In January 1986, the Missouri Board for Architects, Professional Engineers and Land Surveyors voted unanimously to permanently revoke the engineering licenses of Gillum and Duncan and to revoke the certificate of authority for their firm, GCE International.

The Hyatt tragedy attracted widespread public attention because of the large loss of life. The collapse also forced the engineering community to take a new, closer look at the responsibility implied when an engineer affixes his professional seal to a set of project documents. The judge in the Hyatt case made it clear that while the courts would allow the engineer to delegate the job of designing a detail to another party, that engineer could not delegate the ultimate responsibility for that detail to the other party as well.

More than a decade after the Hyatt walkway disaster, the lines of responsibility between a structural engineer-of-record and a project fabricator are still a subject of controversy. Although the Hyatt case seemed to indicate plainly that the structural engineer could be held responsible for errors made by a fabricator, many structural engineers and architects do not want to be held liable for errors made by others and have tried to "write away" responsibility in project specifications and other contractual documents. Many firms also require the fabricator's own engineer to seal shop drawings that come out of that company.

Although all of the issues raised by the Hyatt walkway collapse may never be completely addressed, the tragedy did draw the engineering profession's attention to long-standing problems that had gone unresolved. The collapse inspired countless professional seminars, conferences, and papers and is recognized as a key factor in the American Consulting Engineers Council's decision to institute its peer review process and the American Society of Civil Engineers' push to publish its *Quality in the Constructed Project* manual in 1988.

Where to Learn More

Alm, Rick. "Hyatt Engineers Lose Licenses in Missouri." *Engineering News-Record,* January 30, 1986, p. 11.

"Hyatt Hotel Engineers Cited for 'Negligence'." *Engineering News-Record,* February 9, 1984, p. 14.

breakdown

"Hyatt Hearing Traces Design Chain." *Engineering News-Record,* July 26, 1984, pp. 12–13.

Marshall, R. D., et al. *Investigation of the Kansas City Hyatt Regency Walkways Collapse,* U.S. Dept. of Commerce, National Bureau of Standards, 1982.

"Death Trap in Kansas City." *Newsweek,* July 27, 1981, pp. 30–31.

Petroski, Henry. *To Engineer Is Human*. St. Martin's Press, 1985.

Pfrang, Edward O., and Richard Marshall. "Collapse of the Kansas City Hyatt Regency Walkways." *Civil Engineering,* July 1982, pp. 65–68.

Ross, Steven S. *Construction Disasters*. McGraw-Hill, 1984.

East Chicago, Indiana, highway ramp collapse

East Chicago, Indiana **1982**

by Rita Robison

Poor quality scaffolding and numerous safety violations led to the fatal collapse of a portion of a highway ramp during construction. In addition to the thirteen workers who died, fifteen workers were injured severely as the ramp crashed onto the banks of an adjacent industrial canal.

Background

On April 15, 1982, shortly after 11:00 A.M., thirteen workers were killed in an event that the Indiana Department of Transportation (IDOT) called "the worst construction accident in Indiana history." Two sections of a highway ramp under construction collapsed without warning. While workers were not pouring concrete at the moment of collapse, they were placing slabs of set concrete. Investigators later determined the cause of the accident to lie within the falsework, or scaffolding, rather than in the design of the elevated ramp itself.

An eyewitness described the disaster as happening in slow motion. The first section collapsed without warning; three minutes later he heard a "big boom" and the second section collapsed, catapulting workers into the air. In addition to the thirteen who died, fifteen workers were injured severely as the ramp crashed onto the banks of an adjacent industrial canal. Some went down with the rubble; others were caught underneath. The body of one man was found head down in a pillar of concrete that had hardened around him.

Some seventy-five workers were on the site of the Cline Avenue Extension—also known as the Riley Road Interchange—part of a highway designed to link the steel mills lining the Lake Michigan shore with the city of East Chicago, Indiana. The ramp, which is twenty-eight feet wide to allow for two lanes of traffic and a shoulder, rises over railway tracks and industrial sites.

The ramp was originally designed as a precast segmental concrete bridge by Figg & Muller Engineers of Tallahassee, Florida. In this type of bridge, huge sections are cast in a special yard separate from the site, transported by truck, and lifted into place by crane. The sections are box-shaped, with a bottom slab and top slab connected by sloping webs. Their ends fit together and are "glued" either by epoxy or by concrete poured into the joint. Tendons—cables within the box shape—apply most of the holding force, allowing several segments to span between piers.

Superior Construction Company of Gary, Indiana, was named low bidder, at $13.5 million, for the contract. Its engineers, however, sought and won permission from the IDOT to change the construction method to cast-in-place concrete. The subcontract for installing the reinforcing steel and post-tensioning cables was let to Midwest Steel Company. The change meant that a substantial amount of falsework would have to be constructed in order to form the complex concrete box-shaped superstructure. Superior Construction purchased falsework designed and manufactured by Anthes Industries of Mississauga, Ontario, Canada.

Details of the Collapse

The job went smoothly at first. Workers completed piers for the concrete ramp and began building sections of the superstructure, known as units. The sections were each 180 feet long and terminated in mid-air 42 feet beyond a pier. The concrete for each unit was cast in place (poured) in two steps. The bottom slabs and webs were cast first, followed by the top slab. The ramp was designed as a post-tensioned structure—one in which much of the strength is derived from steel cables that are tensioned (tightened) after the concrete is hardened. In this project, the top slabs were post-tensioned after the concrete had cured to a prescribed strength.

Prior to the post-tensioning, the falsework—a system of steel and wood forms erected to hold the freshly cast concrete—had to bear all the weight. Erecting falsework is a separate and important discipline within the construction industry, as it must be done with great care to ensure the safety of the workers and the integrity of the finished project. Here, the plywood boxes of the formwork rested on longitudinal stringers supported by transverse crossbeams, which in turn were supported by shoring towers located next to the piers and at one-third points of a span.

The shoring towers were prefabricated from welded steel frames joined by bolting on tubular braces. At the top, U-shaped heads met the crossbeams, and at the bottom, the tower legs were supported by individual concrete pads that had been formed with only a small amount of wire mesh instead of heavier steel reinforcing bars. Actually, the tower legs rested on sand jacks, ten-inch-square boxes of two-by-four lumber and sheet metal on top of the concrete pads. These devices enabled the workers to remove the towers by lowering the jacks after a unit was completed and post-tensioned.

Since this project was a ramp rather than a straight elevated highway, it had an uphill slope of 3.6 percent—a 3.6-foot rise every 100 feet. This meant that it was necessary to insert wedges above the U-shaped heads to maintain the slope. The fact that no wedges were found in the debris was one of four major findings listed later by investigators as contributing to the accident.

The original construction drawings had shown towers supported by a guy-wire system such as that used with telephone and other utility poles. The contractor, however, received permission to substitute the tubular X-bracing, even though it provided less stability.

At the time of the collapse, workers were placing concrete for the top slab of unit 4, up to about twenty feet from pier 408. The diaphragm form over this pier was about half full of fresh concrete, and the unit 4 tendons had been attached to unit 3. For a few minutes after unit 4 crashed down, unit 5 stood "teetering," according to witnesses, then also collapsed. The domino effect took all but 20 feet of one 180-foot span and the full length of the other.

Impact

The Indiana DOT lost no time in calling in investigators. Teams came to the site from the Federal Occupational Safety and Health Administration (OSHA), the National Bureau of Standards (NBS), and the Federal Highway Administration (FHWA). Forensic engineering specialists arrived from Concrete Technology Laboratories (CTL), in Skokie, Illinois. These specialists are trained to reconstruct disasters, much like medical specialists are trained to perform autopsies.

Some investigations involved full-scale load tests on the concrete pads and sand jacks, which were found capable of sustaining loads of 160 kips

The first section collapsed without warning; three minutes later the second section collapsed, catapulting workers into the air.

breakdown

(1,000 pounds per square inch) when the design load of the tower leg was 81 kips. Two separate structural analyses were required, because when the bottom slab was cast, the weight of the concrete was transferred to the stringers and crossbeams; when the top slab was cast, the load was distributed to the towers by continuous-beam action of the U-sections. The structural analysts concluded that the collapse had not been triggered by failure of stringers, crossbeams, U-heads, shoring towers, or sand jacks, even though some of the jacks were loaded "critically."

Lawsuit activity began almost immediately. An IDOT inspector who had been injured in the accident filed a $15 million suit against the general contractor. He charged that the scaffolding had been improperly installed and maintained, that guy-wires were not fixed to the falsework, and that the job had been improperly inspected by others. Two ironworkers also filed $15 million suits.

Early speculation about the cause of the collapse centered on the falsework; this was confirmed late in August by a CTL interim report. After a four-month investigation, the forensic engineers pinpointed the area where the collapse started: one of the steel supporting towers. They cited "differential movement at the base of the towers," and "transfer of forces through the system of upper jackscrews, subledgers, and ledgers." The movement, they reported, could have resulted from cracking of the concrete pads or silt settlement beneath them.

After a four-month investigation, the forensic engineers pinpointed the area where the collapse started, one of the steel supporting towers.

Concrete Technology Laboratories found that cracked pads had been reported months before, and that "differential movement at the base of the tower would induce forces in diagonal members. These could exceed the buckling capacities of the individual members." The report noted that a large horizontal force hinted at instability at the top of the towers.

In October 1982, NBS and FHWA together released a 215-page report, shortly after the Indiana OSHA cited the two construction companies and IDOT for sixteen safety violations. One of the violations was that Midwest Steel had not provided adequate escape routes for the workers. The NBS-FHWA report said the IDOT had been most at fault bevause it had not responded to prior reports of cracking in the five-by-five-by-one-foot concrete pads supporting the falsework. This cracking "most likely" had triggered the collapse and occurred because the pads lacked an adequate margin of safety to support the falsework and ramp.

The report also found that the specified wedges had not been used between the stringers and crossbeams at the top of the falsework to compensate for the slope of the roadway. In addition, investigators found that the tops of the shoring towers had not been adequately stabilized against longitudinal movement that developed when the concrete pad cracked and the tower

Poor quality scaffolding and numerous safety violations led to the fatal collapse of this portion of highway ramp during construction. Workers comb through the rubble looking for victims of the disaster.

frame dropped slightly. The report also cited poor quality welds in supports for the falsework crossbeams at the top of the towers, which were inadequate to resist the forces resulting from the longitudinal movement.

The report did not specifically blame any person or company. The researchers did conclude, however, that had any one of the four deficiencies not been present, the collapse would probably not have occurred.

Where to Learn More

Carino, Nicholas J., H. S. Lew, and William C. Stone. "Investigation of East Chicago Ramp Collapse." *Journal of Construction Engineering and Management*, March 1984, pp. 1–18.

"Fallen Ramp Probe Widens." *Engineering News Record*, April 29, 1982, p. 12.

"Probers Eye Concrete Ramp Collapse." *Engineering News-Record*, April 22, 1982, pp. 45–46.

"Ramp Failure Cause Detailed." *Engineering News-Record*, October 28, 1982, pp. 15–16.

"Report Eyes Ramp Failure." *Engineering News-Record*, August 26, 1982, p. 29.

"12 Workers Die in Collapse of Unfinished Bridge Ramp." *New York Times*, April 16, 1982, p. 14.

"U.S. Cites Defects in a Collapsed Road Ramp." *New York Times*, October 21, 1982, p. 23.

breakdown

Mianus River Bridge collapse

Greenwich, Connecticut **1983**

The collapse of one bridge span was caused by several factors, including lack of proper maintenance over twenty-five years. Three people were killed and another three severely injured when the 100-foot-long section, three lanes wide, fell out of the Mianus River Bridge.

Background

On June 28, 1983, three people were killed and another three were severely injured when a 100-foot-long section, three lanes wide, fell out of the Mianus River Bridge in Greenwich, Connecticut. The disaster occurred without warning: one moment motorists were traveling east on I-95 in the usual manner; the next moment all three eastbound lanes vanished. The incident triggered lengthy engineering and scientific investigations that ended in a lawsuit against the company that had designed the bridge twenty-five years earlier. More important, it triggered extensive inspections of bridges in all fifty states, changing inspection procedures in each.

Interstate 95 carries a heavy load of commuter traffic as well as through traffic in southwestern New England, a load estimated to be about one hundred thousand vehicles per day. In June 1983, the seasonal buildup of tourist and vacationer traffic had already begun, putting additional pressure on the

by Rita Robison

Connecticut portion of I-95, which is owned and maintained by the state's Department of Transportation (ConnDot) and known locally as the Connecticut Turnpike.

Parallel to the Long Island Sound shoreline, the turnpike stretches across numerous coves and river outlets, crossing some three hundred bridges in the state and dozens of bridges in Fairfield County alone. The bridge over the Mianus River in the town of Greenwich crosses marshland and tidal flats along its banks. The structure is 2,656 feet—about half a mile—long, and looms seventy feet above the river at mean tide. The design, by Tippetts-Abbett-McCarthy-Stratton (TAMS), was typical of thousands of bridges built during that era.

Details of the Collapse

The bridge collapse involved a 100-foot span on the eastbound side that crashed into the Mianus River and river bank seventy feet below. The span consisted of two 9-inch-deep plate girders, four stringers, and several crossbeams. The girders, made up of plates fastened together in an I-shape with top and bottom flanges, are parallel with the roadway and form its primary support. Crossbeams perpendicular to the girders support the stringers (again parallel to the roadway) that support the deck, a 7.5-inch-deep concrete slab that is in turn topped by two inches of asphalt paving. The entire section weighed about five hundred tons.

Three features of this original design bear examination, for they were central to the controversy about the cause of the failure. The first significant feature was the bridge's skewed appearance. Skewing a bridge reduces the total amount of steel and concrete required but may introduce some structural weaknesses. Oriented on the diagonal between its east- and west-end abutments, the Mianus River Bridge skew was fifty-three degrees.

The second feature of the bridge that received considerable attention was the two-girder design. Using two rather than three or more girders is a popular way to cut total costs in construction of a bridge. As critics point out, though, if one girder fails, so does the other.

The third controversial feature of the bridge was the pin-and-hanger design. The span in question was supported conventionally on a pier at one end, but at the other was hung from the adjoining span, a cantilever anchored at the following pier. The girders of both spans were shaped somewhat like a reverse Z to fit each other at their ends, and a steel strap was fastened to the topmost cantilever girder and to the girder of the hung span below. The fasteners were steel pins, each with a one-inch diameter hole along its axis that received an eleven and one quarter-inch-long bolt with washers and a welded nut at each end.

> Skewing a bridge may introduce some structural weaknesses. The Mianus River Bridge was skewed fifty-three degrees.

As is common in many structural failures, public demand for information conflicted with the engineers' need to undertake a thorough investigation. Newspaper, radio, and television reporters raced to get the story, eager to quote any "authority" they could locate. Local residents said they had heard unusually shrill noises coming from the bridge for several days and insisted that their previous reports of such noises had not been acknowledged by police or highway authorities.

To reassure an alarmed public, Governor William O'Neill immediately ordered an inspection of all other turnpike bridges and the installation of a temporary bridge over the gap left by the failed span. Similar to the Bailey bridges used by the military during two wars, this was delivered on ten trucks and bolted together within days. The temporary span, including ramps on either end, actually weighed one-half as much as the permanent span, so the total weight on the piers was kept well within safety limits. Before traffic could be routed over the remaining spans, however, they were thoroughly inspected and strengthened by temporary "slings" of steel. These were formed by placing girders on top of the deck, threading steel rods through the deck to reinforce the hung span below.

COLLAPSE A RESULT OF SEVERAL FACTORS. Speculation about the cause of the collapse differed widely. Some people thought that the heavy traffic had somehow weakened the bridge. Others said its skew was at fault. Still others blamed ConnDot's maintenance practices, which had allowed parts of the bridge to rust. ConnDot officials bristled. J. William Burns, head of the agency, noted that the Mianus Bridge had been inspected and found safe in September 1982, less than a year before. That pronouncement drew attention to the agency's inspection program. As the investigation proceeded, investigators found that all these theories had some validity.

At the time of the collapse, ConnDot's inspection program fielded only twelve people in six teams to look at all 3,425 bridges in the state. The policy, according to its officials, was to inspect every bridge once every two years. If a bridge was found to be "in danger," it was to be inspected more often. With such a heavy work load, inspectors rarely used X-ray or other sophisticated detection equipment.

In the wake of the disaster, ConnDot called in three New York City consulting engineering firms, one for inspection, one for a detailed forensic analysis, and the third to design a replacement bridge. In the meantime, widely-quoted statements from TAMS officials indicated that the pin-and-hanger design, while not unique for its time (1958), had fallen out of favor in the 1960s because it had become a "maintenance nuisance."

Other investigations were begun by the local and state police, the Federal Highway Administration, and the National Transportation Safety Board

(NTSB). Professor John W. Fisher of Lehigh University, a specialist in metal fatigue, was also consulted. He noted that the remaining hung spans continued to wobble and that the failed pin had come loose despite being constrained from sliding. These observations alarmed officials in other states, who dispatched inspectors to their pin-hanger bridges. In Massachusetts, for instance, inspectors found two broken hangers on the 1,800-foot Harvard Bridge over the Charles River in Boston.

The first consultant's report to ConnDot about the Mianus River Bridge was written by Hardesty & Hanover, New York City engineers. It cited three factors in the bridge collapse: rust buildup on the fourteen-inch washers behind the hangers and on the rear of the hangers themselves; an increase in high bearing stresses of the hanger on the pins as the links moved away from the guide webs; and out-of-plane deformations of the girders under live loads because of the heavy skew.

In September of 1983, hearings were convened by the NTSB, and Conn-Dot released an internal report that called for additional staff and equipment and improved training and supervision in its bridge inspection division. Even so, the report concluded, "inspectors could not have been expected to detect the imminent collapse of the bridge."

That conclusion came under fire, though, as separate probes proceeded. One ConnDot inspector, Jerry White, was arrested for forgery and later convicted of altering, after the collapse, his September 1982 Mianus report. He said he had submitted warnings about the bridge, but ConnDot testified it had logged in no such notes. Actually, the original report, which ConnDot had hailed as finding the bridge "safe," had rated the bridge only "fair. . . . [A] potential exists for major maintenance."

In the NTSB hearings, which took four days, twenty-six witnesses failed to agree about the cause of the collapse. They disagreed, for instance, about the significance of the rust that had accumulated on the underside of the bridge. The forensic engineer, Lev Zetlin of Zetlin-Argo Structural Investigating, New York City, downplayed the rust factor, citing instead the skewed design. Others focused on ConnDot's maintenance practices.

A year later, in June 1984, the official NTSB report did blame ConnDot maintenance and inspection programs, concluding that the probable cause of the collapse was corrosion that caused undetected displacement of the pin-and-hanger suspension assembly. ConnDot contested those conclusions, pursuing the theory of design deficiencies. Yet the agency began to follow NTSB recommendations that included reopening drains that had been paved over, preparing inspection guide manuals, reviewing inspection reports in greater depth, establishing quality control measurements for inspections, and placing catwalks on bridges to facilitate inspections.

As late as February 1985, forensic engineer Zetlin was still blaming the skew of the bridge for the disaster. He released a five-volume report that cost $800,000 to produce. Corrosion of the pins accelerated, but did not cause the accident, he reported, adding that bridge inspectors could not have predicted the accident because the phenomenon of lateral movement of the strap was not widely known and that the movement, only 1/25th of an inch a year, was too small to be detected.

Other engineers disputed the skew theory, contending that if it had been the cause, the pin shift would have taken place gradually rather than in a sudden jarring action. ConnDot, however, sued the original designers in the state's superior court. The suit claimed that because of design negligence, TAMS should reimburse Connecticut for the $25 million cost of settlements with the three survivors and the families of the three dead victims, replacement of the 100-foot collapsed section, and miscellaneous items such as lost toll revenues and police overtime.

During the nineteen-day trial, the jury considered 489 pieces of evidence. They heard expert witnesses on both sides dispute the others' contentions as to the ultimate reasons for the structural failure. The state's forensic consultant blamed the original designers. Weight of the traffic, he said, put pressure on the pin-and-hanger assemblies, causing the hangers to creep slowly off the pins. He demonstrated his theory with a videotape of a laboratory model.

Professor Fisher disagreed, declaring that the collapse was initiated not when the hanger shifted off the pin, but when the edge of the pin, loaded too much by the shifting hanger, failed. His conclusion was that expanding rust had led to the collapse. Other witnesses also zeroed in on the rust. One even argued that the problem could have been rectified fifteen years earlier "if the inspectors had noticed."

Another expert told the jury that paved-over drains and missing gutters let water and road salt flow directly onto the steel. His testimony, coupled with the statements of other witnesses, including some from the state's own witnesses, backed up the defense contention that poor maintenance, not design, had caused the tragedy. Indeed, one state inspector noted that accumulations of bird droppings up to six inches deep had prevented inspectors from walking the beams. Instead, they used binoculars.

On August 14, 1986, the jury exonerated the original designers, ruling that the bridge met the design standards that prevailed in the 1950s. The verdict seemed a recognition that it is exceedingly difficult to hold engineering designers responsible for subsequent discoveries about materials or details that are not known at the time of construction. The jury rejected the state's claim for monetary damages.

Reconstruction of the bridge was accomplished in stages so that traffic could continue without undue interruption. The design, by Frankland & Leinhard, New York City engineers, replaced the original two lines of steel girders on each roadway with seven lines. The eastbound structure was widened fourteen feet. Piles and substructures for the twenty-four spans were completed early in 1988, and Walsh Construction Company of Trumbull, Connecticut, eventually completed the new bridge.

Impact

The collapse of the Mianus River Bridge resulted in an increased emphasis on the institution of better maintenance procedures. Even before the final jury decision in 1986, though, ConnDot had embarked on a ten-year infrastructure renewal program. Expected to cost $5.5 billion over the decade, the program included inspection and maintenance of all bridges and highways around the state.

Other states were prompted by Connecticut's experience to inspect their pin-and-hanger bridges and make plans to eliminate any potential problems. As of 1992, nearly all have been strengthened by one means or another. One

One state inspector noted that accumulations of bird droppings up to six inches deep had prevented inspectors from walking the beams. Instead, they used binoculars.

breakdown

common method has been to eliminate the pin-and-hanger assembly and replace it with a stronger, bolted connection.

Nearly all states adopted more stringent bridge inspection programs in the aftermath of the Mianus River Bridge collapse. Much of this work is contracted out to private consulting engineering firms. In this way, state transportation departments can have their thousands of bridges inspected by trained professionals without having to build up enormous staff. Connecticut has been a leader in offering such contracts, and continues the practice. Ongoing bridge upkeep and maintenance programs have also proliferated in recent years. As one highly regarded bridge authority once noted, "The best protection for any bridge is to send out a crew with mops and brooms. Keep it clean and painted. Keep the gutters cleaned out. Attend to problems while they are very small."

Where to Learn More

"Collapse Review Continues." *Engineering News-Record*, September 22, 1983, pp. 11–12.

"Collapse's Cause Questioned." *Engineering News-Record*, February 28, 1985, p. 12.

"Designers Cleared in Bridge Collapse." *Civil Engineering*, October 1986, p. 10.

"Failed Pin Assembly Dropped Span." *Engineering News-Record*, July 7, 1983, pp. 10–12.

Failla, Kathleen S. "Anatomy of Fracture: Mianus River Bridge." *Engineering News-Record*, February 19, 1987, p. 48.

"Fallen Span Had Design Ills." *Engineering News-Record*, August 4, 1983, p. 12.

"Girder Flaw Eyed in Span Collapse." *Engineering News-Record*, July 14, 1983, pp. 10–11.

"Hearings on Collapsed Span Focus on Rust, Skewed Plan." *Engineering News-Record* September 29, 1983, pp. 35–6.

"New Bridge for Mianus." *Engineering News-Record*, August 11, 1988, p. 14.

"New Mianus Bridge Report Disputes Earlier Study." *Civil Engineering*, April 1985, p. 10.

"State Blamed for Failure." *Engineering News-Record*, July 5, 1984, pp. 27–8.

Tomasson, Robert E. "Study Says Bad Design Was a Factor in Bridge Collapse." *New York Times*, July 30, 1983, p. 23.

Zetlin, Lev, and James M. Hinckley. "Learning from Failure." *Consulting Engineer*, June 1985, pp. 52–7.

Stava
Dam failure

Stava, Italy **1985**

by Neal J. Gruber

The failure of a pair of mining dams in Italy unleashed a flood that killed 269 people, buried villages under tons of mud, and drew attention to national policy issues.

Background

On July 19, 1985, near the resort community of Stava, Italy, a pair of mining dams failed. The failure occurred during the lunch hour, when large numbers of tourists and visitors returned to Stava for their mid-day meal. The resulting flood wave—which survivors estimated at 100 feet high and 150 feet wide—washed away everything in its path as it traversed the Stava River valley. The villages of Stava and Tesoro took the hardest hits: hotels, businesses, homes, and roads were buried under tons of mud. All told, 269 people were killed.

The two dams were part of a fluorspar mining operation and were located, one directly above the other, 40 feet above and less than a mile upstream from the village of Stava. Also called fluorite, fluorspar is a translucent mineral used to manufacture opalescent glass. The dams were necessary to dispose of the wash water and mine tailings (residues) from the process used to extract fluorspar from mined material.

Mine tailings were separated into clays and sands. The heavier sandy material was evenly deposited on the upstream embankment faces, while the finer clay material was deposited in the upper basin of water. These sediments settled out first in the upper embankment and then in the lower embankment as the wash water passed through. The filtered water was then discharged to an old river bed that flowed into the Rio Porcellini ("rio" is the Italian term for "river"). The embankments had grown over the years. At the time of failure, the basins measured 150 x 300 feet and rose 165 feet from the toe of the lower to the crest of the upper embankment.

The dams were built in 1961. The mining complex was originally owned and operated by two Italian chemical companies, Edison and Montecatini, that later merged to form Montedison. The mine and tailings dam operation changed ownership several times. In 1979, the complex was sold to two units of the Italian state energy company, Enil. In 1981, the property was sold again to the firm Prealpi Mineraria, the owner at the time of the failure.

The location for the dams was selected without sufficient consideration of its geological aspects. The site, named "Pozzoli," was at an elevation of 4,425 feet above sea level on the west side of the Stava River. The dams were built on top of sand, gravel, and cobble deposits formed by the movement and meltwater of glaciers.

The damsite was near the Rio Porcellini, which exists as a surface stream uphill of the dams and resurfaces downstream from the dams as a spring. Investigations at the failure site also revealed calcareous deposits directly beneath the dam site. Calcareous deposits are made up of calcium and/or magnesium carbonates (dolomites or limestones) that are easily eroded by water action. As a result, the site contained many subsurface caves, sinkholes, and springs. Some surface water courses and springs at the site were filled and partially covered. After the failure, several of these springs reappeared just as they existed before construction began in 1961.

In 1984, the year before the failure, the townspeople in Stava and Tesoro complained to the mine owners and local authorities that the Rio Stava water was increasingly dirty. This indicated that the silts in the wash water were not completely settling out in the dams before the water was discharged into the old river bed. The villagers protested on ecological grounds when mine owners applied for a permit to again enlarge the embankments.

Details of the Failure

At 12:23 P.M. on July 19, 1985, the residents and tourists in Stava felt a rumbling in the ground, which was followed by a white cloud that some mistook for smoke. A few believed they had experienced an earthquake, which are common in the area. Several minutes later, everything was engulfed by a surging mass of water, white-gray mud, and debris. Without warning, the

A few believed they had experienced an earthquake, which are common in the area. Several minutes later, everything was engulfed by a surging mass of water, white-gray mud, and debris.

Prealpi Mineraria's two dams had failed, leading to widespread destruction in Stava and, to a lesser degree, in the downstream village of Tesoro. The flood reached Tesoro, four kilometers downstream from the dam, in five to six minutes. All together, it deposited approximately 200,000 cubic meters of mud and debris in the Stava Valley.

Although the dam failure occurred in a matter of minutes, several events during the previous six-month period had suggested serious problems. In January 1985, for example, an earth slide occurred in the lower portion of the upper dam, where decant pipes passed beneath it. The slide appeared to be the consequence of water freezing in and/or around the service pipe. Water continued seeping from this area until March 1985.

In June 1985, the decant pipe beneath the lower dam broke, and the water and liquid mud in the lower basin was released through the broken pipe, creating a crater above the break point. The mine operators plugged the failed decant pipe and installed a bypass pipe. During this repair period, the water level in the upper basin was lowered as much as possible to excavate embankment material for the repairs.

On July 15, both ponds were filled and on a modified basis returned to service. At 11:30 A.M. and again at 12:15 P.M. on July 19, the day of the disaster, power failures occurred in an electrical line running across the Rio Porcellini depression, about 660 feet (200 meters) downhill from the lower dam. The failures were not understood at the time. At 12:23 P.M., the dams gave way.

Impact

The failure of the Stava tailings dams was the worst of its type in European history. Initial speculation about the cause of the failure focused on damaging runoff from recent heavy rains, liquefaction of the embankment, and/or piping and subsurface erosion, all compounded by poor operation and maintenance and lack of regulatory oversight. Liquefaction occurs when water pore pressure increases to the point that the liquid acts as a lubricant, and any additional stress causes movement in the earth material. Piping is a subsurface erosion that occurs when a very small leak in a dam face slowly enlarges to a critical size, at which point it enlarges rapidly. This erosion can be accelerated by sudden increases in reservoir water depth and any actions causing the embankment to settle, compact, or shift.

The enormous loss of life and property involved in the accident led to a complete judicial investigation under the direction of the District Attorney. A group of experts attempted to establish whether or not the failure of the dams could have been foreseen and prevented. The lack of before-failure data about the dams made their task very difficult. A large part of the history of the dams

had to be reconstructed on the basis of assumptions about embankment composition, material placement quantities and characteristics, and general mining operations.

The construction of the lower embankment was based on rough outlines drawn up by a Montecatini engineer who had studied at the Colorado School of Mines. The engineer subsequently wrote a paper that delineated specific steps that were necessary to improve the embankment design, but such modifications were never undertaken. Moreover, the upper basin was added and then expanded without adequate attention to engineering ramifications and construction norms. Thus, the original Montecatini engineer was cleared early in the court investigation of any responsibility for the failure.

The investigating team made several important determinations about the tailings dams' operation:

1. The dams were constructed without any prior geologic, hydrogeologic, geotechnical, or hydrologic investigations. This seemed to be common practice during the early 1960s.

2. Neither the formulation of a comprehensive plan nor a systematic stability analysis was ever undertaken. Construction and operation were makeshift.

A huge chasm at Stava, Italy, cut by the rush of water following the collapse of two mining dams above the town.

3. The dams' reserve stability was always very low. While the factor of safety (FS) started out above 1.0, the FS was estimated to have fallen by the middle of the 1970s to between 0.75 and 1.0, well below acceptable minimum standards.

4. The dams were never instrumented to monitor stress, pore water pressure, or earth movement.

5. No tests were ever performed to ascertain the quality or characteristics of the sediments in the ponds, despite the use of the "upstream construction method" that hinges on those sediment characteristics.

6. Sufficient sediment-filtering could only be achieved by using both ponds in series and at very high water levels. This brought water into contact with the dam crests over large portions of their lengths, which is extremely hazardous to an upstream method dam.

7. No measures were taken to effectively divert surface runoff from the ponds or to drain springs.

Overall, then, the tailings dams were haphazardly engineered, badly constructed, and improperly maintained. The experts concluded that a high failure potential must have existed in these two dams as soon as they reached certain dimensions (which were not specified), and that the structures would be prone to failure given any trigger mechanism. The potential trigger mechanisms, perhaps acting in combination, included: movement in the embankment zones; excess pore water pressure from refilling ponds too quickly; water contact with the dam crests; the decant pipe failure; and the excavation of slope material. Some experts believed that excess pore pressure in vulnerable parts of the foundation was the most likely trigger mechanism, and could alone explain the explosive power and extent of the failure.

The investigators determined that the disaster could have been avoided, observing caustically that the dam collapsed "because it was projected, built, and operated in such a way that it did not offer the kind of safety civilized society expects from works that put the lives of human beings at risk." Italy's lax environmental and dam safety laws, which created conflicting inspection and enforcement responsibilities among various levels of government, also contributed to the disaster. The tragedy at Stava thus revealed the need for national policy and regulatory reform.

The Italian court found all current and past owners of the mining operation, as well as local politicians and safety officials, negligent and guilty in the failure. Some were sent to prison, including ten of the mining operation's owners and employees. All are liable in the court-assigned damage payments.

Where to Learn More

"Actions and Omissions." *Time*, August 5, 1985, p. 41.

"Basin Owners Convicted." *Engineering News Record*, August 11, 1988, pp. 17–18.

"Dam Collapse Analyzed." *Engineering News Record*, July 24, 1986, p. 11.

Hallenstein, D., and D. MacKenzie. "Design Faults Revealed in Stava Dam." *New Scientist*, July 25, 1985, p. 18.

Manson, Tycho. "A Valley of Death." *Maclean's*, July 29, 1985, p. 27.

"More Than Rain at Fault in Failure." *Engineering News Record*, July 25, 1985, p. 10.

Palmer, Jay D. "The Mountainside Exploded." *Time*, July 29, 1985, p. 28.

Van Zyl, D. J. A., and S. G. Vick. "Hydraulic Fill Structures." *Proceedings from a Specialty Conference at Colorado State University. Geotechnical Special Publication No. 21*. American Society of Civil Engineers, 1988.

Schoharie Creek Bridge collapse

New York State 1987

by Rita Robison

Two long-standing bridge engineering problems—scour and lack of redundancy—converged to destroy a New York State Thruway bridge. When the center span of the 540-foot Schoharie Creek Bridge suddenly collapsed without warning, ten people plunged to their deaths in the water below.

Background

At opposite ends of the state of New York, New York City and Buffalo are linked by the 550-mile-long New York Thruway. For thirty-one years, the toll road operated without encountering significant structural problems on any of the 819 bridges along its lengths. That streak of good fortune came to an unfortunate end on April 5, 1987. On that morning, at 10:45 A.M., the center span of the 540-foot Schoharie Creek Bridge suddenly collapsed without warning, plunging ten people to their deaths in the water below.

The highway, known formally as the Governor Thomas E. Dewey Thruway, crosses the Schoharie Creek about forty miles west of Albany, near the town of Ft. Hunter. At thirty to forty-five feet wide, the "creek" could more aptly be called a river. That April day, it was raining, but in the rural area flooding from the storm seemed manageable even though the Schoharie was running thirty feet deep under the eighty-foot-high bridge, a good twenty feet higher than usual. The heightened water level was due to flood control measures initiated nearly forty miles upstream. Still, the high water was not seen by Thruway officials as a particular source of concern. After all, the Schoharie Creek Bridge and other bridges in the area had survived a devastating flood in 1955. On this day, however, the bridge would fail, succumbing to the force of the rushing water flowing under its belly.

Operators of the Blenheim Gilboa Pumped Storage Power Project about forty miles upstream from the Schoharie Creek Bridge, fearing damage to the reservoir, had released flood waters into the Schoharie. The flow was later reported at a record 65,187 cubic feet per second; the previous record had been 55,000 cubic feet per second, recorded during the 1955 flood that left Ft. Hunter under five to six feet of water. The town was spared during the reservoir release because of a levee that had been constructed along its north side. The levee kept the creek within its banks, but further intensified the flow. Witnesses later said that the water "seemed to boil over on the rocks below and tear at tree trunks leaning out over the banks of the creek."

The high flow of the Schoharie caused state highway officials to close a bridge about a half mile downstream from the Thruway, but other bridges in the region were left open to traffic. It was on one of these other bridges, located just downstream from the Thruway, that a stunned fifteen-year-old boy witnessed the collapse of the Schoharie Creek Bridge at 10:45 A.M. "All of a sudden I heard this noise. Water splashed up high, and the road and the concrete just fell in," he told reporters. The boy watched as a truck plunged straight into the creek. Other drivers were ensnared as well. A small car hurtled into the void, spinning upside down. A large white car that was later found downstream with its top ripped off followed, sailing off the ruined bridge and into the water. At least two other cars also disappeared.

When asked about the collapse, nearby residents related that a sound like an explosion was audible from the area of the bridge, followed ten minutes later by a noise that "sounded like a bomb going off." These two noises, investigators determined, signaled the collapse of two spans of the highway. The two spans were swept some eighty feet downstream, while the others dropped when their piers failed within a few hours.

State trooper Peter Persico had crossed the bridge a short time before the collapse, but turned back after witnesses called the police. He found several cars and trucks parked on the partly collapsed bridge, "their drivers gawking." With the help of other troopers, he evacuated the bridge just before the second section collapsed. By nightfall, police had located the two lost cars and a tractor trailer, but the rescue efforts were curtailed by high water and the threat of further collapse.

The boy watched as a truck plunged straight into the creek. Other drivers were ensnared as well. A small car hurtled into the void, spinning upside down. A large white car that was later found downstream with its top ripped off followed, sailing off the ruined bridge and into the water. At least two other cars also disappeared.

THE INVESTIGATION BEGINS. Thruway officials were astounded when they learned of the Schoharie Creek Bridge collapse. Chief engineer Daniel S. Garvey said, "We were just totally shocked. We're nonplussed about the whole thing. We don't understand it." James A. Martin, deputy executive director, was stunned as well. He noted that the thruway's bridges were designed to withstand the most violent of storms.

Martin recognized that an examination of other bridges needed to be set in motion at once. He ordered an immediate inspection of all 819 Thruway bridges; 100 were inspected within the first day. Senator Daniel Patrick Moynihan flew in by helicopter and promised to ask the federal Department of Transportation for $10 million to rebuild the bridge. (The Schoharie Bridge had only been insured for its construction cost of $8.8 million, with a $2.5 million deductible.) By the end of that day, three separate investigations into the disaster had been arranged. Two forensic engineering firms were brought in to determine the cause of failure: Wiss, Janney, Elstner Associates of Chicago, and Mueser Rutledge of New York City. The National Transportation Safety Board also began a full investigation. Their reports led the New York State Commission of Investigation to fix blame for the tragedy on the Thruway Authority (NYTA) as early as August, four months after the collapse.

The bridge, which in 1987 carried an average of 16,000 vehicles per day, was constructed in 1952 of five spans. The reinforced concrete deck sections each rested on a pair of steel girders about seven feet high and one hundred to one hundred twenty feet long. The transverse floor beams were fifty-five feet wide. Below, four piers consisted of two columns supported by a single shallow spread footing. The columns, nine feet wide at the bottom and tapering to seven feet wide at the top, were connected near their tops by a beam that gave the pier an H shape. Two piers were planted in the creek bed and two on the banks; the superstructure also rested on two abutments.

The bridge had been rehabbed five years earlier and had been inspected last in April 1986, according to Robert C. Donnarums, Thruway deputy chief engineer. In the yearly inspections before that, no problems with the piers had been found, though one inspector, in 1977, had recommended replacement of the riprap that seemed to be missing on the upstream sides of the bridge. Riprap consists of large broken stones that are piled around the pier bases to protect them. Rehab plans made between 1981 and 1982 called for repairs and repaving of the four-lane deck, but included no mention of the riprap. Donnarums added that, in light of the collapse, investigators "would pay close attention" to the flow of water around the bridge supports.

Despite the existence of rehab plans, Thruway and state officials soon learned that their records were in disarray. Construction details were lacking and officials recognized that they had no idea how many other Thruway bridges were of the same steel plate, two-girder design. When they did locate

breakdown

the records, they found that no underwater inspection had been made of the Schoharie Creek Bridge, although the precaution had been urged at the time of the rehab.

Details of the Collapse

Investigators initially blamed the failure on the bridge's lack of redundancy (lack of back-up, load-bearing systems in case of component failure). Each of the five spans was supported independently, and the two-girder design provided no alternative load paths in case one horizontal member failed. The lack of frame-action reinforcement in the concrete piers was also considered as a factor that contributed to the sudden nature of the collapse. But within two or three days of the collapse, investigators began to focus almost exclusively on hydraulics—the behavior of flowing water—and its effect on pier foundations. Dr. David Axelrod, state health commissioner who also headed the State Disaster Preparedness Commission, contended that "a whole series of unusual factors" impacted the water flow in Schoharie Creek.

One investigation uncovered a report—written by a state engineer who had reviewed the bridge design before its construction—warning that the proposed design did not take into account the frequent occurrence of ice jams in the Schoharie Creek and the possibility of extremely severe floods. The report further claimed that the 540-foot-length of the bridge might prove too constrictive given the nature of the river. The report recommended lengthening the span to 775 feet. This report had been disregarded, and the construction of the bridge, along with the erection of the levees, had narrowed the river channel sufficiently to greatly increase the velocity at which the stream's water passed through. The rapid flow of water, in turn, had caused a great deal of erosion. After the collapse, it was found that scour, the erosion of the streambed by the force of the currents, had washed nine feet of the streambed out from under the upstream side of one of the piers. When the pier finally tipped into this hole, the spans of the bridge above disengaged from their supports and fell into the river as well. Had the bridge been constructed with concern for redundancy—with one continuous span across the river rather than five independent spans—some experts maintained that the girders would have merely sagged at the point of the pier failure instead of collapsing. The slump of the bridge would have provided a visual warning that the bridge was in danger of collapsing. The bridge could then have been closed for repairs, preventing any loss of life.

While the lack of redundancy and reinforcements contributed to the severity of the collapse, investigators determined, based on the evidence in the streambed, that scour was the primary cause of the disaster. This was not an unusual finding. During that same spring of 1987, scour was blamed for the failure of seventeen other bridges in the northeastern United States alone. Two years later, the Hatchie River Bridge on U.S. Route 51 in Tennessee failed when material was lost from around a pier because the channel shifted laterally. But while scour is recognized as a dangerous threat to bridges, it is not easy to track. The same water that scours out the streambed promptly refills the hole with loose silt and gravel. Without probing, even a diver cannot see the effects. Scour recurs over time as well.

While scour was found to be the culprit in the collapse, The New York State Commission of Investigation castigated the Thruway Authority (NYTA), noting that "while the bridge design and construction may well have been deficient, with proper inspection and maintenance, this bridge would not have collapsed." The commission then recommended a complete overhaul of the state's bridge inspection program, urged bridge inspectors to review drawings before site visits—a practice not rigorously enforced—and urged the state legislature to intervene by funding bridge repairs for needy localities.

The final verdict came in April 1988, just a year after the collapse, when the National Transportation Safety Board accepted a staff report that also blamed the NYTA for not maintaining the riprap. The report cited "ambiguous

While scour is recognized as a dangerous threat to bridges, it is not easy to track. The same water that scours out the streambed promptly refills the hole with loose silt and gravel. Without probing, even a diver cannot see the effects.

breakdown

plans and specifications for the original construction, an inadequate inspection and inadequate oversight by NYDOT and FHWA."

Impact

Reconstruction of the bridge began soon after the collapse. Traffic was jammed on all other available roads through the area, so re-establishment of the Schoharie Creek Bridge was important to the region. Thruway officials quickly retained the New York City firm of Hardesty & Hanover, who redesigned the bridge for quick reconstruction as well as for durability. The new blueprints called for fourteen plate girders placed continuously over the piers and spaced a conservative eight feet apart. The stiff girder design allowed the contractor to pour the concrete deck span by span rather than wait for all steel on the entire bridge to be in place.

Due to the growing traffic problems, design and construction of the new pier foundations had begun before the cause of the collapse was determined. Mindful of possible causes of the collapse, however, the firm had settled on foundations specifically designed to "make the system independent of scour." Steel-plated boxes, called sheetpile cofferdams, extended from the surface to twenty-three feet below the river bottom—eight feet below the foundation bottoms—to permit the construction crew to pour the pier foundations in dry conditions. When it was completed, the replacement bridge boasted deeper foundations and steel H-piles that extended down to bedrock and rigidly connected to the foundations. With proper riprap, the design effectively protected the pier bases from scour.

The Schoharie tragedy prompted new concerns and new regulations, both at the national level and within various states. In 1988 Charles H. Thornton of Thornton-Tomasetti, a New York City engineering firm, published what he called a "powerful plea for better bridge inspection practices" in *Civil Engineering*. He recommended that a bridge inspection program be implemented that would specify the degree of experience and familiarity with bridge design required of an inspector, the need for periodic evaluation of each bridge's complete structural and foundational system, and numerous other measures to ensure that a failure such as the Schoharie Creek Bridge tragedy did not repeat itself.

The danger of the scour phenomenon to the nation's bridges continued to receive a great deal of attention as well. In 1989 a study found that 494 of the 823 U.S. bridge failures from 1951 to 1988 occurred as a result of hydraulic conditions, primarily scour of foundation material. In 1988 the FHWA instituted a requirement that initial screening and review processes be undertaken to identify bridges most likely to be vulnerable to scour damage. Each state was to develop its own plan. While the FHWA provided procedures for predicting potential scour depths and designing countermeasures, its main emphasis concerned the need for more sophisticated measurement devices for gauging bridge fitness.

The state of New York was among the first to bring in an independent task force to devise its plan. The task force devised a simple, straightforward method for scour screening and priority procedure. It evaluated nearly 20,000 bridges in composing the priority list. Interim countermeasures—creation of riprap and guide banks to withstand scour action, increased underpinning support, bridge closure during storms—were implemented at several sites. Finally, New York's Department of Transportation, which once, according to one critic, had to "rummage through boxes in the basement" to locate specific bridge records, created the post of state bridge inspector general to bring order to archives, supervise the inspection process, and review new bridge designs.

Where to Learn More

"Can You Top This? (Schoharie Creek Bridge Reconstruction)." *Civil Engineering*, January 1988, pp. 61–2.

Green, Peter. "Feds Blame State Agency for Schoharie Failure." *Engineering News-Record*, May 5, 1988, p. 16.

Huber, Frank. "Update: Bridge Scour." *Civil Engineering*, September, 1991.

Lane, Kate. "Schoharie Bridge Probe Yields Inspection Changes." *Engineering News-Record*, May 14, 1987, p. 11.

Murillo, Juan A. "Scourge of Scour." *Civil Engineering*, July 1987, pp. 66–69.

"Schoharie Report Offers Guidance on Inspection." *Engineering News-Record*, December 10, 1987, p. 11.

Thornton, Charles H., et al. "Lessons from Schoharie Creek." *Civil Engineering*, May 1988, p. 46.

"Thruway Blamed for Collapse." *Engineering News-Record*, August 13, 1987, pp. 13–14.

L'Ambiance Plaza collapse

Bridgeport, Connecticut 1987

The twin towers of a half-completed apartment building collapsed during construction and fell like a gigantic stack of concrete pancakes, killing twenty-eight workers and injuring sixteen.

by Loretta Hall

Background

Shortly after lunch on April 23, 1987, the twin towers of the half-completed L'Ambiance Plaza apartment building fell like a gigantic stack of concrete pancakes, killing twenty-eight workers and injuring sixteen. The second-worst construction accident in American history focused attention on the importance of designing for construction loading as well as the static conditions of completed structures.

The state of Connecticut had financed the building as part of an economic revival effort for the city of Bridgeport. The $17 million project would provide 218 apartments in thirteen above-ground stories atop three levels of underground parking.

In the interests of economy and (ironically) safety, designers chose the lift-slab technique to build the structure. Once the first level of concrete flooring was poured on the foundation, slabs for the remaining floors and the roof were poured in layers atop the base. After each slab had hardened sufficiently,

2
4
1

it was post-tensioned—meaning that high-strength steel wires embedded in the concrete were tightened—to increase its strength.

When all of the slabs were ready, they would be lifted in groups of about three by jacks positioned atop each of the building's steel columns. As lower-level slabs reached their destination heights, they were welded to the columns; upper-level slabs became working platforms from which column extensions were erected to permit raising floors to higher levels.

This procedure of pulling buildings up by their own bootstraps is economical, because the concrete is formed and poured essentially at ground level. It reduces the amount of work that must be done on scaffolding, diminishing the risk of workers falling or being hit by falling tools or other material. Post-tensioning allows for longer spans (fewer columns) and thinner slabs, reducing materials costs.

Texstar Construction Corporation was selected to lift the slabs for L'Ambiance Plaza. It had already built 800 lift-slab structures without a fatality, although there had been a few mishaps during the 37-year history of the procedure.

WARNING SIGNS ABOUNDED. Two incidents within the first six years of lift-slab construction helped formalize essential safety measures. In 1954, a 250-ton slab fell sixteen feet while being lifted at a site in San Mateo, California. This accident demonstrated the need for cribbing (supporting the slab with temporary posts until attachment to the columns was completed) and sway bracing (keeping the unstable structure from shifting sideways by anchoring it with temporary cables). The necessity of sway bracing was underscored two years later when a partially completed eight-story garage in Cleveland, Ohio, leaned eight feet from vertical before being winched back into position.

A succession of problems had plagued L'Ambiance Plaza even before the structure's ultimate collapse. In one instance, an automobile jack was braced against one column and used to move another column back into vertical. In another, workers attached jacks to four slabs at one end of the building and to only three slabs at the other end; when lifting operations began, one slab cracked and was subsequently patched. There were also difficulties with fitting columns together, problems with jacks, and incidents involving deformed shearheads.

Shearheads, consisting of steel channel sections cast into the concrete slab to form a frame around each column, were critical to the structure's integrity. They provided attachment points for the lifting rods that linked each slab to the jacks above. They were also the connection points at which slabs were welded to the columns. Just a year before the L'Ambiance Plaza

breakdown

collapse, a shearhead failure at another Texstar project in Stamford, Connecticut, had allowed a slab to fall fifteen inches, injuring a worker.

Details of the Collapse

Work seemed to be proceeding normally on April 23, 1987. L'Ambiance Plaza's two rectangular towers were offset, so that they shared half a wall. Columns in both wings extended through the ninth-floor level, and a stack of upper-floor slabs sat parked at the top awaiting extension of the columns. Another set of three slabs—the ninth, tenth, and eleventh floors—had just been raised to the top of the west tower, and workers were preparing to secure the set's bottom slab to the columns.

Suddenly, a loud metallic bang rang out. With an ominous rumble, cracks spread through the ninth-floor slab as through a shattering sheet of ice. The slab collapsed, pulling the ones above down with it. As the upper floors dropped, each lower floor crashed in succession in what is known as "progressive collapse." The attached east tower was wrenched into failure as well. Within five seconds a heap of crumbled concrete punctuated with twisted steel was all that remained of the structure.

The catastrophe apparently began at column E4.8, which stood in front of slab cutouts for an elevator shaft centered on the twin towers' shared wall. Post-tensioning wires curved around the cutouts. The building's original design had included an additional column nearby; a redesign, however, eliminated the extra column, leaving E4.8 the most heavily loaded column in the building. Inexplicably, no changes in the jacking plan accompanied the redesign. Hydraulic jacks placed atop the columns to lift the slabs had a capacity of 178 kips (178,000 pounds). At some locations, superjacks with a capacity of 300 kips were substituted. The jack atop E4.8 was the smaller type.

As workers prepared to secure the crucial package of three 320-ton slabs prior to the collapse, they evidently realized that the slabs were not quite level. Raising them a fraction of an inch at column E4.8 put additional strain on the jack at that location. A superjack atop next-in-line column E3.8 was apparently used to help in the leveling effort.

What failed, however, was not the jack atop E4.8, but its connection to the ninth-floor slab. Sections of ninety-degree-angle steel were welded to opposite sides of each shearhead, extending into the channels of the column's steel I beam. A threaded rod connected to the jack above extended through a slot in the horizontal section of each of these "lifting angles." A nut screwed onto the end of the rod provided a surface on which the lifting angle rested.

As workers attempted to level the slabs, the lifting angle at column E4.8 twisted upward, allowing the nut to slide toward the column. The rod then

Suddenly, a loud metallic bang rang out. With an ominous rumble, cracks spread through the ninth-floor slab as through a shattering sheet of ice.

swung out of its slot, slamming into the column with a thunderous 75,000 pounds of force. Without support at that location, the seven-inch-thick slab began to sag and crack. The sudden loss of connection between the slab and the jack overburdened jacks at neighboring columns. In the ultimate wreckage, the surrounding columns bent toward E4.8 like accusing fingers.

Several other factors may have contributed to the difference in severity between the L'Ambiance Plaza shearhead failure and the episode in Stamford. Construction of concrete shear walls in strategic locations, which would have provided stability to the column-and-slab skeleton, improperly lagged several floors behind slab placement. The builders had not installed any cribbing or sway bracing, further contributing to the structure's instability.

Moreover, inadequate safety factors in Texstar's shearhead design and construction increased the likelihood of that component failing. O'Kon & Company, the Atlanta-based engineering firm that designed L'Ambiance Plaza, reviewed the shearhead connection design only for postconstruction loading, not for loads imposed during the lifting operation. Although American National Standards Institute specifications called for a minimum safety factor of 2.5 in jacking assemblies, subsequent laboratory tests of this shearhead design revealed a safety factor between 1.1 and 1.3. That is, the shearhead and lifting angle assemblies began to deform under a load of 160 kips; they would have had to support 375 kips to meet the 2.5 safety factor.

Impact

Precise details of what caused the disaster have never been established conclusively. A team from the National Bureau of Standards (NBS) investigated the incident on behalf of the federal government. Upon release of its report, the U.S. Occupational Safety and Health Administration (OSHA) announced record fines totaling $5.11 million against the prime contractor, TPMI/Macomber, and the lift-slab subcontractor, Texstar. Each entity was assessed 238 willful violations for inadequate lifting angles. They and two other subcontractors were also cited for inadequate lateral support and inadequate inspection, testing, and correction of weld problems.

In late October 1987, all of the known victims of the accident jointly filed suit against the city of Bridgeport and two of its employees who were responsible for issuing the building permit and inspecting the project. Attempting to avert an unwieldy number of separate lawsuits lingering interminably in the court system, a two-judge panel engineered a mediated $41 million settlement among all parties.

For the defendants, the agreement had mixed consequences. On the positive side, OSHA dropped all but $430,000 of its proposed fines, settling for

recovery of the investigation's costs. On the other hand, over twenty parties involved in the ownership, design, and construction of the structure were assigned some level of responsibility for the disaster. Some felt that a longer, more extensive investigation might have exonerated them.

For the plaintiffs, the settlement meant a quick resolution of their claims. Payments and annuities for survivors and families of those killed in the collapse totaled $30 million. In addition, it was decided that L'Ambiance Plaza would be rebuilt; ownership of the completed building would be transferred to the plaintiffs, who would subsequently receive a portion of the future earnings of the facility.

For the construction industry, the settlement meant that the exact causes of the catastrophe might never be fully identified. While further investigation was not barred by the settlement, the lack of court proceedings to apportion liability removed much of the impetus for additional analysis.

Within days after the accident, the city of Bridgeport hired Thornton-Tomasetti, a New York City–based structural engineering firm, to conduct an investigation. Four years later their report suggested that the catastrophe had been triggered by the loss of a wedge holding the slab in place at column E4.8, resulting in a sudden sagging that initiated the collapse sequence. The report

L'Ambiance Plaza collapsed during lift-slab construction, probably due to an inadequate method used in connecting the floor slabs to the column-mounted lifting mechanisms.

also charged that the NBS team's misidentification of elements of the debris when they were moved from the site hindered efforts to analyze the accident.

The American Society of Civil Engineers (ASCE) annual convention in October 1991 included three sessions relating to the L'Ambiance Plaza disaster. The most heated discussions involved Neil M. Hawkins, an engineer who had worked as a consultant to Texstar. He argued that the collapse had originated when pressure from dirt filled in behind an adjacent retaining wall caused poorly designed lower-level slabs to crumble. He disputed the laboratory tests showing inadequate shearhead safety factors, and charged that OSHA had rushed to blame Texstar without allowing other investigators prompt access to the debris.

COLLAPSE REVERBERATES THROUGH CONSTRUCTION INDUSTRY. The spectacular failure, with its heavy loss of life, generated some changes in construction procedures and law. For example, OSHA directed contractors to meet the 2.5 safety factor criterion on all lift-slab jobs. In response to the fact that almost half of those who died at L'Ambiance Plaza had been working on tasks unrelated to the jacking process, OSHA also obtained an injunction banning the presence of nonessential workers underneath slabs during the lifting operation at a subsequent Texstar job site. Two weeks after the collapse, an ironworkers' union in Massachusetts adopted a policy prohibiting its welders from working underneath concrete slabs as they were being lifted.

The L'Ambiance Plaza collapse was the third major structural or construction failure in the state of Connecticut in a decade. Based on recommendations from a governor-appointed committee, the state enacted a new construction safety law in 1988. Key provisions included improving the qualifications, visibility, and power of building inspectors and requiring that building plans and specifications for large projects be reviewed by an independent engineering consultant.

The disaster underscored the need for designers to evaluate connections as well as the major elements of a structure. It also focused attention on the fact that temporary loads and stress during construction must be analyzed when determining the adequacy of a design. Because of construction accidents such as the one at L'Ambiance Plaza, ASCE formed a committee to write a new standard on structural design loads during construction. The collapse of L'Ambiance Plaza showed that small details can be the most critical elements in large construction projects.

Where to Learn More

Godfrey, K. A., Jr. "After L'Ambiance Plaza." *Civil Engineering*, January 1988, pp. 36-9.

Korman, Richard. "Changes Asked in Safety Law as L'Ambiance Pact Is Signed." *Engineering News-Record*, December 8, 1988, pp. 13–14.

—. "Column May Help Locate Cause of Fatal Collapse in Bridgeport." *Engineering News-Record*, April 30, 1987, pp. 10–12.

—. "Flawed Connection Detail Triggered Fatal L'Ambiance Plaza Collapse." *Engineering News-Record*, October 29, 1987, pp. 10–12.

—. "Mediated Settlement Seeks to Close the Book on L'Ambiance Plaza." *Engineering News-Record*, November 24, 1988, pp. 10–11.

—. "L'Ambiance Plaza Won't Rest Easy." *Engineering News-Record*, November 4, 1991, pp. 14–16.

—, and Kathleen S. Failla. "Lack of Temporary Bracing Studied." *Engineering News-Record*, May 7, 1987, pp. 12–13.

Levy, Matthys, and Mario Salvadori. *Why Buildings Fall Down*. W. W. Norton & Company, 1992, pp. 173–82.

Vogel, Shawna. "The Domino Building." *Discover*, January 1988, p. 88.

Index

A

Adams, Robert 126
AEA (Atomic Energy Authority) 138
Agency of Natural Resources and Energy
    (ANRE) 148, 149
Air Route Traffic Control (ARTC) 12
Albacore-type hull 87
ALCOA 45–46
Alyeska 99, 100–101, 104
American Consulting Engineers Council
    214
American National Standards Institute
    244
American Society of Civil Engineers 214,
    246
Ammann, Othmar 193
Anderson, George W. 82
Andrea Doria–Stockholm collision 73–78
Andrew, Charles E. 192
Anoxia 26
ANRE (Agency of Natural Resources and
    Energy) 148, 149
Anthes Industries 217
Apollo 1 capsule fire 17–22
Apollo-Soyuz Test Project (ASTP) 27
Arkin, Kenneth 191
ARTC (Air Route Traffic Control) 12
Atlanta Beacon Journal 121

Atlantis 82–83
Atmospheric electrical discharge 9
Atomic Energy Act 134
Atomic Energy Authority (AEA) 138
Audi 5000 sudden acceleration 124–129
Audi Victims Network (AVN) 127
Auto-restow system 50, 51
Automatic pilot 100
AVN (Audi Victims Network) 127
Axelrod, David 237
Axene, Dean L. 80

B

Babcock & Wilcox 141, 142
Ballard, Robert D. 70
Ballasting 73, 78, 83, 84, 92, 93, 96
Basic Law on Atomic Energy 148
Belt separation 118
Bends 26
Bhopal Claims Act 165
Bhopal toxic vapor leak 159–165
Billah, K. Yusuf 193
Bioremediation 101
Blenheim Gilboa Pumped Storage Power
    Project 235
Bloch, Byron 112
Boston Building Department 187
British Board of Trade 68, 71

British Gas Board 199
Brittle fracture 70
Bronx–Whitestone Bridge 192
Brush discharge 9
Bureau of Air Commerce 11
Burns, J. William 223

C

CAA (Civil Aeronautics Administration)
11, 12, 15
CAB (Civil Aeronautics Board) 12
Calamai, Piero 74–75, 77
Carter, Jimmy 145
Center for Auto Safety 109, 110, 115,
119, 126, 127
Chaffee, Roger B. 18, 19, 20, 22
Challenger explosion 29–36
Chernobyl accident 173–179
China Airlines 747-200 59
Civil Aeronautics Administration (CAA)
11, 12, 15
Civil Aeronautics Board (CAB) 12
Claybrook, Joan 122
Coatsworth, Leonard 191, 192
Cockpit Resource Management (CRM) 48
Cold War 89
Collier, John 138
Collision rules 74–75
Connecticut Department of Transportation
222, 223, 225, 226
Consumer Reports 118, 121
Containment booms 101
Containment shell 175
Control failure 90
Corrosion 57, 58, 59, 61
Cosentino, Michael 113
Cousins, Gregory 100
Cronin, David 40
Crown Center Redevelopment Corporation
212
Crush depth 79, 83, 90
Cumbria Area Health Authority 138

D

Deep Submergence Rescue Vehicle (DSRV)
84, 90–91
Department of Commerce 12

Department of Environmental Protection
102
Department of Transportation (DOT) 16,
236
Deutsch, James B. 213
Dewey Thruway (Thomas E.) 234
Dispersants, chemical 101, 104
Ditlow, Clarence M. 119, 128
Dobrovolsky, Georgi 24, 25
Donnarums, Robert C. 236
DOT (Department of Transportation) 16, 236
Double-hulled ship 66, 99, 103–104
DSRV (Deep Submergence Rescue Vehicle)
84, 90–91
DSRV-1 84, 90
DSRV-2 84, 90–91
Duncan, Daniel M. 212–214

E

East Chicago, Indiana, highway ramp
collapse 216–220
Eckener, Hugo 3–4, 5, 10
Edison 229
El Al Boeing 747-200 crash 57–62
Electrical malfunction 21
Electronically controlled thrust reversers
49
Environmental Protection Agency (EPA)
167
EPA (Environmental Protection Agency)
167
Erosion 230
Excitation 194
Explosive bolts 23
Exxon Corporation 99, 102, 104
Exxon *Valdez* oil spill 98–105

F

FAA (Federal Aviation Administration)
15–16, 39, 41, 42, 46, 48, 51, 52,
53, 55, 58–59, 60, 61
Farquharson, Frederick B. 191
Federal Aviation Act 15
Federal Aviation Administration (FAA)
15–16, 39, 41, 42, 46, 48, 51, 52,
53, 55, 58–59, 60, 61
Federal Communications Commission 71

Federal Highway Administration (FHWA) 218, 219, 223
Federal Motor Vehicle Safety Standard "301" 111
Federico, Mario A. Di 119
FHWA (Federal Highway Administration) 218, 219, 223
Figg & Muller Engineers 217
Final machining 46
Firestone 500 steel-belted tire failure 117–123
Fisher, John W. 224, 226
Floberg, John F. 119
Fluorescent penetrant (FPI) 46
Flutter 193
Forced resonance 194
Ford Motor Company 109–115
Ford Pinto rear-impact defect 109–116
Fracture 185, 186
Frankland & Leinhard 226
Frye, Ralph 185
Fuchs, Isaac 60

G

"Galloping Gertie" 190–194
Garvey, Daniel S. 236
General Electric Corporation 148
General Motors Corporation 115
Ghandi, Rajiv 165
Gillum Colaco Associates 209
Gillum, Jack K. 212–214
Ginna power plant radioactive release 153–158
Gorbachev, Mikhail 175
Gore, Al 122
Gowing, Margaret 138
Graf Zeppelin 3–4, 7, 10
Grissom, Virgil I. "Gus" 18, 20, 21, 22
Ground settlement 199

H

Haeusler, Roy 113
Hammond Iron Works 183, 184
Hardesty & Hanover 239
Hartigan, Neil 126
Harvey, John W. 81
Hatchie River Bridge 238

Havens Steel Company 212
Hawkins, Neil M. 246
Hazelwood, Joseph 100
Hindenburg crash 3–10
Hindenburg, Paul von 4
Hitler, Adolf 5
Hodge, Ivy 198
House Subcommittee on Oversight and Investigations 118
Howell, Dan 127
Hyatt Regency Hotel walkways collapse 208–215

I

Iacocca, Lee 109–110
Idaho National Engineering Laboratory 144
IDOT (Indiana Department of Transportation) 216
Indiana Department of Transportation (IDOT) 216
INPO (Institute of Nuclear Power Operations) 145, 157
Institute of Nuclear Power Operations (INPO) 145, 157
Institute, West Virginia, toxic vapor leak 166–172
Institution of Structural Engineers 200
International Ice Patrol 71
Ismay, J. Bruce 65, 66

J

Japan Atomic Power Company (JAPC) 148, 150, 151
Jarvis, Gregory 31

K

Kamanin, Nikolai 27
Kemeny Report 145
Kovatch P-18 water-supply vehicle 45

L

L'Ambiance Plaza collapse 241–247
Larsen and Nielsen prefabrication system 197
Lauda Air Boeing 767-300 crash 49–56

Lauda, Niki 53, 54
Lienhard, Fred 189
Lifeboats 76, 95–96
Lift-slab construction 241, 242
Liquefaction 230
List 76, 77, 78, 92, 93, 94
Load, dead 211
Load, design 211
Load, dynamic 200
Load, live 211
Load, static 200, 241
Load, temporary 246
Load-bearing walls 199, 200
Loading capacity 198
Loading, construction 241, 244
Loading, floor 198
Loading, postconstruction 244
Loading, wind 198
Lovell, Malcolm 122
Lowery, Lee 211
LZ 129 4–5
LZ 130 7

M

Martin, James A. 236
McAuliffe, Christa 29, 31, 33
McDonnell-Douglas Corporation 45, 47, 48
McNair, Ronald 31
Meltdown 140, 143, 156, 176
Metal fatigue 193, 224
Methyl isocyanate 159, 160, 161,
    162–164, 166, 167, 168
MGM Grand Hotel fire 202–207
Mianus River Bridge collapse 221–227
Michelson, Carl 142
Midwest Steel Company 217, 219
Ministry of International Trade and
    Technology 148
Missouri Board for Architects, Professional
    Engineers and Land Surveyors 212
Mizar 87–88, 89
Moisseiff, Leon 189, 190, 192
Molasses spill 183–188
Montecatini 229, 231
Montedison 229
Morgan, J. Pierpont 65
Morrison, Herb 10

Morton Thiokol 32, 35
Mother Jones 109, 111–112, 115
Moynihan, Daniel Patrick 236
Murray, P.F. 122

N

Nader, Ralph 110, 113, 119, 126
NASA (National Aeronautics and Space
    Administration) 17–18, 20–21, 27,
    29–30, 32–36
National Aeronautics and Space
    Administration (NASA) 17–18,
    20–21, 27, 29–30, 32–36
National Bureau of Standards (NBS) 211,
    218, 219, 244
National Highway Traffic Safety
    Administration (NHTSA) 109, 110,
    112, 119, 120, 124–126, 127, 128
National Radiological Protection Board
    138
National Traffic and Motor Vehicle Safety
    Act 115
National Transportation Safety Board 41,
    43, 47, 48, 54, 96, 223, 225, 236,
    238
NBS (National Bureau of Standards) 211,
    218, 219, 244
Neal, James F. 113
New York Department of Transportation
    240
New York State Commission of
    Investigation 236, 238
NHTSA (National Highway Traffic Safety
    Administration) 109, 110, 112, 119,
    120, 124–126, 127, 128
NR-1 84, 91
NRC (Nuclear Regulatory Commission)
    142, 144, 145, 156, 157
Nuclear-powered submarine 79–80, 83,
    84, 86–87, 91
Nuclear reactor 79, 80, 84, 87, 88, 91
Nuclear Regulatory Commission (NRC)
    142, 144, 145, 156, 157

O

Occupational Safety and Health Act 160,
    171

Occupational Safety and Health
Administration (OSHA) 167, 218,
219, 244
Ocean Drilling & Exploration Company
(ODECO) 93, 97
Ocean Ranger oil-drilling rig sinking
92–97
Offshore oil-drilling rig 92, 93, 94
Oil Pollution Act 103
O'Kon & Company 244
O'Neill, William 223
Onizuka, Ellison 31
OPEC (Organization of Petroleum
Exporting Countries) 148
Organization of Petroleum Exporting
Countries (OPEC) 148
(OSHA) Occupational Safety and Health
Administration 167, 218, 219, 244

P

Patsayev, Viktor 24
Patty Berkebile Nelson Duncan Monroe
Lefebvre Architects Planners 209
Persico, Peter 235
Petroleum Industry Response
Organization 104
Petroski, Henry 210
Pfrang, Edward O. 211
Philips Consultants 197, 198
Pike, Charley 198
Pin-and-hanger design 222, 223, 225,
226–227
Piping 230
Pore water pressure 232
Portman, John 209
Post-tensioning 217, 242, 243
Prealpi Minearia 229, 230
Prefabricated construction 196, 197,
199–201
Pressure equalization valve 23, 25
Pressurized-water reactor 141, 153–154,
155–156, 157
Progressive collapse 199, 243
Pruss, Max 7, 8, 10
Public Works Administration 190
Purity Distilling Company 183, 184, 185

R

Radar 73, 74, 77–78
RBMK reactor 174–175, 176, 178
Redundancy 234, 237, 238
Resnick, Judith 31
Rickover, Hyman G.91
Riley, Richard A. 119
Riprap 236
Robertson, Thomas A. 118
Rochester Gas & Electric Company (RG&E)
153, 157
Rogers Commission 34, 35, 36
Rogers, William B. 34
Rogovin Report 145
Ronan Point tower collapse 196–201

S

Safety of Life at Sea (SOLAS) 71, 78
St. Elmo's Fire 9
Salyut 1 23–24, 25
Scanlan, Robert H. 193
Schoharie Creek Bridge collapse 234–240
Scobee, Francis 31
Scorpion sinking 86–91
Scour 234, 238, 239–240
Sea Cliff 41
Seaforth Highlander 95
Securities and Exchange Commission 122
Shatalov, Vladimir A. 27
Shirasawa, Tomiichiro 151
Shot-peening 46
Sixty Minutes 126
Skewing 222
Skimmers 101
Skipjack class 86, 87–88
Skylark 82
Slattery, Francis A. 87
Smith, E. J. 67–68
Smith, Michael 31, 33
Smith, William Alden 71
Society of Automotive Engineers 111
SOLAS (Safety of Life at Sea) 71, 78
SOSUS underwater listening system 88
Soyuz 10 24
Soyuz 11 reentry disaster 23–28
Soyuz 12 27

Staffeldt, Harold 114

State Disaster Preparedness Commission 237

Stava Dam failure 228–233

Steed, Diane 128

Stewart, Jimmy 122

Stress 58, 184, 187, 209, 212, 230, 232

Stress, temporary 246

Structural failure 208

"Subsafe" program 89, 90

Sudden acceleration 124–128

Superior Construction Company 217

Suzuki, Shunichi 151

System building 197, 199, 201

Systems Review Task Force (SRTF) 47

T

Tacoma Narrows Bridge collapse 189–195

TAP (Trans-Alaska Pipeline) 99

Taylor-Woodrow-Anglian 197

Tennessee Valley Authority 142

Texstar Construction Company 242, 244, 246

Thermal shock 156–157

Thornburgh, Richard 144

Thornton, Charles H. 239

Thornton-Tomasetti 245

Three Mile Island accident 140–146, 151, 156, 157, 175, 179

Thresher sinking 79–85, 89, 90

Threshold limit value 160

Thurner, Josef 51

Tippetts-Abbett-McCarthy-Stratton (TAMS) 222, 223, 225

Tire Industry Safety Council 122

Titanic sinking 65–72

Torsional forces 194

TPMI/Macomber 244

Trans-Alaska Pipeline (TAP) 99

Tread separation 119, 120, 121

Trieste 82, 83

Tsuruga radioactive waste spill 147–152

TWA Super-Constellation and United Airlines DC-7 collision 11–16

Two-girder design 222

U

Underinflation 119, 122

Union Carbide 159, 162, 164–165, 166, 169–170, 171

United Airlines Boeing 747 explosion 37–42

United Airlines DC-10 crash 43–48

United States Coast Guard 96, 99–100, 101, 103

V

Vibration 194

Visual flight rules (VFR) 12

Volkov, Vladislav 24

Volkswagen of America 124, 128

Vortex shedding 193

W

Walsh Construction Company 226

Washington State Toll Bridge Authority 190

Webb, Sam 201

Weight capacity 211

Welch, Thomas 51, 52

Westinghouse Electric Corporation 153

White, Edward H. 18, 19, 20, 22

White, Jerry 225

Wigner effect 134–136

Wigner, Eugene 134

Wind dynamics 189

Windscale reactor complex fire 133–139

Woods Hole Oceanographic Institute 70

Z

Zetlin, Lev 225